THEORY AND INTERPRETATION OF NARRATIVE
James Phelan, Peter J. Rabinowitz, and Robyn Warhol, Series Editors

NARRATING SPACE / SPATIALIZING NARRATIVE

WHERE NARRATIVE THEORY AND GEOGRAPHY MEET

MARIE-LAURE RYAN, KENNETH FOOTE, AND MAOZ AZARYAHU

THE OHIO STATE UNIVERSITY PRESS / COLUMBUS

Copyright © 2016 by The Ohio State University.
All rights reserved.

Library of Congress Cataloging-in-Publication Data
Names: Ryan, Marie-Laure, 1946– author. | Foote, Kenneth E., 1955– author. | Azaryahu, Maoz, author.
Title: Narrating space/spatializing narrative : where narrative theory and geography meet / Marie-Laure Ryan, Kenneth Foote, and Maoz Azaryahu.
Other titles: Theory and interpretation of narrative series.
Description: Columbus : The Ohio State University Press, [2016] | "2016" | Series: Theory and interpretation of narrative | Includes bibliographical references and index. Identifiers: LCCN 2015038944 | ISBN 9780814252635 (cloth : alk. paper) | ISBN 0814212999 (cloth : alk. paper)
Subjects: LCSH: Space perception in literature. | Geography in literature. | Narration (Rhetoric)
Classification: LCC PN56.S667 R93 2016 | DDC 808/.036—dc23
LC record available at http://lccn.loc.gov/2015038944

Cover design by Martyn Schmoll
Text design by Juliet Williams
Type set in Minion Pro

∞ The paper used in this publication meets the minimum requirements of the American National Standard for Information Sciences—Permanence of Paper for Printed Library Materials. ANSI Z39.48-1992.

CONTENTS

List of Illustrations   vii

Chapter 1   Introduction and Overview   1
Chapter 2   Narrative Theory and Space   16
Chapter 3   Maps and Narrative   44
Chapter 4   From Cognitive to Graphic Maps   75
Chapter 5   Space, Narrative, and Digital Media   101
Chapter 6   Street Names as Story and History   138
Chapter 7   Landscape Narratives   160
Chapter 8   Museum Narratives   181
Chapter 9   Into the Future   207

References   227
Index   247

ILLUSTRATIONS

Figures

3.1	A map of spatial form: Franco Moretti's analysis of character relations in Flaubert's *L'Education sentimentale*	49
3.2	Maps from Jonathan Swift's *Gulliver's Travels*	51
3.3	Map from Robert Louis Stevenson's *Treasure Island*	56
3.4	Spontaneous reader's map: Francis Scott Fitzgerald's *The Great Gatsby*	63
3.5	Vladimir Nabokov's map for Franz Kafka's *The Metamorphosis*	65
3.6	Page from *River Guide to the Grand Canyon*	68
3.7	Charles Joseph Minard's map of Napoleon's Russian campaign of 1812	70
3.8	Mattias Quad, *Geneva Urbs*	72
3.9	Redrawing the map of Europe	74
4.1	Master map of *Chronicle of a Death Foretold*	80
4.2	Itinerary map: Pure plan	90
4.3	Symbolic map: Iconic plan	91
4.4	Storyspace map: Mixed picture-plan	92
4.5	Predominantly pictorial representation	93
5.1	*Ms. PacMan*: Abstract playfield	106
5.2	*World of Warcraft*: Playfield as world	107
5.3	*Zanzarah*: Design document from Funatics	108
5.4	Map of *World of Warcraft*	113
5.5	Memory Maps: Carnock, Scotland, annotated by Diarmid Mogg	116
5.6	Telling stories through Google maps: *The 21 Steps*, by Charles Cummins	118
5.7	Itineraries from *Les Trucs*, by Microtrucs	122
5.8	[murmur] online archive	130

6.1	Story St., Cambridge, Massachusetts	142
6.2	Street signs in Berlin and Paris	146
6.3	Street names in central Tel Aviv	147
6.4	A corner where two philosophers meet, Berlin	149
6.5	Renaming a street after David Ben-Gurion, Ramat Gan, Israel, 1986	151
6.6	Belle-Alliance Apotheke, Mehringdamm, Berlin-Kreuzberg	152
6.7	Leninova: A nameplate on display in the Museum of Communism, Prague, Czech Republic	158
7.1	Common strategies for using signs and inscriptions to present stories	162
7.2	Little Bighorn Battlefield in Montana	168
7.3	The two- and three-hour automobile tour routes of the Gettysburg, Pennsylvania, battlefield	172
7.4	The Mormon Trail across Iowa	174
7.5	The intersection of several thematic narratives on Beacon Hill, Boston, Massachusetts	175
7.6	Tours of the Buchenwald concentration camp near Weimar, Germany	176
8.1	Tourist guide to the Israel Defense Forces History Museum, Tel Aviv	188
8.2	Design sketch of the Palmach Museum, Tel Aviv	190
8.3	Plan of the Jewish Museum, Berlin	192
8.4	"Crossroads of Czech and Czechoslovak Statehood" exhibition at the National Memorial on Vítkov Hill, Prague	195
8.5	Holocaust History Museum at Yad Vashem	201
8.6	Street name in Lidice bearing the date of the massacre: June 10, 1942	206

Tables

4.1	The most often mentioned items on the maps	86
4.2	Representation of spatial relations	88
4.3	Map styles	90

CHAPTER 1

Introduction and Overview

THIS BOOK FOCUSES on the intersections of space and narrative. Interest in this topic has grown rapidly as narratology has expanded from literary forms and oral discourse, to a broader concern for storytelling across many domains of human action and experience, as well as across many types of media. Space has traditionally been viewed as a backdrop to plot, if only because narrative, by definition, is a temporal art involving the sequencing of events. Against this traditional conception, this book advances the argument that space serves other narrative roles: it can be a focus of attention, a bearer of symbolic meaning, an object of emotional investment, a means of strategic planning, a principle of organization, and even a supporting medium. The two parts of our title—narrating space and spatializing narrative—suggest that space can intersect with narrative in two principal ways. On one hand, it can be an object of representation, on the other, it can function as the environment in which narrative is physically deployed, or, to put it differently, as the medium in which narrative is realized. While narratologists are best equipped to deal with the first of these issues, geographers can make significant contributions to narratology by drawing attention to the second. By bringing these two issues together, and thereby building a bridge between narratology and geography, this book should yield both a deepened understanding of human spatial experience and a greater insight into narrative theory and forms.

Bridges can be crossed in two directions. Moving from geography into narratology means continuing along what Fredric Jameson (1991) and others have called the "spatial turn" of late twentieth-century culture. The spatial turn is the recognition of the material dimensions of society and culture and, in particular, of the importance of space and place in theory and method. Moving in the other direction from narratology to geography, we extend the "narrative turn" that began in the 1980s and has grown to encompass the manifestations of narrative in many disciplines and life situations, as well as in many different communicational media. The result has been the extension of narrative theory into fields as varied as the law, medicine, historiography, education, the natural sciences, and music.

Chapters 2, 3, 4, and 5 address the first part of our title by focusing on topics that we see as central to developing the spatial turn in narrative theory—what we view as a more encompassing analysis of the role of space in narrative. Chapters 6, 7, and 8 address the second part by focusing on how some narratives use space as a medium through the disposition of their inscription in physical objects and locations. Given these concerns, three caveats are in order.

First, not all work that deals with aspects of space in a narrative text can be considered narratological. As a theoretical and descriptive project, narratology is not the interpretation of individual works but the exploration of regularities found in multiple narrative texts. It is only when it develops concepts both original and generalizable that a study of, say, Proustian or Joycean space or cartographic narrative can be considered a genuine contribution to narratology. Our efforts concentrate on sharpening this focus and exploring the potential overlap between narrative and geography to advance theory in both fields.

Second, not all texts are narrative, nor is narrative synonymous with discourse. Narratology is concerned with one type of discourse but does not necessarily encompass all the work being done in geography that questions the discursive foundations of its theory, method, and practice (Barnes and Duncan 1992; Duncan and Ley 1993). We mention this issue because, at the moment, the concept of narrative is applied somewhat loosely in geography. Terms like "narrative" and "storytelling" are used increasingly, but inconsistently. Sometimes narrative is substituted for "theory" to emphasize the tentative, situated, and contingent nature of explanations in poststructuralist theory (Price 2010). In other areas of geography that employ ethnographic methods, it is a substitute for "oral history" or "autobiography" (Cameron 2012). These uses are not necessarily applied incorrectly, but narrative theory has more to offer geographers than these ideas alone. It offers a range of analytical tools that can aid geographers in analyzing stories and text across many media in new and inventive ways.

Third, not all discourse about the role or the theme of space in narrative represents a convergence of geography and narratology. Many geographers see their discipline as offering some of the most advanced concepts and theories for addressing the spatial dynamics of natural, social, economic, cultural, and political phenomena and processes, but geography has no monopoly on the concept of space. Disciplines across the arts, humanities, and the natural and social sciences (such as philosophy, mathematics, physics, architecture, and the visual arts) also deal with space in a variety of ways. Therefore, attempts to deal with the manifestations of space in narrative can be inspired by several disciplines other than geography, such as phenomenology, linguistics, and cognitive science.

Although narratology and geography can gain from cross-fertilization, these caveats suggest some of the obstacles to closer contact between them. While acknowledging the differing perspectives and interests of narratology and geography, our aim is to showcase the complementarity of their concerns in ways that allow geographers to learn from the narratological approach, and narratologists to benefit from the geographic approach.

POINTS OF CONTACT BETWEEN GEOGRAPHY AND NARRATOLOGY

By tracing an arc from narratology to geography and back, our aim is to build a more encompassing theory of space, place, geography, and narrative, one in which space and narrative intersect not at a single point, but rather converge around four somewhat interrelated issues.

1. Narrative space

This is the space (and the places) providing the physical environment in which the characters of narrative live and move (Buchholz and Jahn 2005). This environment, which can be conceived as a "storyworld," has received the greatest attention in both narratology and geography. It will be discussed from two perspectives: the textual perspective of how narrative resources are used to guide its perception; and the symbolic/functional perspective of its role in the plot.

We concentrate on narrative space early in this book, in chapters 2, 3, and 4, because it is the most important for understanding the cognitive processing of stories and the role of space in narrative structure. Many stories cannot be followed without mentally simulating the movements of characters, whether physical or mental, through the storyworld.

2. The space that serves as context, and occasionally a referent, for the text

Narratives not only describe space, they involve storytellers and audiences who are situated in physical space. The act of storytelling and the use of narrative devices are deeply affected by the spatial and temporal distance between storyteller or narrator and the audience for a story, as well as by whether or not they are located on the scene of the events. Space can also affect narrative by taking on a referential function. Again, this is a topic that has received considerable attention in geography and narratology. It has been explored from the standpoint of what are termed "place-defining novels," travel literature, and nature writing. In addition, location-specific content occurs in such projects as stories inscribed on plaques at historical sites, signs pointing out sights at tourist locations, street names inspired by historical events, and, more recently, stories about certain landscape or cityscape features downloadable on cell phones only within a certain distance from their referent.

But relation to real-world locations is not limited to factual narratives; it can also occur in no-longer-believed stories, such as myth and legends. These genres might tell etiological stories about how certain striking landscape features have come into existence, or they might take the form of make-believe reference (or should one say pseudo-reference?), as when the characters of a fictional story visit counterparts of real-world locations, such as Hamlet's castle in Denmark or Reichenbach Falls in Switzerland, where Sherlock Holmes fell to his death (only to be resurrected later). In recent years, researchers have also drawn increasing attention to the "situated" position of narrator and audience in both time and space (Herman 2013). Much of this work focuses on examining how certain types of narrative form are tied to particular places and historical moments in all their social and political complexity.

These approaches to space in narrative will be addressed in chapters 5, 6, 7, and 8, where we focus on narratives inscribed in specific locations, rather than being transportable, like book-based stories.

3. The space taken by the text itself

Narrative texts can be transmitted by objects of variable dimensions: zero dimensions for purely temporal forms, such as radio plays, books on tape, and, to some extent, oral storytelling (if one ignores the facial expression and gestures of such performances); one dimension for moving lines of texts used in ticker-style news banners on television or in public displays; two dimensions for the printed page or the image; two dimensions plus time for film or computer games; three dimensions for text positioned on signs and markers at historical sites; and four dimensions for live performances (McAuley 1999). As long as narratological attention was limited to literature, the dimensionality of the text was taken for granted—wasn't it always two-dimensional? The move to digital formats on computer screens, iPads, and other electronic devices has not really changed this two-dimensional assumption, even though researchers are becoming attentive to the expressive potential of different types of material supports and frames for storytelling, such as the ability of digital devices, now referred to as "screens," to augment this two-dimensional world with three-dimensional images and animations.

One of the innovations we develop in this book is to consider texts and narratives that move off the page and screen entirely and are positioned in the environment. Such texts are found at historical sites and in museums, especially in museums that have been designed expressly to tell particular stories. This means that our approach to the space taken by the text, as well as issue 4 (below) about the spatial form of text, are new ways of addressing these topics. In chapters 6, 7, and 8, we are conceiving of stories told "on the ground," so to speak, sometimes across large areas like cityscapes and historical sites but also within the small areas occupied by museums. We argue that organizing stories in such places involves issues of spatial form that are different from those involved in using books, e-books, or even computer screens for storytelling. In some cases, the text is embedded in a graphic or cartographic design, which can blur in space the distinctions among textual, graphic, cartography, and even multimedia storytelling.

4. The spatial form of the text

Literary theorists occasionally use space in yet another sense: the "spatial form" of a text—a term that was introduced by the literary critic Joseph Frank (1991 [1945]) to describe a type of narrative organization characteristic of modernism that deemphasizes temporality and causality through compositional devices, such as fragmentation, montage of disparate elements, and juxtaposition of parallel plot lines. The notion of spatial form can be extended to any kind of design formed by networks of semantic, phonetic, or, more broadly, thematic relations between nonadjacent textual units. When the notion of space refers to a formal pattern, it is taken in a metaphorical sense, since it is not a system of dimensions that determines physical position but a network of analogical or oppositional relations perceived by the mind. It is the synchronic perspective necessitated for the perception of these designs and the tendency to associate the synchronic with the spatial that categorize them as spatial phenomena. We will occasionally refer to spatial form in the literary sense (e.g., figure 3.1 is called a "map of spatial form"), but most of the time, when we talk about "spatial form" (e.g., in chapters 6, 7, and 8), we mean the particular disposition of nonmoveable material supports of narrative in physical space. Our use will be literal rather than metaphorical.

Let us stress the point that in these chapters we are concentrating on location-specific texts that have some sort of narrative structure. Words and texts, such as advertising, road and traffic signs, logos, commercial marquees, posters, and more, are commonplace elements of everyday environments. While all these texts are meaningful for disciplines such as marketing, advertising, and urban design, we are interested here only in texts that attempt to tell stories, however loosely or tightly these stories might be structured in physical space.

SPACE, PLACE, AND SENSE OF PLACE: CONTEXTS AND DEFINITIONS

The next chapter provides an extensive analysis of the use of "space" and "place" in narrative theory, but it is important to begin here, in the first chapter, with a few words about how our approach fits into some of the broader debates surrounding the use of these terms, particularly those of space, place, and "sense of place." At issue is the fact that these concepts are used in a number of ways across the sciences and humanities. That is, in addition to the uses of the term space in physics, mathematics, philosophy, and logic, many geographers and researchers in nearby fields have come up with a variety of not-always-compatible schemes for describing and classifying space, such as Yi-Fu Tuan's (1977) distinction between space and place; Deleuze and Guattari's (1987) concepts of smooth and striated space; David Harvey's (2006) absolute, relative, and relational spaces; Henri Lefebvre's (1991 [1974]) differentiation between spatial practice (perceived space), representations of space (conceived space), and representational space (lived space); and, in narratology, Linde and Labov's (1975) contrast between map and tour and Franz Stanzel's (1984 [1979]) concepts of perspectival and aperspectival spaces. All of these methods of defining and classifying space do, of course, have value within the research domains where they were developed, but they also suggest the difficulty of finding common ground among such varied definitions.

In this book we use space to denote certain key characteristics of the environments or settings within which characters live and act: location, position, arrangement, distance, direction, orientation, and movement. These are also characteristics of the real-world locations that are sometimes used in narratives as settings or referents. Space can be important in both a relative sense—the position of characters with respect to each other in a particular scene or setting—and an absolute sense—actual positions, distances, and directions in either the real world or the storyworld. Space might also have allusive, figurative, and connotative meaning in a given narrative.

We use place to refer to the way environments and settings have been shaped and molded by human action and habitation, the qualities that make spaces distinctive or unique. There is a close relationship between place and the concept of sense of place, the latter referring to the affective, emotive bonds and attachments people develop or experience in particular places and environments on a variety of scales, from the microscale of the home (or even room), to the neighborhood, city, state, or nation. Writing and narratives are often influential in shaping people's sense of place and a means by which authors express their own or their characters' attachments to place.

In some cases, sense of place is used to describe the unique or distinctive qualities that give an identity to particular areas and regions. From this perspective, sense of place is related to other concepts like the "spirit of place" or *genius loci*. For the Romans, *genius loci* described the protective spirit of a place, a spirit that belonged to a particular location, irrespective of human use. In this sense, the term is related to practices of geomancy and divination such as *ilm al-raml* (Arabic) and *fengshui* (Chinese). In modern usage, however, the term refers not to a supernatural essence of places but to the distinctive character of a place that grows out of human use and experience. This means that sense of place can refer to positive bonds of comfort, safety, and well-being engendered by place, home, and dwelling, as well as negative feelings of fear, disorientation, and dislike. In this use of the term, sense of place is related to the process of place making, through which individuals as well as social groups shape the environment and invest space with meanings.

FROM LITERARY TO NARRATIVE GEOGRAPHY

Space, place, and sense of place are central to the work of geographers, but the connections to narrative theory have not been a focus of geographical research. By this we mean that although there is a long-standing interest in what might be termed "literary geography" as well as to cinematic and media geographies, this research has generally been concerned with different issues than those we address in this book. Previous research has focused on the storyworlds of particular writers such as Thomas Hardy's Wessex (Darby 1948; Radford 2010); Faulkner's Yoknapatawpha County (Aiken 2009), and Tolkien's Middle Earth (Fonstad 1991), as well as on the storyworlds of science fiction and fantasy (Kitchin and Kneale 2002). Other research has focused on place-defining novels and sense of place in literature (Hones 2008; Shortridge 1991). Some attention has also focused on how novels are rooted in particular socioeconomic contexts (DyLyser 2005; Saunders 2010, 2013) and how writers depict real places and landscapes, particularly in travel and nature literature that revels in local color (Caviedes 1996; Lando 1996; Lutwack 1984; Mallory and Simpson-Housley 1987). These interests have extended beyond literary geography to film, television, and mass media (Adams 2009; Aitken and Zonn 1994; Burgess and Gold 1985; Lukinbeal and Zimmermann 2008; Zonn 1990).

These lines of research have been very productive but, as we noted, are not directly related to narrative theory and the topics we explore in detail in this book. Douglas Pocock's work (1981a, 1988) is perhaps closest to our concerns and touches on two of the four central issues of this book: (1) the form of narrative space; and (2) the space that serves as context and occasionally referent for the text. His article on place and the novelist (1981b) is prescient in this regard, but its major emphasis is on issues of sense of place in literature. Our aim, however, is neither to reassess the entire field of literary geography nor to redefine the terms space, place, and sense of place. Instead, our goal is to highlight some areas of overlap between narrative theory and geography that have not been as thoroughly investigated.

ORGANIZATION OF THE BOOK

Chapter 2, "Narrative Theory and Space," provides a common narratological background for the chapters to come. Using James Joyce's "Eveline" as an example of how space is configured by narrative, we dissect the multiple layers of narrative space (issue 1 above), from the transitory spatial frames that surround characters, to the multiple worlds that constitute a narrative universe. Turning to the textual presentation of space, and adapting to literary narrative observations made by the sociolinguists Charlotte Linde and William Labov about oral storytelling, we distinguish two major structures, both found on the microlevel of individual description, as well as on the macrolevel of the general organization of the text. The first is the tour, a description of space from the point of view of a moving, embodied observer who visits locations in a temporal sequence; the second is the map, a representation of space as seen from a fixed, elevated point of view that affords the observer a totalizing, simultaneous perception of the relations between objects. A reading of William Least Heat-Moon's *PrairyErth* illustrates the macrolevel implementation of this rather rare, highly experimental mode of presentation.

But space is not merely a static background for narrative events, it is also actively involved in those events. After discussing the abstract model of plot proposed by Jurij Lotman, who posits the crossing of spatial boundaries as a universal condition of narrativity, we turn to the variations on this general pattern created by individual narratives, singling out two relations to space (and place) that play a particularly important role in shaping narrative content. One of them is the emotional relation that links characters to certain places within space (or occasionally to space as a whole) on the basis of stories, memories, and lived experience; the other is a strategic relation that associates space with movement, and values places not on the basis of how they speak to the heart but on the basis of what actions they allow, and of how important their control is to one's particular goals. Both of these relations, which will surface over and over again in the coming chapters, are illustrated through a reading of Homer's *The Odyssey*.

The concept of map, one of the most popular of contemporary theory (Mitchell 2008) has been used in literary studies in both a figural and a literal sense: talk of "mapping the territory" and of "mental maps" at one end of the figural-literal axis; designing visual diagrams to represent various aspects of texts at the other end. Adopting a definitely literal perspective on narrative cartography, we propose in chapter 3, "Maps and Narrative," a survey of the various ways in which narrative have been associated with maps. After mentioning maps devoted to the spatial context and to the spatial form of narrative, we devote the bulk of the chapter to maps of narrative space proper. A detailed analysis of the maps found in *Gulliver's Travels* and *Treasure Island* contrasts extradiegetic maps, which are not part of the storyworld but are added to the text for the benefit of the reader, with intradiegetic maps, which exist as objects in the storyworld, are accessible to the characters, and play a role in the plot. Next we turn to maps spontaneously drawn by readers, discussing how a sketch drawn by a consummate reader, Vladimir Nabokov, and another by a high school student serve as interpretive tools.

The last section of the chapter is devoted to an issue that has recently attracted considerable attention in geography: how can maps be turned into a narrative medium? By this we mean not just the insertion of maps in text-based narratives, nor the use of maps in multimedia databases, but the narrative exploitation of the specific "language" (i.e., semiotic resources) of maps.

The question now becomes: how can one tell a story with a visual representation drawn from a vertical perspective that limits textual annotations to names, legends, titles, and brief captions? Multiple frames, as we find in historical atlases representing military campaigns or the evolution of national boundaries, would greatly increase the storytelling power of maps; but if single-frame cartoons can tell stories, why couldn't individual maps do the same? Acknowledging the possibility of telling stories through standard cartographic resources does not mean, however, that maps are able to tell *any kind* of story: our analysis of four narrative maps highlights both the distinctive possibilities and the limitations of cartographic storytelling.

In chapter 4, "From Cognitive to Graphic Maps," we tighten the notion of cognitive mapping, which has been so loosely used in literary criticism and narratology that it has become something of a theoretical cliché, by conceiving it as a mental model of the movements of characters through the storyworld. While it seems evident that narrative comprehension requires some kind of mental model of space, the issue of the form and content of this model remains to be explored. What are the relations between cognitive maps and graphic maps? To what extent and in what detail do mental maps of textual worlds need to represent spatial relations between objects? Through what strategies do texts facilitate the conceptualization of these relations? Is a totalizing, bird's-eye view mental image of narrative space necessary to a proper understanding of plot, or do readers work from cartographic fragments that replace each other in short-term memory? What, more generally, are the relations between the vividly imagined scenes held in short-term memory, and the global image of the story that audiences gradually built in long-term memory? In this chapter, we try to answer some of these questions through an empirical investigation of reader reconstructions of the world of Gabriel García Márquez's novella *Chronicle of a Death Foretold*. More precisely, we compare our own "master-map" of the text, a map reconstructed through close attention to spatial cues, with maps drawn by high school students who do not construct narrative space for its own sake, but as a background for the understanding of plot. The maps provided by the subjects are analyzed in terms of several criteria: which locations important in the plot are shown; how accurately are the relations between these locations represented; and what is the dominant cartographic styles (i.e., pure plan, image, image-plan, etc.). The results are then discussed in view of more formal psychological studies of narrative processing. Though drawings made at the request of an investigator should not be confused with purely mental maps, they provide important clues as to what constitutes for the reader the salient features of the plot and the landmarks of the fictional world.

Spatiality is widely recognized by theorists as being one of the distinctive properties of digital media, but rather than designating a specific feature of these media, the term is used to cover a variety of different phenomena. Chapter 5 surveys these many forms of spatiality and shows how they lead to new narrative genres and narrative experiences. The first part of the chapter is devoted to the virtual worlds of games, especially of multiplayer online games. We discuss, among other topics, the relationship between strategic design (the underlying organization of gameworlds into discrete zones of activity) and mimetic design (the visible display that places players in smooth, more or less realistically rendered landscapes); what kinds of stories lend themselves to active participation by the player; the use of "little stories" embedded in multiplayer gameworlds in the form of folklore, gossip, and backstory; and how players develop an emotional attachment to gameworlds.

Then we turn to digital maps, discussing three artistic projects that use their distinctive features—being easily updated, interactive, animated, responsive to live data, and customizable—to generate stories: the personal memories collected as map annotations on the web site Memory Maps; the web-based narrative *The 21 Steps*, which tells a story through animated Google maps; and Les Trucs, a French project that inscribes on a map the trajectory of objects being passed from player to player like hot potatoes, and then, posts the stories of the exchanges on the Web. The last two sections are devoted to locative narrative and alternate reality games (ARGs), two types of projects that connect participants directly to real space. The locative narrative [murmur] gathers stories told by ordinary people about urban features, and makes them available on-site through mobile technology. A close reading of two of the [murmur] stories reveals how telling in the presence of the spatial referent leads to distinctive narrative techniques. While locative narratives aim to create or tighten emotional bonds to places by giving participants an appreciation of their rich narrative legacy, the much more strategically oriented ARGs use the real world as a springboard—or rabbit hole—into the imaginary world of a fictional story that is reconstituted by the players. The computer emerges from the contrast between ARGs (as well as online games) and [murmur] as a technology equally capable of taking us into virtual realities and of capturing the *genius loci* of real places.

At this point our argument changes direction to focus on modes of inscription that are not commonly associated with storytelling. Although dealing with quite different topics, chapters 6, 7, and 8 all address the question of how stories can be told by positioning text in real-world settings, such as those of streetscapes, historical sites, and museums. In leading off the set, chapter 6 explores the spatial textuality and narrativity of street names. Belonging to the language of the cityscape, the primary function of street names is to signify locations in the city. Their institution by municipal authorities is understood as a regulatory matter, designed to produce a rational system of orientation in the urban maze. Inscribed on street signs and nameplates, street names are a visual and seemingly trivial aspect of streetscapes. Street names belong to the geographies of everyday life. They have much to tell about ideology and power, culture and history, but obviously, regardless of its fame and significance in the urban texture, a single street name inscribed on street signs is not a narrative in any conventional sense of the term. The spatial configuration of street names in a city is ostensibly devoid of any inherent sequential structure, let alone of a coherent storyline. However, as this chapter shows, street names, and commemorative street names in particular, are rich in narrative potential. Street names are bound up with stories, and also abound in stories. In particular, when invested with a commemorative function, street names belong to master-narratives of national and local history, while each commemorative street name is also the "title" of a life-story of a (exemplary) person or an account of a (dramatic) event.

Following a brief discussion of the surge of academic interest in the critical study of place names since the 1980s, the first section of this chapter expands on street names as commemoration and on the history-telling capacity of commemorative toponymic inscriptions. The second section offers insights into the narrative structure of a synchronous spatial configuration of commemorative street names as a city-text of "toponymic history." The last three sections address different issues pertaining to the narrativity of street names: street names as news, as literature, and the "stories behind" street names, which feature their ostensibly "'hidden" history.

Chapter 7 examines how narratives are draped across real spaces, such as the large-scale landscapes of historical and heritage sites. Rather than applying text as a toponym to particular points in space, landscape narratives divide text into pieces and place these fragments within a particular environment. Insofar as the "setting" of the narrative text coincides with the real setting of the story being told, a direct connection is created between narrative and space, and space can be considered the material medium through which the story is told. Drawing on some of our earlier work (Azaryahu and Foote 2008), we focus on the strategies most frequently used to configure stories in space.

Four types are discussed. "Point narratives" involve telling a story from a single point in space, reducing the telling of events to brief inscriptions in often formal or formulaic prose. The text at such sites is often set off from its surroundings by a fence or wall, or with gates sometimes used to separate the narrative space from the surrounding area. "Sequential narratives" are linear arrangements of narrative content along trails or paths with clear starting and ending points and a chronological progression from point-to-point along the way. Some sites invite visitors to begin anywhere along a route, others have a single entry point and fixed order, but since rigid control of visitor movement is nearly impossible over larger sites, repetition or overlap of content will often be needed to facilitate comprehension. "Areal narratives," the third type, are used for stories extending over large areas or encompassing stories that involve long periods of time, such as military campaigns or major social, economic, or political transformations (as for instance the rise and fall of U.S. slavery). Since no one point, path, or trail can provide an effective spatial perspective for telling the story, other techniques are used to simplify and present the story as a coherent sequence. Instead of telling a continuous story, areal narratives highlight key moments in a sequence of events, key places where events took place, or key themes that connect disparate events and place them into a unified storyline. The fourth type includes hybrid forms that involve using combinations of the other three types. Such hybridizations are used at places that are the locus of multiple stories (such at Arlington National Cemetery in Virginia) or at sites commemorating events that can be interpreted in several ways (such as the Sixth Floor Museum in Dallas, Texas, which focuses on the assassination of President John Kennedy).

Chapter 8 examines how stories are told in history museums, emphasizing how narratives are configured in exhibition space and possibly constituted through architectural design of interior spaces. The narrative turn in museum design has had a substantial impact on the shaping of exhibition spaces in museums. In contrast to traditional collection-based museums (such as art, ethnographic, or archeology museums, where the public display of the collection predominates), in a contemporary narrative museum, the display of artifacts is subordinated to the poetics of storytelling, while issues of exhibition sequence and museum architecture underlie and direct the spatial configuration of narratives.

A basic question with regard to storytelling in exhibition space is whether the arrangement of the display along a circulation path corresponds to a coherent storyline. As this chapter argues, permanent exhibitions at contemporary history museums vary across a wide spectrum in the way they employ narrative as an organizing principle. At one end of the spectrum are collection-based museums, where the display of artifacts reigns supreme and the spatial arrangement of displays does not follow a timeline. At the other end of the spectrum is the chronological approach to narrative, which is based on the continuous passage of time as a structural principle. The spatial arrangement of the exhibition is predicated on a storyline that flows along the circulation path. In such a case, the exhibition is built upon a preconceived narrative framework, and movement in space corresponds to progression in time. Along the spectrum are hybrid forms of history museums that combine displays of artifacts belonging to the museum's collection with chronological and thematic approaches to storytelling within museum space.

The chapter further expands on how architecture is employed to shape the museum's interior as narrative environment. The popular view of the museum as a storytelling institution accords with innovative architectural designs for newly commissioned history museums that concur with the museum's story. Prominent examples of architecture in the service of narrative are offered by three landmark historical museums that feature or revolve around the Holocaust: the United States Holocaust Memorial Museum in Washington, DC; Berlin's Jewish Museum; and the Holocaust History Museum at Yad Vashem in Jerusalem. The chapter concludes with some preliminary thoughts on how beginnings and endings are featured in museum narratives.

Chapter 9 is less as a summary than an outline of future research. Our aim is to bring our book full circle by considering how the themes of the individual chapters extend beyond the scope of our argument but also, and more importantly, how the themes of our book extend outward toward new intellectual frontiers. Our argument runs in two directions, one leading from geography to narratology and the other extending from narrative theory to geography. In the first section of the chapter, we focus on some of the most promising opportunities for extending the topics addressed in chapters 2 through 5, so as to promote a more encompassing geographical narratology. The second section considers the promising paths for advancing narrative geography and extends a number of themes presented in chapters 6, 7, and 8.

In the third and final section of chapter 9, we consider topics that crosscut both geographical narratology and narrative geography and suggest research paths for the future. Perhaps the most important of these is how our arguments might be applied to a wider range of nontemporal and temporal media. Although we chose to confine our argument to certain narrative forms, it is important in closing to acknowledge some of the connections to related work on other media, such as film and cinematic landscapes. It is also clear that innovations in digital and cybernetic storytelling crosscut just about all of the themes we have addressed in this book and present many avenues for research. We close by suggesting how our work relates to the rising interest in the digital and spatial humanities and how the themes of this book open new opportunities for collaboration across disciplines.

COLLABORATION IN WRITING

We raise this issue of collaboration because the expansion of narrative theory into new domains has created an urgent need for cross-disciplinary interaction between representatives of the narratological "homeland," who tend to come from literature, and specialists of other disciplines, such as geography. The stakes in such collaborations are high: it gives narratology a chance to expand its scope to narrative forms not found in literature; and conversely, it gives nonliterary disciplines a chance to gain new perspectives by selectively borrowing concepts from the extensive toolbox of literary narratology. Yet a genuine transdisciplinary collaboration in narratology remains problematic. It often takes the form of a collection of chapters independently written by specialists of various fields, with an editorial preface highlighting the common theme of the essays. A less frequent form of transdisciplinary collaboration is a book with multiple authors that blends their individual voices, so that the reader can only guess what comes from one author and what comes from another.

Our book is the product of a different, still relatively rare type of collaboration: it juxtaposes, without blending them, the contributions of a narratologist (Ryan) and of two geographers (Azaryahu and Foote). We were all responsible for developing specific chapters: Foote and Ryan (1 and 9), Ryan (2, 3, 4, and 5),[1] Azaryahu (6), Foote (7), and Azaryahu and Foote (8). But, in contrast to conventional collections of independent essays, we wrote as a team from the earliest drafts. Each of us was able to add his or her own expertise to the contributions of the others. In this respect, perhaps our writing team was unusual insofar as we have all written in the various areas that bridge the issues of space and narrative: narratology, semiotics, cultural and human geography, electronic textuality, cyberculture, place-name geography, multimedia and hypermedia theory, literary theory, and landscape history. This eclecticism has allowed us to offer a strongly interdisciplinary on how space is narrated and how narrative is spatialized.

---

1. Marie-Laure Ryan is indebted to the Guggenheim Foundation for a Fellowship in 2001–2 that allowed her to start working on maps, space, and narrative.

CHAPTER 2

Narrative Theory and Space

SPACE IS A RELATIVELY NEGLECTED DIMENSION of narrative, especially when compared to time. Though Kantian philosophy regards time and space as the two fundamental categories that structure human experience, most definitions of story, by insisting on a sequence of events and changes of state, foreground time at the expense of space. Typical of this approach is Paul Ricoeur's oft quoted formula: "I take temporality to be that structure of existence that reaches language in narrativity, and narrativity to be the language structure that has temporality as its ultimate referent" (1981, 165). The famous sequence of events proposed by E. M. Forster as fulfilling the basic conditions of plot, "The king died, then the queen died of grief," (1990 [1927], 87) does not mention any spatial setting. Yet events are changes of states that affect, or are initiated by, individual existents, and these existents have bodies that both occupy space and are situated in space. If narrative is "a blueprint for constructing a world," as David Herman describes it (2009, 105), then space is an essential part of the mental act of narrative world (re)construction, since the imagination can only picture objects that present spatial extension. An image, after all, requires at least two dimensions. This spatial bias of the imagination explains why language tends to represent time in terms of spatial metaphors, such as "life is a journey," "the past is behind us," or, as in James Joyce's "Eveline," "evening invades the avenues" (1914, par. 1).

Literary critics have long been aware of the symbolic potential of spatial representation, but the concept is either absent or only implicit in the classical texts of early narratology (e.g., Barthes [1972], Genette [1972], Rimmon-Kenan [1983], Todorov [1969]). The only exceptions are Bal (1985)[1] and Chatman (1978).[2] It was not until narratology expanded from the investigation of literary forms toward the narratives of other media, disciplines, and life situations that space received a theoretical attention that went beyond the interpretation of individual texts (e.g., Herman 2002; see Dennerlein 2009 for an extensive survey of narratological treatments of space). But many of the spatial concepts proposed in conjunction with narrative tend to be metaphorical and fail to account for the physical existence of characters, objects, and setting. Among such uses are Gilles Fauconnier's (1985) mental spaces, which are constellations of meanings held together in the mind; his notion of mapping (1997), whose origin in the visual representation of space has been overshadowed by its extension to any kind of analogical thinking; or Susan Stanford Friedman's "spatial reading" of narrative (1993), an approach that she describes as paying attention not only to a "horizontal axis" of plot but also to a "vertical axis" standing for a variety of other literary dimensions: author-reader relations, literary-historical considerations, and intertextual allusions. Mark Turner's concept of "spatial stories" (1996) is metaphorical for another reason: the term designates expressions based on space-implying movements

---

1. Bal regards location as a constitutive element of *fabula* (i.e., story), because events must take place somewhere (1985, 2). In a highly condensed section titled "From Place to Space" (93–99), she discusses several other topics, many of which are treated in more detail in the present chapter: (a) the senses through which characters experience space: sight, hearing, and touch; (b) how spatial frames are filled with objects; (c) how these objects create an atmosphere; (d) how character movements mediate between spatial frames; (e) the intrinsic symbolic value of some kinds of places, such as the mountaintop or the *locus amoenus*; (f) description as the communication of spatial information; (g) actions that are performed not merely in space but with space, such as "walking into a wall" (see the discussion below of "strategic space").

2. Chatman (1978, 96–107) discusses the presentation of space in film through the eminently spatial medium of the image. In the domain of verbal narrative, he proposes a distinction between "story space" and "discourse space," through which he tries to transpose into the spatial domain the well-established distinction between "story time" ("the duration of the purported events of the narrative") and "discourse time" ("the time it takes to peruse [i.e., read or listen to] the discourse"; 62). "Discourse time" is a useful concept because language is a temporal medium. But Chatman's notion of "discourse space" does not involve space in the same way as "discourse time" involves time, for it does not concern the space physically occupied by narrative discourse, such as pages (i.e., what is called "space 3" in chapter 1), but rather, refers to the disclosure by discourse of the space in which the story takes place. In other words, Chatman's "discourse space" is not a physical space, it is rather another term for description of the storyworld. This may explain why the term has not established itself in narratology.

(e.g., "the stock market sank") and it is "story" rather than "spatial" that functions metaphorically.

As a prelude to the discussion of narratological approaches to space, we will begin *in medias res,* with an analysis of James Joyce's "Eveline," a short story from *Dubliners* that packs within its four pages a remarkably rich evocation and symbolic use of space. The spatial structure revealed in the course of our reading will serve as the foundation for a survey that will cover both story and discourse, the two elements whose conjunction narratologists regard as constitutive of narrative.[3] Discourse will be represented by an analysis of the textual strategies through which space is presented in narrative, and story through a discussion of the spatial categories that underlie its semantics.

NARRATIVE SPACE: A CASE STUDY

The story concerns a young woman, Eveline, who is trapped in a joyless, caged existence. Her father is a violent man (probably an alcoholic) who physically abuses his children. Her mother has died insane after a life of suffering and subordination. Before her mother died, Eveline promised her to keep the family together. This is what she does, working at a drab sales job, giving her paycheck to her father (as does an older brother), and taking care of the house and of the younger children. But now she has a chance to escape from her humdrum life. She met a sailor, Frank, who wants to take her to Buenos Ayres (Joyce's spelling), where he now lives, and marry her. As the story begins, she is sitting by the window, mulling over her decision to leave. Her thoughts swing back and forth between her attachment and duty to her family and her right to the happiness that she expects from a new life with Frank, even though she is not sure that she loves him. She hears a street organ that reminds her of the night when her mother died, and she makes up her mind: she must, at all cost, escape from her present condition. She meets Frank at the dock, but when time comes to board the ship, she holds tight to the railing rather than following Frank, and she ignores his frantic calls for her. As the ship's bridge is lifted, her eyes give him "no sign of love or farewell or recognition" (par. 26).

Two metaphors stand out in the human imagination's attempt to come to grips with the abstract notion of space: space as a container, and space as

---

3. Gerald Prince defines story as: "The content plane of narrative . . . the what of a narrative . . . the *fabula*," (itself defined as "the set of narrated situations in their chronological sequence") (1987, 91, 30) and discourse as "the expression plane of narrative as opposed to its content" (21).

a network.[4] As Lakoff and Johnson (1980) observe, the container metaphor presents space as a bounded environment that encloses the subject; it can therefore stand either for security and attachment to one's surroundings, or for passivity and entrapment. While space as container is delimited by boundaries often imposed on the subject, space as a network is a dynamic system of relations that allows movement, and that is often actively created by the subject. Because of this inherent dynamism, and also because it is better able to deal with problems of urbanization (for what is a city, if not a system of relations between distinct neighborhoods, public spaces, work spaces, and leisure areas), the network metaphor is the favorite of poststructuralist theories of space, especially of those inspired by Marxism. But the container metaphor is a powerful way to express a sense of place, and it cannot be dismissed as inert and theoretically unproductive, as some scholars have done, since we are dealing here with the functioning of the imagination, rather than with the practical organization of real space. The gripping dramatic tension of the plot of Eveline can indeed be attributed to the interplay between the container and the network conceptions of space, as well as to the inherent ambiguity of the container metaphor: emotionally fulfilling sense of place *versus* freedom-depriving prison.

In "Eveline," as indeed in most literary texts, the container schema works in two directions. Through a process of metonymic implication, some of the spatial objects explicitly named in the text invite the reader to imagine the larger spatial unit of which they are a part: for instance, the window mentioned in the first sentence, "She sat at the window watching the evening invade the avenue" (par. 1) implies a room, which itself implies a house or apartment. Conversely, the room implied by the window is described through the objects that fill it: a broken harmonium and yellowed pictures on the wall.

In contrast to the mention of generic types of location, the use of place names borrowed from real-world geography situate the story in a specific spatial setting. The most important of these actual places is Dublin, even though the name is only implied by the title of the short story collection in which "Eveline" appears (*Dubliners*). Among the place names explicitly mentioned

---

4. These two conceptions of space underlie the contrasting cosmologies of Newton and Leibniz. As Mary Jane Rubenstein writes (2014, 123), "Newton [argued] that 'absolute space' is an inert, extended background through which objects may or may not move. Similarly, he insisted that 'absolute time' flows universally and inexorably, 'without regard to anything external.'

Gottfried Leibniz (1646–1716) rigorously contested Newton's 'absolute' view of space and time, insisting that these terms were just descriptions of relations between objects. Space and time, Leibniz argued, have no independent existence: they are, as he wrote to the Newtonian Samuel Clarke in 1716, 'purely relative' to each other and to the matter 'within' them."

in the story are Belfast, Melbourne, England, Italy, and Buenos Ayres. Through what Ryan calls the principle of minimal departure—a principle that urges readers to build their mental representations of fictional worlds on the basis of their life experience and knowledge of the world, as long as this knowledge is not contradicted by the text (1991)—the referents of actual place names enter the storyworld with most of their real-world properties: readers will imagine Italy as sunny, England as foggy and industrialized, Belfast as the Protestant rival of Catholic Dublin, and Buenos Ayres as far, far away. (The only real-life property of these places modified by the text is that they are objects of thought for Eveline, who does not exist in the real world.) Moreover, though only a small number of real-world locations are mentioned, one must assume that the storyworld encompasses all existing real-world geography. The standard procedure for imagining the world of fictional texts that combine real-world and imaginary locations is to locate the latter in unspecified areas of real-world geography. For example, we imagine that Eveline's house is squeezed into Dublin, but that the map of Dublin remains otherwise unchanged.

While minimal departure entitles readers to imagine that the storyworld is a continuous space, the text directs attention to discrete locations within it. One way for the text to select what is shown and what is not is the narrative device of focalization. Gérard Genette (1972) defines focalization as the answer to the question "who sees" (or, more generally, "who perceives") as opposed to the question "who speaks." The "who" marks the difference between point of view and focalization: point of view stands for a purely spatial position from which a scene is observed (e.g., from above or below, from afar or close by), whether or not this position is occupied by somebody, while focalization suggests that the scene is inscribed in somebody's consciousness. Throughout most of the story, Eveline functions as the focalizer; what the reader sees of the storyworld is what constitutes the objects of Eveline's mental activity. It is only in the last sentence that the text abandons Eveline's mind and presents her as an object, rather than as a source of perception: "Her eyes gave him no sign of love or farewell or recognition." Here the focalizer could be either Frank, or the anonymous third-person narrator.

An effect of the technique of focalization is to create a distinction between events that take place on stage (in the narrative here and now) and events that take place off stage (in a space located elsewhere, mediated by the consciousness of the focalizing character). There are only two scenes that take place in the "narrative now": the scene where Eveline sits at the window and the scene at the harbor; everything else is presented either retrospectively or prospectively through Eveline's mental activity. Whether an event takes place on stage or off stage does not necessarily reflect its importance to the plot. While the scene at the harbor has decisive consequences for Eveline, the scene at the window matters narratively not for what happens there but for the backgrounded events that appear on the screen of Eveline's mind: the death of her mother, her meeting with Frank, and her plan to leave home.

The topographical configuration of Eveline's world is fairly easy to construct, because the only spatial relations that play a strategic role in the story are the relations that link together the locations borrowed from real-world geography. It matters that Buenos Ayres is a long sea voyage away from Dublin, or that Belfast is relatively close; but it does not really matter where exactly Eveline's house is situated with respect to the harbor or to the store where she works. While the real-world sites can be located on the readers' mental map on the basis of the reader's knowledge of geography, the text-specific sites can be located anywhere within Dublin.[5]

If there is one phenomenon that facilitates the conceptualization of the intimate connection between space and time, this phenomenon is movement, since it takes time to move from one point to another. This explains why, inspired by Bakhtin's notion of the chronotope—itself inspired by Einstein's conception of time as the fourth dimension of a so-called "spacetime"—Gabriel Zoran (1984, 315) calls the emplotment of narrative space through character movement the "chronotopic level." While on the topographical level, space is a container for all the sites mentioned in the story, on the chronotopic level these sites are linked into a network. The movements that connect the sites of a narrative network are not only physical but mental; a character "thinking" of a place can make this place a significant part of the story, even if it is not physically accessible to the characters. It is therefore possible to have plots without actual movement.

In "Eveline," as in most narratives, character movement can be either unique or repetitive. For instance, Eveline's commute to the store where she works is part of her daily routine, while her (projected) trip to Buenos Ayres would be a singular and irreversible event that will definitely change her life. Some movements are physical and actual, while others are the content of mental representations directed toward either the past (remembering) or the future (planning/fearing/projecting). (Perceiving, by contrast, remains anchored in the here and now; but perception can lead to either remembering or projecting.) While actual movement plays a minimal role in the time span framed by the story (Eveline only goes from her house to the harbor;

---

5. In chapter 4 we will analyze a story where the location of imaginary places with respect to each other plays a crucial role in the understanding of the plot, and where, consequently, the process of mental mapping requires much more precise operations.

and this trip is not represented but implied), the story's dramatic force resides in a tension between actual and virtual movement. This tension is relieved when running away with Frank is cut off from the tree of open possibilities and passes into a definitive state of counterfactuality. The opportunity slowly trickles away when Eveline clings to the shore while Frank follows the call to board the ship, giving the last scene a poignancy of almost unbearable intensity.

While the chronotopic level connects the various sites of the storyworld through movement, the symbolic level structures narrative space by dividing it into distinct areas, and by associating these areas with various kinds of values. In "Eveline," these values are mostly emotional. (As we will see later, they can also be strategic.) The window mentioned in the first sentence establishes a contrast between the inside and the outside, which in turn stands for the closed versus the open, containment versus freedom, and passivity versus activity. On the outside, Eveline sees a housing development recently built by a man from Belfast (i.e., by an outsider to the neighborhood). The row of new houses, where people are seldom seen, reminds Eveline of what the area used to be in her youth: an open field where a community of children, now dispersed and grown up, used to meet and play.

The public space of the playfield contrasts not only with the private spaces of the present urban development but also with the closed space and loneliness of the apartment. As metonymic representatives of the closed space that holds them, and therefore as manifestations of the container schema, the objects that decorate the room inspire ambiguous feelings in Eveline: on one hand, a feeling of emotional security, of human warmth, of attachment to her family; on the other hand, a feeling of being trapped, as in a spider web. These objects have become so much a part of Eveline that "she had never dreamed of being divided" from them. The dust that covers everything—and that she removes every week, only to see it return—stands for the accumulation of time and the repetitiveness of her life. One can easily imagine what Eveline's future will be like if she declines the opportunity to escape with Frank: a life of passivity and submission, a repetition of her mother's sad fate. On the walls, yellowing pictures of a saint and a priest speak of the hegemony of the Catholic Church, and through the Church, of the Law of the Father: not only is the priest a friend of Eveline's father, but Catholic priests are addressed as "Father." We are told that the priest in the picture is now in Melbourne; does Eveline think of him as somebody who was cut off from his roots against his will, or as somebody who managed to free himself from his former life? Her indecision leaves both interpretations open.

The antithesis to the stifling atmosphere of the apartment, which stands for life in Dublin in general, is represented by all the faraway, almost mythical places that Frank tells about—Patagonia, the Straights of Magellan, and especially Buenos Ayres, a city whose name suggests the breath of fresh air that would be needed to blow away the dust of Eveline's life. As interconnected goals of imaginable movement, these places represent the network conception of space. But is Frank a mere storyteller, or can one believe what he says when he speaks of taking Eveline to the New World? Frank, the savior who could free Eveline from her present condition, remains a vague figure in the text; so vague, in fact, that until the harbor scene, the reader might wonder whether he actually exists, or is a figment of Eveline's imagination: isn't he too much of a fairy tale prince charming to be real? But to give the story a quasi-religious interpretation, one could say that even when a new life becomes miraculously possible, even when a forking path opens itself in her seemingly predetermined destiny, Eveline lacks the faith to seize the opportunity.

From a plot-functional point of view, the harbor is the setting of the most important event—in fact, of the only event directly told by the text—but from an emotional point of view, it is much less a place than the apartment, the playfield, or even Buenos Ayres because Eveline and Frank have no intent to stay there. It is one of these countless sites of transit that anthropologist Marc Augé (1995) describes as "non-places." While the harbor is the *site* of a highly emotional event, it is not itself the *object* of an affective experience. Within the harbor, two objects stand out as powerful symbolic of opposite attitudes toward life. One of them is the railing, which represents solidity, stability, and anchoring in the Dublin soil; the other is the sea, which represents the onrush of the unknown. By clinging to the railing, Eveline protects herself from drowning in the open future toward which Frank wants to take her, and she resigns herself to the predictable destiny that life in Dublin offers. As she rejects the turbulence of the sea, an image of becoming, she kills her emotional self, and she turns from a sentient being, a vibrant source of perception, into a passive object: "She set her white face to him, like a helpless animal. Her eyes gave him no sign of love or farewell or recognition." With this last sentence, Eveline becomes reified as a piece of the landscape and of the social order that she does not dare to escape.

LAYERS OF NARRATIVE SPACE

One of the reasons space has been a relatively neglected topic in narratology is the wide range of phenomena that can be considered spatial: narrative space extends from the individual object described in a narrative to the cosmic order in which the story takes place. We propose five basic levels of narrative space, and we illustrate them with data from "Eveline" (Ryan 2009):

(a) *Spatial frames*: the immediate surroundings of the characters (cf. Zoran's [1984] "fields of vision"). Spatial frames are shifting scenes of action, and they may flow into each other: a "salon" frame can turn into a "bedroom" frame as the characters move within a house. As the term "frame" suggests, spatial frames are filled with individual things, and they are defined by the set of objects that they contain. For instance, as characters move from the salon to the bedroom, the reader will imagine—or the text will describe—different pieces of furniture. Spatial frames are hierarchically organized by relations of containment (a room is a subspace of a house), and their boundaries may be either clear-cut or fuzzy (for instance, a landscape might slowly change as characters move through it). In "Eveline" spatial frames do not blend into each other, because Eveline is never shown moving along a path. The transition between the scene by the window and the scene at the harbor is the kind of abrupt cut that film has made familiar, and it is left to the reader to infer Eveline's trip from one place to the next.

(b) *Setting*: while spatial frames vary during the plot, what we call setting is a relatively stable socio-historico-geographic category that embraces the entire text. According to this view, the setting of "Eveline" is early twentieth-century, lower-middle-class Dublin.

(c) *Story space*: the space relevant to the plot, as mapped by the actions and thoughts of the characters (Zoran's chronotopic space). It consists of all the spatial frames plus all the locations mentioned by the text that are not the scene of actually occurring events. In "Eveline," the story space comprises not only Eveline's house and the Dublin harbor but also all the real-world locations referred to by proper names.

(d) *Storyworld*: the story space completed by the reader's imagination on the basis of the principle of minimal departure. While story space consists of selected places separated by voids, the storyworld of realistic texts is conceived by the imagination as a coherent, unified, ontologically full, and materially existing geographical entity. In Eveline's world, we assume that Dublin and South America are separated by the Atlantic, even though the ocean is not mentioned by name. In a story that refers to both real and imaginary locations, the storyworld superimposes the locations specific to the text onto the geography of the actual world. In a story that takes place in wholly imaginary landscapes (e.g., J. R. R. Tolkien's *Lord of the Rings*), readers assume that the storyworld extends beyond the locations named in the text and that there is a continuous space between them, even though they cannot fill out this space with specific geographic features.

We do not, however, want to exclude the possibility of narratives projecting impossible spaces or discrete frames that do not cohere into a full world.

An example of a novel with an impossible space is Mark Z. Danielewski's *House of Leaves,* which concerns a house that is smaller on the outside than on the inside and serves as a portal to an infinite labyrinth contained in a finite area. An example of a novel whose space presents unbridgeable gaps is Kafka's *The Trial.* The impossibility for the reader to understand the law of the Court, which sentences Joseph K. to death, and to connect the realm of the Court to the realm of everyday life, where K. leads a normal, presumably crime-free existence, is not a matter of missing information but a matter of radical ontological difference.

(e) *Narrative universe*: the world presented as actual by the text, plus all the counterfactual worlds constructed by characters as beliefs, wishes, fears, speculations, hypothetical thinking, dreams, fantasies, and imaginative creations (Ryan 1991). The narrative universe of "Eveline" contains two worlds: one, imagined by Eveline, where she boards a ship to South America and lives happily ever after with Frank; and another, corresponding to facts, where she is emotionally unable to leave Dublin. For a possible world to be part of the narrative universe, it must be textually activated and relevant to the story. On these criteria, for example, we can eliminate from the universe of "Eveline" the world where Eveline becomes Queen of England.

Another phenomenon that contributes to the diversification of a narrative universe is the potential multiplicity of diegetic levels, or levels of fictionality. In a standard narrative ontology, stories are told as fact for a certain world, and they posit consequently their own actual world. Whenever a fictional story embeds another fiction, this new level of fictionality introduces a new planet in the narrative universe, corresponding to the actual world of the embedded story. In a standard, realistic ontology, the various levels of a narrative universe are kept neatly separate, but in fantastic texts, characters native to one level occasionally migrate to another level through a narrative device known as "metalepsis." The result is an entanglement of diegetic levels. A classic example of metalepsis is the story *Continuity of Parks* by Julio Cortázar, where a reader is murdered by a character in the story he is reading. Narrative universes, consequently, may or may not be ontologically coherent and logically possible (Alber 2013).

THE TEXTUALIZATION OF NARRATIVE SPACE: MICROLEVEL

The Austrian narratologist F. K. Stanzel was one of the first literary scholars to pay attention to the presentation of space in narrative. In his book *A*

Theory of Narrative (1984 [German original 1979]), he suggests two strategies of spatial description: perspectivism and aperspectivism. Perspectivism is a highly immersive representation of space that "encourages the reader's illusion of being directly and vividly presented with fictional reality" (123). In a perspectivist description, the narrator (or the focalizing character) occupies a certain point in space, and the scene is described from this particular point of view. This strategy enables the reader to grasp the locations of objects with respect to each other. Stanzel's example is a passage from James Joyce's *A Portrait of the Artist as a Young Man*, in which a Jesuit father discusses with Stephen Dedalus, the hero, the possibility of Stephen's entrance into the order. While the story is narrated in the third person, it uses Stephen as a focalizer, presenting the Jesuit father as Stephen sees him: a dark shape in front of the window that blocks the sunlight. The reader, consequently, can mentally map the spatial relations between Stephen, the Jesuit father, and the window. In an aperspectivist description, by contrast, "the interior of a room is never depicted in such a way that a graphic sketch can be made, even if the reader is given a more or less complete inventory of the objects in the room" (120). A good example of aperspectivism is this description from David Mitchell's novel *Cloud Atlas* (2012 [2004]):

> My new room is big enough for badminton doubles; has a four-poster bed from whose curtains I had to shake last year's moths; century-old Cordova peels off the walls like dragons' scales, but it's attractive in its way; indigo witch ball; armoire inlaid with burr walnut; six ministerial armchairs, and a sycamore escritoire at which I write this letter. (66)

Another way to conceive aperspectival description would be to attribute it to a position freely floating in space (Dennerlein 2009, 151). For instance, if a description begins by showing the front of a house, then the back, then the garden, then the inside, and alternates between a bird's-eye view and a horizontal view, the perspective cannot be attributed to an embodied human being located on site, but rather, belongs to a disembodied consciousness unconstrained by time and space, a consciousness that works from memory or from the imagination. In this type of description, each individual element may be seen from a particular perspective, but the whole is aperspectivist. Stanzel suggests that perspectivist description is typical of third-person narrative with character focalization ("reflector-character narration," in his terminology), while aperspectivist description is more frequent in first-person narration, but this observation is based on a very limited sample. We would rather suggest that the choice between perspectivist and aperspectivist description is dictated by the contrast between a strategic and a symbolic conception of space. (We return to this contrast at the end of the chapter.) When objects have an intrinsic emotional or aesthetic value, or when the purpose of the description is to evoke an atmosphere (as in the Mitchell example above), it is not necessary to specify how they relate to each other, but when the configuration of space determines the range of actions that can be taken, and consequently impacts the unfolding of the plot (as it would in a murder mystery) then a perspectivist description becomes preferable.

Within perspectivist description, an important distinction can be made on the basis of whether the narrator/observer occupies a fixed or a moving point of view (Dennerlein 2009, 155). In a study of how people describe their apartment, Linde and Labov (1975; see Herman 2002 for narratological applications) identified two basic cognitive strategies, which they called the "tour" and the "map." In the tour strategy, the speaker moves through the apartment as if it were a maze (though apartments have much simpler spatial structure than mazes), typically entering it from the front door, following hallways and describing the rooms situated on the right or the left. Sometimes speakers enter the room by means of a verb of motion, sometimes they just glance at it from the hallway. In this example of tour strategy, as Linde and Labov note, "the spatial representation is transformed into a temporal sequence—a pseudo-narrative":

> You walked in the front door
> There was a narrow hallway
> To the left, the first door you came to was a tiny bedroom.
> Then there was a kitchen,
> and then bathroom,
> and then the main room was in the back, living room, I guess.
> (Linde and Labov 1975, 927)

While in the tour strategy speakers look at the apartment from the inside, in the map strategy they occupy an external, elevated, static perspective:

> I'd say it's laid out in a huge square pattern, broken up into four units.
> If you were looking down at this apartment from a height, it would be like—like I said before, a huge square with two lines drawn through the center to make like four smaller squares.
> Now, on the ends—uh—in the two boxes facing out in the street you have the living room and a bedroom.
> In between these two boxes you have a bathroom.

> Now between the next two boxes, facing on the courtyard, you have a small foyer and then the two boxes, one of which is a bedroom and the other of which is a kitchen and then a small foyer—ah—a little beyond that.
> (Linde and Labov 1975, 929)

Judging by the hesitations, marked with "uh" and "ah," this description involves a greater cognitive effort than the tours. It is, indeed, the only example of map strategy in Linde and Labov's database, while tours are numerous. The tour is obviously the preferred strategy, thanks not only to its inherent narrativity, which makes it more lively, but also because it makes it easier for the speaker to remember all the rooms. The Roman mnemonic techniques of the *loci*, or memory palaces, typically took the form of a mental walk through a building. Each object encountered during the walk was associated with one of the items to be remembered through a made-up story. Apartment descriptions do not associate rooms with lists of items to be remembered; rather, it is the rooms themselves that are retrieved during the walk-through.

In written texts, however, the mnemonic advantages of the tour are much less significant, because the author does not need to remember items on short notice; in narrative fiction, moreover, the author makes up rather than remembers the spatial configuration. Map-like descriptions should therefore be more common in written than in oral communication, and in fiction than in descriptions of real-world spaces.

In the following example from William Faulkner, the focalizing character's location on a high point detaches him from the landscape and provides a substitute for the bird's-eye point of view of maps (Duvert 1986). The map-like perspective is reinforced by the absolute directional terms east, west, and south. The reader can not only locate the elements of the landscape with respect to each other but also situate them within real-world geography:

> [From a vantage point at the eastern edge of Yoknapatawpha County, Charles Mallison saw] his whole native land, his home . . . unfolding beneath him like a map in one slow soundless explosion: to the east ridge on green ridges tumbling away toward Alabama and to the west and south the checkered fields and the woods flowing on into the blue and gauzed horizon beyond which lay at last like a cloud the long wall of the levee and the great River itself flowing not merely from the north but out of the North. (Faulkner 1948, 151)

Another example of map strategy in narrative fiction comes from the French New Novelist Alain Robbe-Grillet. His stated literary goal was to purify description of any human element, especially of anthropocentric metaphors that attribute a mental "depth" and intention to inanimate objects. Instead of writing "the village is tucked away [French original: *blotti*] at the bottom of the valley," why not, argues Robbe-Grillet, simply say "the village is located"? (1963, 60). His insistence on presenting things in their exteriority reminds us of the phenomenological project of capturing the world in its radical otherness; yet even this otherness cannot be apprehended without the mediation of a reflecting consciousness. In the description quoted below, the eye of an anonymous observer wanders around from an elevated point to present a panoramic view of the landscape:

> From the far side of the bedroom the eye carries over the balustrade and touches ground only much further away, on the opposite slope of the little valley, among the banana trees of the plantation. The sun cannot be seen between their thick clusters of wide green leaves. However, since this sector has been under cultivation only recently, the regular crisscrossing of the rows of trees can still be clearly followed. The same is true of almost all the property visible from here, for the older sectors—where confusion has gained the ascendency—are located higher up on this side of the valley, that is, on the other side of the house.
>
> It is on the other side, too, that the highway passes, just below the edge of the plateau. The highway, the only road that gives access to the property, marks the northern border. A dirt road leads from the highway to the sheds and, lower still, to the house, in front of which a large cleared area with a very slight slope permits cars to be turned around. (Robbe-Grillet 1981, 40)

While the Faulkner description conveys the exhilaration of a traveler who reaches a high point and discovers the world anew—an experience familiar to mountain climbers—the much longer and more detailed Robbe-Grillet description, which fills a page and a half, provides a set of precise, and (to this reader) somewhat tedious instructions for building a mental map of the setting. But does it really succeed? Even though the text pays great attention to spatial relations ("on this side"; "higher up"; "on the other side"; "in front of"), it overwhelms the reader's mind with objects that chase each other in memory, preventing the imagination from forming a global visualization that encompasses simultaneously every described element. It would take a reader equipped with pen and paper to gain a comprehensive, panoramic view of the landscape. Maybe inciting the reader to draw a map was Robbe-Grillet's intent. But the perspective is not literally cartographic, since it is not elevated enough to prevent objects from hiding each other (cf. the insistence on visibility).

While Robbe-Grillet's text is an experiment in extreme writing whose value lies in its originality rather than in its ability to stimulate the imagination, a much more immersive way to textualize space lies in a combination of the map and the tour strategies. In Balzac's *Eugénie Grandet* (1955), the text pulls the reader into the storyworld through a second-person address that casts her in the role of the wandering observer: the four-page description of the town of Saumur that opens the novel takes the reader on a walk through the town, letting her peek into courtyards and stores on her way, until she reaches the actual stage of the novel: "When you have followed the windings of this impressive street whose every turn awakens memories of the past, and whose atmosphere plunges you irresistibly into a kind of dream, you notice a gloomy recess in the middle of which you may dimly discern the door of Monsieur Grandet's house" (37). While the general movement of the description enacts a tour, the lengthy evocations of the views encountered along the way adopt a more map-like strategy.

Even more tour-like is the description of the Buddenbrook family house in Thomas Mann's eponymous novel (1961 [1901]). Here the tour is not performed in make-believe by the reader, but rather literally implemented as a narrative event. At the end of a house-warming party, the host, Consul Buddenbrook, takes his guests around the new house, inviting them to inspect the various rooms:

> "So you live up there, Buddenbrook?" asked Senator Langhals. To the right a broad white staircase with a carved baluster led up to the sleeping-chambers of the Consul's family in the second storey; to the left came another row of rooms. The party descended the stairs, smoking, and the Consul halted at the landing.
>
> "The entresol has three rooms," he explained, "the breakfast-room, my parent's sleeping chamber, and a third room which is seldom used. A corridor runs along all three. . . . This way, please." (27)

Though the Consul acts as a tour guide through the house, his description of the entresol is brief and map-like, because he does not want to take his guests to the private parts of the house. The tour resumes with detailed narratorial descriptions of the passage to the courtyard, and of the courtyard itself, the most public space in the house.

The ultimate in dynamic perspective may be W. G. Sebald's landscape description from what might be called a roller-coaster point of view:

From Bad Kissingen the road to Steinach goes by way of Grossenbrach, Kleinbrach, and Aschach with its castle and Graf Luxburg's brewery. From there it climbs the steep Aschacher Leite, where Lazarus (Luisa writes) always got down from his calèche so that the horses would not have so hard a job of it. From the top, the road runs down, along the edge of the woods to Höhn, where the fields open out and the hills of the Rhön can be seen in the distance. The Saale meadows spread before you, the Windheim woods nestle in a gentle curve, and there are the tip of the church tower and the old castle—Steinach! Now the road crosses the stream and enters the village, up to the square by the inn, then down to the right to the lower part of the village, which Luisa calls her real home. (1996, 194)

In this pure example of the tour strategy, the wandering observer is replaced, metonymically, with a road that seems to move across space—climbing the hills, descending into the valleys, and revealing along the way an ever-changing view. The invention of high-speed transportation has made us familiar with how landscape evolves in relation to the observer's position. Film experiments, such as Dziga Vertov's use of a camera mounted on a car, or video games, in which the computer updates the display according to the player's position, have been able to capture this experience. But language is ill-fitted for doing so, because when it reports movement, it does not show moment-to-moment progression, but rather reports quasi-instantaneous displacement from an origin to a destination, as if the agent were teletransported: "Mary went from Paris to London." Through its dynamic description of space, Sebald's example stretches language as far as it can go toward emulating film's and computer games' ability to convey a sense of traveling through a changing landscape. It does not ask the reader to map the world, but rather, to experience the journey.

THE TEXTUALIZATION OF NARRATIVE SPACE: MACROLEVEL

The tour and the map and their various hybrids appear not only on the microlevel of individual descriptions, they can also be used as global structuring principles of narrative space. Here again the tour is by far the more common strategy. When practiced on the macrolevel, it is much more than a certain way of presenting space—it becomes the thematic foundation of a type of plot. We find a tour structure whenever a story follows the travels of a solitary hero: in the epic narrative (as opposed to the dramatic narrative, which focuses on a network of human relations); in the medieval romance; in the picaresque novel; in the *Bildungsroman;* in most computer games; and, of course, in travel writing. The tour might be one of the oldest forms of narrative (strangers telling about their travels, according to *The Odyssey,* were a favorite form of entertainment in oral cultures), but it has never fallen out of favor. From *The Odyssey* to *Don Quixote* and from Jack Kerouac's *On the Road* (a novel depicting multiple traversals of the United States by car) to the recent *The Selected Works of T. S. Spivet* by Reif Larsen (where a 12-year-old genius cartographer, who has been awarded a prize by the Guggenheim Foundation, runs away from home and hops on various vehicles to travel from Montana to Washington, DC), the tour structure has proven over and over again its ability to express the diversity of human experience. As the hero moves from place to place, making chance encounters, meeting new people, traversing diverse landscapes, discovering new cultures and customs, experiencing various highly tellable adventures, and learning along the way, the tour literalizes the popular spatiotemporal metaphor "life is a journey" (Mikkonen 2007). This narrative structure is so widespread and familiar to readers that we can dispense with a discussion of specific examples.

The map structure, by contrast, is a highly experimental and mostly postmodern form of organization. Rather than visiting space through the linear itinerary of a traveler, it divides it into distinct sections and evokes each of these sections in an order determined by a formal algorithm. Whereas the tour treats space as an expanse to be traversed, stopping at various points where significant events occur, the map regards it as a surface to be thoroughly covered by language. An example of this spatial form is William Least Heat-Moon's *PrairyErth*, a text of creative nonfiction.

William Least Heat-Moon (*nom de plume* for William Trogdon) made his name in literary circles with a highly tour-like book, *Blue Highways*, which describes a car trip through the backroads of the United States. In *PrairyErth* (1991), he switches to the opposing strategy of spatial representation. The book courts the impossible by attempting a verbal mapping of Chase County, Kansas, which leaves no part and no aspect of the territory uncovered. Starting from a graphic map[6] and dividing it, rather arbitrarily (but in accordance with standard cartographic practice) into twelve quadrants (reproduced at the beginning of each chapter), the author explores the geography, fauna, flora, history, economy, agricultural practices, and social life of each quadrant in an

---

6. Though *PrairyErth* contains graphic maps, it is not this feature that makes it into a map-narrative, but rather how the text as a whole covers space, and how the stories that relate to this space are presented in a sequence that has nothing to do with time. Tour-narratives may also contain maps to show the travels of the hero.

rigid order inspired by Japanese writing: from top to bottom and from right to left. Yet there is no compelling reason to read the text in this order. The reader can open the book anywhere to explore one of the quadrants; and instead of following the textual trail through a given quadrant, can freely jump across the whole territory. This freedom of movement stems from the arbitrariness of the map's divisions.

Why Chase County and why Kansas? Because this sparsely populated grassland in a state that most people tend to regard as pitifully deprived of exciting features and natural attractions reveals, on close inspection, the diversity of the seemingly uniform. As a reader comments on Amazon.com: "You couldn't believe how much a book on an insignificant Kansas County can be so haunting." Yet, as Kansas goes, Chase County is not truly run-of-the-mill: it is a hilly county in a generally flat state; it attracts ecologists because it contains the last remnant of the tall grasses that once covered the great plains; and it is the site of one of the most memorable events of American sports history, the 1931 plane crash that took the life of Knute Rockne, the legendary Notre Dame football coach. These features explain in part why Heat-Moon has chosen Chase County for his "deep map"—a map that accounts not only for the present but also for the past that lies buried under the surface of the land, be it as geological formations, archeological sites, or country cemeteries. Through the act of writing, Chase County becomes much more than a special place in a state that symbolizes the ordinary, it becomes the center of the world, as it is naturally for its inhabitants. This center is both absolute and relative: absolute with respect to U.S. geography, because Chase County is situated at the intersection of a line that runs from Seattle to Miami and another that runs from Boston to San Diego, and relative, because wherever the narrator moves, he is situated at the intersection of a meridian and of a parallel that can be followed all around the world and back to the starting position. This imaginary trip suggests that no matter where we are, we are at a place connected to everywhere else in the world, a place where all the roads come together. As one of the countless places that function for their inhabitants as the center of the world, Chase County is both unique and ordinary.

A passage in which Heat-Moon describes his attempt to record every thought that crosses his mind in the time span of one minute reveals the impossible dream that inspires the whole text—the dream of providing an exhaustive image of the territory, a kind of 1:1 map: "The telling on tape of that minute took, of course, sixty seconds, but listening to it, I realized that for an audience other than myself all the important information was missing. . . . I took up a pencil and paper and began trying to give a description of those sixty seconds as a novelist might, and when I hit six pages I stopped—not because I was finished but because I was so far from finishing" (1991, 334–35). Here language, a temporal medium, is unable to keep track of thought, a temporal phenomenon. Even greater is the gap between language and the four-dimensional space-time of the quadrants, because the medium of representation is incommensurable with the represented. The text can only reveal shards and fragments—a recurrent image in *PrairyErth,* as Russell (2000) has shown—of the reality of Chase County. In its mapping of Chase County, *PrairyErth* is both complete and selective: complete because every area of the territory is textually accounted for, and selective in what it chooses to represent.

How can the quadrants of the graphic map of Chase County be turned into language? The idea of the map provides the author with a way to organize the shards of materials he has already dug up from the soil. In the first chapter of the book, he describes how he climbs the highest hill in Chase County, Roniger Hill, and sees the land stretch below like a map. Its (visible) grid of roads reminds him of the invisible grid of maps, "arbitrary quadrants that have nothing inherently to do with the land, little to do with history, and not much to do with my details. . . . Would coordinates lead to connections? Were they themselves the only links we can truly understand? Could they lead into the dark loomings that draw me here?" (15). Yet the project of creating a "topographic map of words" (15) driven by the quadrants is not without its problems, because some quadrants are full of features, while others are largely empty. The blank spaces on the map might be the magnet that attracts Heat-Moon to Chase County (as they attracted the hero of Joseph Conrad's *Heart of Darkness* to Africa), but they are difficult to turn into stories—stories require human agents, and where humans exercise their activity, they leave traces on the land, and the map is no longer blank. On the other hand, the quadrant that contains the only real town in the county, Cottonwood Falls, has so many stories to tell that it cannot be treated in the same framework—that is, a chapter—as the other quadrants. The author solves this problem by appending a section about the town and its rich history to every chapter, somewhat breaking the global pattern. As for the more empty quadrants of the map, they are occasionally filled by importing stories that straddle several areas. For instance, here is how Heat-Moon evokes the Homestead quadrant, whose only feature recorded on the graphic map is an unappealing physical grid of country roads: (1) he imagines what the countryside looks like from studying the map and concludes, from the predominance of the road grid, that he will not like it; (2) he narrates his walk on these roads (by night, to avoid seeing the fences that borders them), his midnight encounter with cops, and his return to a motel in another Kansas county; (3) he describes the habits of the prairie chicken, a bird found in the area; (4) he reports an interview with a farmer who lives outside the quadrant but whose fields are located inside it (the farmer tells about his experiences in France and Germany as a soldier in World War II); and (5) he narrates the plane crash that killed Knute Rockne, though the monument that marks the plane crash is situated in an adjacent quadrant. These slight deviances from an organization that respects the arbitrary grid lines make it possible to achieve what any good topographic or road map should: represent areas of comparable size in the territory by areas of comparable size on a map, or in the case of a word map, by a text of comparable length. Moreover, as the stories send tendrils toward other quadrants, other counties, and other countries, they reveal the connections that the author hoped to discover by letting an arbitrary grid organize his text, and they turn Chase County, Kansas, into the center of a network that stretches far beyond any arbitrary borders, be they political, administrative, or cartographic.

SPACE AS A UNIVERSAL FEATURE OF PLOT

The role of space in the layer of meaning that constitutes the properly narrative content of texts can be conceived on two levels: the general and the particular. On the general level, space can be regarded as an indispensable element of plot, as we will call the medium-independent cognitive structure that defines narrativity. It was Jurij Lotman who first theorized plot in terms of spatial categories. His argument is worth summarizing in some detail because it anticipates the work of present-day cognitive scholars such as Lakoff, Johnson, Fauconnier, and Turner on the importance of spatial metaphors for human thought. Lotman begins by observing that the "language of spatial relations" (such as "high-low," "left-right," "near-far," or "open-closed) is a "basic mean of comprehending reality" (1970, 218). The human mind operates by associating these conceptual pairs with nonspatial ideas, using them as empty signifiers capable of being filled with a wide variety of meanings. The contrast "high-low" can, for instance, stand for good vs. evil, far vs. near, movement vs. immobility, freedom vs. slavery, culture vs. nature, or harmony vs. strife. This spatial imagery operates in literature in both archetypal, culture-transcending ways and in idiosyncratic patterns characteristic of individual writers.[7]

---

7. While Lotman concentrates on verbal art, Lakoff and Johnson (1980) and Mark Turner (1996) focus their attention on spatial metaphors frozen into ordinary language. True to phenomenological doctrine, these authors believe that the most fundamental human experience consists of apprehending oneself as a body located in space. The embodied nature of the mind is reflected in language by families of metaphors that concretize abstract concepts in terms of

The conceptual pairs that underlie narrative (as well as lyrical) texts are made possible by what Lotman regards as an even more fundamental spatial concept—namely, the topographical concept of boundary, which structures storyworlds into differentiated zones obeying different rules. Boundaries forbid crossing, but they are generally not impermeable enough to prevent violations. This ambiguity is fundamental to eventfulness, the cornerstone of narrativity. Lotman contrasts "plotless" texts, which define and respect a topological system of boundaries (e.g., purely descriptive texts), and "plotted" (or narrative) texts, in which these boundaries are violated. But even plotted texts presuppose the static structure that Lotman regards as plotless: "The movement of the plot, the event, is the crossing of that forbidden border which the plotless structure establishes. It is not an event when the hero moves within the space assigned to him. A plot can always be reduced to a basic episode—the crossing of the basic topological border in the plot's spatial structure" (1970, 238). Eventfulness is dependent on the strength of the boundary: a poor girl marrying a rich man is an event capable of generating narrative interest in societies with strongly stratified social classes, but much less so in egalitarian societies. Not particularly eventful episodes can, however, start a causal chain that leads to a narratively significant event. The crossing of boundaries that characterizes eventfulness can happen any number of times during the course of a story, often reversing the consequences of a previous crossing and restoring a previous order: "If we interpret the plot as an expanded event, the crossing of a semantic border, then the reversibility of plot becomes evident: the surmounting of the same barrier within the limits of the same semantic field can be extended into two plot chains running in opposite directions" (238).

This spatial conception of plot does not limit narrative to stories in which the hero travels across the regions of a physically or politically divided world; boundaries can be literally spatial, but they can also be social (rich vs. poor), ontological (gods vs. humans), or biological (animals vs. humans; living vs. dead). Since spatial categories are able to model concepts that are not themselves spatial in nature, any plot can be visually diagrammed in set-theoretical terms—for instance, through a Venn diagram augmented with arrows. Yet even when the boundaries are social or ontological in essence, they tend to

---

bodies moving through or situated in space. Words like "up" and "down," "front" and "back," "high" and "low," organize space using the body as a point of reference. Due to the erect position of the body, up and down are the most prolific sources of metaphors: for example, happy is up, sad is down; more is up, less is down; and so on. Front and back are mainly used as metaphors of time: in our culture, the future is ahead and the past is behind. Other spatial schemata that provide important sources of metaphors are the conduit, the journey, the path, and the container. See Dannenberg (2008) for an analysis of some narrative scenes and plots in terms of these frozen metaphors.

be associated with physical regions: for instance, humans live on the earth and the gods in heaven; the rich live in the Hamptons and the poor live in the slums; the living inhabit the surface of the earth and the dead dwell in the underworld. The spatiality of plot thus presents an "oreo-cookie" structure: on the highest level of abstraction, plot presupposes a world structured by the spatial concept of boundary; the areas delimited by these boundaries can be associated with any kind of concept as long as these concepts enter into binary oppositions, and the spatiality of these concepts is often metaphorical. But on the surface, these concepts frequently receive what Lotman calls "spatial realization," and it is by means of physical travel that the hero crosses forbidden boundaries.

Like all formal models of narrative, Lotman's conception of plot is not a schema that can be applied to texts like a cookie cutter, automatically and unambiguously revealing their semantic structure; it is rather a flexible analytical instrument whose application to a given text depends on interpretative decisions and yields variable results. "Eveline," for instance, can be modeled in at least two ways: as the story of an actual near-crossing, which takes Eveline out of her home but stops at the boundary (the harbor), followed by an expected future crossing back to her home and everything that it symbolizes; or as the story of a nonactualized crossing, in which Eveline escapes from her life in Dublin and moves to Buenos Ayres. In the first analysis, there are two crossings, but one lies in a disnarrated future; in the second analysis, the text is plotless on the factual level, since no change really happens, but it embeds a virtual plot. The usefulness of Lotman's model depends, however, on whether or not the text's relevant semantic features (or themes) are associated with distinct spatial areas. When spatial concretization takes place, the concept of boundary crossing can be applied quite literally; but when it does not, the idea of crossing becomes a metaphor so thin that one might just as well replace it with a "change of state" or "switch of value of a semantic feature."

SPACE AS A PARTICULAR FEATURE OF PLOT

While the approach sketched above uses spatial concepts to build a universal model of plot, an approach concerned with the particular will focus on those texts that make the characters' experience of space into a prominent narrative theme, as well as on the attribution of symbolic meaning to the various regions and landmarks of the storyworld.

In the cosmology of traditional societies, space is ontologically divided into a profane world (the realm of everyday life) and a sacred world (inhabited by supernatural beings) with holy sites functioning as portals between the two. The narrative response to these cosmologies and topologies is a symbolic geography diversified into regions where different events and experiences take place—where life, in other words, is governed by different physical, psychological, social, or cultural rules. In fairy tales or computer games, for instance, the symbolic map of the narrative world might associate the castle with power, mountain tops with communication with the sacred, open areas with danger, closed areas with security, and so on. This symbolic organization of space is not limited to fantastic texts: narrative worlds can be structured by oppositions between colonizing countries and colonized regions; between life in the capital and life in the province (Balzac's *Human Comedy*); between home and away from home (*The Odyssey*); between the knowable and the unknowable (the town vs. the castle in Kafkas's *The Castle*); or between landscapes that speak differently to the imagination (Swann's way vs. Guermantes's way in Proust's *Remembrance of Things Past*).

Architecturally, as well as plot-functionally, narrative space can be described in terms of the partitions, both natural and cultural, that organize it into thematically relevant subspaces: walls, hallways, political boundaries, rivers, and mountains, as well as in terms of the openings and passageways that allow these subspaces to communicate: doors, windows, bridges, highways, tunnels, and passes. Besides horizontal partitions, narrative can also present vertical ones, corresponding to what Thomas Pavel (1986) calls "salient ontologie." These ontologies can oppose the world of everyday life to a world of magic, dreams to reality, images to existents, or, in narratives with embedded stories, higher to lower levels of fictionality. Whereas horizontal partitions divide the geography of the storyworld, vertical partitions create ontological layers within the narrative universe.

The lived experience of space offers a particularly rich source of thematization. Some stories present space as closed and confining (prison narratives; Anne Frank's diary), others as open and liberating (narratives of exploration; many travel narratives), and still others as open and alienating (stories of wandering aimlessly in a hostile environment; modern representations of the city). Confined space occasionally turns into a field of endless discoveries, as does Robinson Crusoe's island. Through its immensity, space might be perceived as separating (narratives of exile; *The Odyssey*) or its existence might be denied by technology (telecommunications; travel through teletransportation). Narrative may also highlight the importance of our sense of embodiment for the experience of space by featuring a protagonist whose body grows or shrinks out of human proportions. Novels like *Gulliver's Travels* or *Alice in Wonderland* de-automatize our relation to space by showing how movement, navigation, the handling of objects, and interpersonal relations are affected by a change of scale. The most radical thematizations of space are those that involve alternative or logically inconsistent worlds. An example of experimentation with the dimensionality of space is Edwin Abbott's 1884 novella *Flatland*, a narrative that depicts everyday life and cognition issues within worlds of two, and then one, dimensions. But when the narrator is finally transported into a three-dimensional world, and asks its inhabitants to take him to a four-dimensional world, the three-dimensional creatures tell him that no such thing exists. The imagination can subtract dimensions from, but not add them to, our three-dimensional perception of reality.

EMOTIONAL VERSUS STRATEGIC SPACE

To conclude this chapter, we would like to outline two contrasting relations to space that play a major role in shaping narrative content: emotional and strategic. In the emotional relation, spatial objects matter for what experiences they afford, for what aesthetic feelings they inspire, and for what memories they bring to mind. Emotional space has a special affinity with stories and with memories—it is because they are linked to stories that spatial objects inspires special feelings, either positive or negative. For instance, legends relating to a certain landscape create an emotional attachment to this landscape, even for people who do not believe these legends. Since emotional space involves a lived, embodied experience, it is best represented by pictures taken from a horizontal perspective, because this perspective represents the perspective of the human body.

While emotional space typically takes the form of an appealing or frightening landscape, strategic space is best symbolized by a chessboard. The squares on a chessboard have no intrinsic emotional value for the player; they only matter because of the actions that they allow to perform. For instance, you want to move your rook to a certain square because by doing so you can capture one of your opponent's pieces. In strategic space, it is very important to see how objects relate to each other. Strategic space is best represented in map view as a vertical projection in which no object hides any other.

For the majority of us, the most deeply emotional conception of space is the opposition between home and away from home. This is why *The Odyssey* has never ceased to move readers. Far from enjoying his nine-year trip through the known and the unknown world as a tourist eager to discover new countries, Odysseus has only one goal in mind: getting back to Ithaca, because returning to his homeland and restoring the order that was destroyed during his absence is a matter of fulfilling his destiny. When Odysseus is believed dead by the people on Ithaca, his fate strikes them as particularly miserable because his body will not rest in his native soil, where his ancestors are buried. When he is asked by the king of Scheria (his last stop before returning home) to identify himself, he does so in terms of name, ancestry, and place of origin: "I am Odysseus, son of Laertes, known to the world / for every kind of craft— my fame has reached the skies. / Sunny Ithaca is my home" (1997, Book 9, ll. 21–23). Yet it is not as a particularly sunny spot offering easy living that Odysseus yearns for Ithaca. If settling down in a beautiful and fertile landscape were his prime objective, he would have remained on Calypso's island, a lush paradise where a beautiful goddess offers him immortality. While he finds at night some amorous pleasures with the goddess, Odysseus spends his days on a barren rock overlooking the sea, pining for Ithaca, and rendered thoroughly passive by his captivity. On this barren rock, he finds a landscape reminiscent of Ithaca's, which he describes to the king of Scheria as "a rugged land but good for raising sons / —and myself, I know no sweeter sight on earth / than a man's native country" (Book 9, ll. 30–32). Offering few opportunities for agriculture, suitable for raising goats but not cows, Ithaca builds character through the difficulty of eking a living out of its harsh, rocky landscape.

In *The Odyssey*, as in many other narratives, emotional relations to space are the projection of affective relations to people;[8] in the case of Odysseus, his attachment to Ithaca cannot be separated from his love for his wife, Penelope, his son, Telemachus, and his aging father, Laertes. When Calypso asks him how Penelope compares to herself, the goddess, and why he is refusing her offer of immortality, Odysseus cannot find any other explanation than the simple desire to return home: "Look at my wise Penelope. She falls far short of you, / your beauty, your stature. She is mortal after all / and you, you never age or die.... / Nevertheless I long—I pine, all my days— / to travel home and see the dawn of my return" (159). The connection between love and attachment to Ithaca is beautifully symbolized by the marital bed that Odysseus built for himself and Penelope before his departure for Troy. After Odysseus slays all of Penelope's suitors in the Great Hall of his palace in Ithaca, Penelope refuses

---

8. Nowhere is this more evident than in Proust's (1981 [1913–27]) *A la recherche du temps perdu*: for Marcel, the hero and narrator, the village of Combray or the Champs Elysées in Paris are magical places when, as a child, he is in love with the women he sees there: Gilberte Swann and the duchess of Guermantes, whose aristocratic lineage brings history to life in the child's imagination. But years later, when Gilberte has married and he has become a regular in the duchess's social circle, seeing her as a betrayed wife rather than as the incarnation of a glorious past, these places inspire in him only boredom or indifference. They will regain their aura when, after stumbling on uneven pavement, Marcel recaptures his past, together with the spaces that served as its stages (Lutwack 1984, 63–66).

to recognize him as her husband until he gives her a sign known only to the couple. To test Odysseus she asks him to move her bed to another room. This is impossible, replies Odysseus: he built it on the trunk of an ancient olive tree, and its feet are the roots, inseparably attached to Ithaca's soil. The roots that stretch into the earth also signify where people properly belong. Love, family, ancestry, identity, and memory: these are the values that bind Odysseus to Ithaca and that make his return home necessary for him to truly be who he is.

Emotional space is not necessarily linked to happy memories, a sense of security or pleasant discoveries—the kind of positive emotions that Gaston Bachelard explores in his seminal *Poetics of Space,* associating them with intimate places, such as the house, drawers, chest, wardrobes, nests, shells, and miniatures. Yi-Fy Tuan's book *Landscapes of Fear* (2013 [1979]) complements Bachelard's geography of happiness with the opposite. Odysseus is familiar with such landscapes: before returning to Ithaca he must pass the test of Charybdis and Scylla, and descend into the Land of the Dead. The fear inspired by the six-headed monster of Charybdis and the whirlpool of Scylla is only temporary, at least for those who survive the tests; but the Land of the Dead instills a much deeper fear, since it reveals a fate that no mortal escapes. The ghastly discovery of the permanent mode of existence of the dead—spectral beings, lacking bodies, starved for news of their loved ones, and living in a world deprived of stories, because nothing ever happens in it—retrospectively puts in proper perspective Odysseus's refusal of the immortality later offered later by Calypso. (Retrospectively for the reader, for Calypso's offer is narrated before the visit to the Land of the Dead, though these episodes take place in opposite order.)

Odysseus is not only an emotional man who longs and frequently weeps for his home and family, he is also a "cool tactician" (as one of those famous Homeric epithets describes him) who knows how to design schemes that take advantage of the particular configuration of the environment. He entertains, in other words, a strategic relation to space. In the episode where Odysseus slays the suitors of Penelope, his strategic planning takes the form of a keen attention to doors, rooms, and passageways. Let's review the situation. Penelope (who might or might not be aware that Odysseus has returned to Ithaca—the text is compatible with both interpretations) has agreed to marry the suitor who is able to string the bow of her husband. About eighty suitors gather in the Great Hall of the royal palace for a banquet and for the test. Shortly before the beginning of the trial, Odysseus, who has taken the appearance of a beggar, slips out into the courtyard with the swineherd and the cowherd, the only men in Ithaca faithful to him (beside his son), and reveals his identity. They burst into tears, but Odysseus puts an end to their effusions and orders them back into the Hall, for fear somebody might hear them while they are outside. The slaughter that is going to take place must be kept secret, because society is dominated by family feuds, and the relatives of the suitors could come to their aid if they knew what is going on. Then Odysseus locks the door of the courtyard to prevent possibilities for escape. He also orders the door of all the servants' rooms shut, so that they will not come out when they hear the screams of dying men. Finally the "games" begin, the suitors each taking their turn trying to string the bow. Everybody fails. The beggar (Odysseus) is allowed by Telemachus and Penelope to give it a try, despite the loud opposition of the suitors, but first Telemachus sends his mother back to her quarters to spare her the sight of the coming massacre. Odysseus easily strings the bow and then directs his arrows toward the suitors, who are trapped without weapons inside the Hall. Soon Odysseus runs out of arrows and Telemachus must retrieve weapons from an upstairs storeroom. But he forgets to lock the door. The goatherd (a traitor) manages to sneak into the storeroom through a shaft in the rafters and provides weapons to the suitors. Through a switch of momentum worthy of Hollywood, the outcome seems for a while uncertain; but Athena directs the blows of the suitors away from their targets, and all of them are killed; only the bard and the messenger are spared by Odysseus. The women who served as concubines to the suitors are made to clean the Hall of the blood before being hanged in the courtyard. The cruel punishment is justified within the text as a rite of cleansing that purifies Ithaca of the "varmint" that has accumulated during Odysseus's absence. To our contemporary sensibilities, however, the atrocities that Odysseus performs in order to purify Ithaca stand as a warning against an excessive emotional attachment to one's lineage and place of origin.

Strategic plotting of narrative space is not only an activity in which characters engage, it is also an integral part of the creative process. Homer designed the layout of Odysseus's palace to allow the defeat of the suitors, but he also gave them access to the storeroom to create narrative suspense. In other examples, when Proust plotted Marcel's discovery of the lesbian activities between Mlle Vinteuil and her friend, he conveniently arranged an open window and a hidden post of observation; and when Conan Doyle plotted the case of the "Speckled Band" (where a snake kills the victim), he configured the crime scene as a closed room that makes the intrusion of a murderer impossible.

The contrast between strategic and emotional space bears strong affinities with the contrast between space and place. While emotions typically relate to specific locations within space, rather than embracing space as a whole, strategic planning concerns possible movement, and movement requires spatial extension. But the two dichotomies are not entirely equivalent, and they can be cross-classified. Our discussion of *The Odyssey* has already illustrated the combinations of emotion + place and strategy + space. Though rarer, the other two possibilities are not inexistent. Place acquires strategic significance when there is a certain location that needs to be controlled in order to win a battle or a game, such as the Bosphorus in World War I or the inside of the goal in a game of soccer. As for space, it combines with emotion when it allows movement, and this movement elicits positive or negative feelings. An example of an emotionally positive relation to space is the sense of freedom that the heroes of Jack Kerouac's *On the Road* (1997 [1957]) attain as they travel through the U.S. or the experience of the nomad in Deleuze and Guattari's rather romanticized conception of nomadic existence. Another kind of space invested with emotions is the labyrinth, a space where you get lost. The theme of disorientation, which plays a major role in twentieth-century literature, illustrates an emotionally negative relation to space (Bernaerts 2012).

Divide and conquer: this is how the human mind deals with the immensity and abstractness of space and turns it into an instrument of discovery— whether in geography or narratology. As we mentioned in chapter 1, many of the thinkers who have focused their mind on space (Deleuze and Guattari, Harvey, Lefebvre, Tuan) have come up with dichotomies or trichotomies. Our distinction between emotional and strategic relations to space is yet another example of this tradition. It would be easy to provide multiple illustrations of the dichotomy in literature and other narrative media, but in keeping with the narratological spirit of this book, we are less interested in the interpretation of individual texts than in the elaboration of analytical tools that can reveal regularities in the role of space and place across many different narratives. Our survey can be thought of as a map with a very large scale; we hope that it will inspire narratologists and geographers to zoom in and discover features of the territory that could not be observed from the distance we chose.

CHAPTER 3

Maps and Narrative

MAPS ARE AMONG THE MOST BELOVED and the most critically scrutinized of cultural artifacts. Postmodern theory has put them in the crosshairs of a critique of knowledge and representation. The impossibility of creating a perfectly accurate 1:1 map is sometimes invoked as an argument against scientific objectivity and the dream of total knowledge.[1] The "deconstruction" of

---

1. The impossibility of a map both complete and accurate has been "demonstrated" by both Lewis Carroll and Jorge Luis Borges. In *Sylvie and Bruno* (1982, 727) Carroll argues that a map of a 1:1 scale (the only scale that allows a complete duplication of information) would cover the entire world. It would consequently block the sun, and the grass would die, to the consternation of the farmers. Since this map, by definition, must represent everything, including every blade of grass, it would be necessarily unfaithful to the territory. The question of the 1:1 map is also taken up by Borges in "On Exactitude in Science," a text attributed by Borges to the seventeenth-century author Suárez Miranda. In a certain empire where the art of cartography reaches perfection, a map is made whose size is that of the empire and coincides "point for point with it" (1998, 325). But the following generation, "who were not so fond of the study of geography as their Forebearers had been, saw that that vast Map was useless" (1998, 325). They consequently let the sun and wind destroy it. In "Partial Magic in the Quixote," Borges demonstrates the impossibility of a complete map regardless of scale: if such a map existed, it should contain "a map of the map, which should contain a map of the map of the map, and so on to infinity" (1983, 196). Both of these arguments can be defeated if one allows the map to be located outside the territory, for instance on another planet, but then the argument can be repeated on the scale of the universe. The debates about the impossibility of a 1:1 map ignore, however, the fact that creating such a map would be a pragmatic aberration: if maps are useful it is because they are transportable and easily consultable, and

maps as instruments of power undercuts their claim to truth. But lovers of maps remain legion and put them to multiple uses other than territorial domination: travelers and hikers depend on them for orientation; graphic designers treasure their ability to represent a wide variety of data; semioticians are fascinated by their complex mode of signification, which includes all three types of signs—icons, indices, and symbols (Bertin 1998; Schlichtmann 1999a, 1999b); artists turn them into raw material for collages and world-creation (Harmon 2004, 2009); art lovers view them as objects of beauty; authors write novels about map-making;[2] and just about everybody, from children to would-be poets, uses them as springboards for the imagination. No type of image induces more powerful dreams than a map, because as the eye travels the map, the mind travels the territory. As Miguel de Cervantes put it so well: one can "journey over all the universe in a map without the expense and fatigue of travelling, without suffering the inconveniences of heat, hunger, and thirst" (Muehrcke and Muehrcke 1974, 324).

It is therefore not surprising that maps have long been associated with stories, another powerful catalyst of imaginative activity. When narrative uses the dual modalities of language and maps, each of these modalities expresses what the other cannot do by itself—or can only do very inefficiently. Maps, because they represent a vertical, disembodied perspective—what philosopher Thomas Nagel has called a "view from nowhere"—are not well suited to express a subject's lived experience in an environment, while language-based narrative, because it relies on a temporal medium, is not well suited to convey a mental image of what we have called "strategic space" in an earlier chapter, namely a network of relations between objects. But when language and map complement each other, space can be represented in both its emotional/phenomenological and strategic dimensions.

---

if they present these two properties, it is because they leave out some information—this is why we have road maps and topographical maps and tourist maps—and because they present the selected data in reduced form.

2. Relatively recent novels and plays about map-making include: *Translations* by Brian Friel (1981), about the translation of Gaelic place names in the British Ordnance Survey Maps of Ireland in the nineteenth century; Thomas Pynchon's *Mason and Dixon* (1997), about the land surveyors who traced the line between Pennsylvania, Maryland, Delaware, and West Virginia; James Cowan's *A Mapmaker's Dream* (1996), about the meditations of Fra Mauro, a late medieval cartographer at the Court of Venice; Andrea Barrett's *Servant of the Map* (2002), about the creation of geological maps of the Himalayas by the British in the nineteenth century; Reif Larsen's *The Complete Works of T. S. Spivet* (2009), about a genius child cartographer whose drawings fill the novel; and Michel Houellebecq's *La carte et le territoire* [The Map and the Territory] (2010), about an artist who becomes famous by taking photos of Michelin maps. In his view, the map is much more interesting than the territory—and an image of the map much more interesting than the map itself.

MAPPING THE VARIOUS KINDS OF TEXTUAL SPACE

The relations between graphic maps and narrative can be mapped in a number of ways. First, maps can be used to represent three of the four kinds of narrative space defined in the introduction. The only kind that does not inspire mapping is the third, the space taken by the text itself, because this space is simply the number of dimensions occupied by the text, from zero to three (or four if we take time into account), and it is the same for entire categories of texts. What differs from text to text is how this space is used and perceived by the reader, rather than its intrinsic configuration.[3]

Maps of the Spatial Context of the Text

These maps are drawn by literary historians to show how literary texts are anchored in actual geography. Since the focus is on the nurturing role of the real world in the production of literary texts, not on the storyworld, *per se,* they consist of marks drawn by the historian on preexisting geographic maps. A good source of this type of map is *The Atlas of Literature,* edited by Malcom Bradbury (1998), or Franco Moretti's *Atlas of the European Novel, 1800–1900* (1998). Here are two examples of the phenomena which are mapped in these books:

Cultural landscapes: A map in *The Atlas of Literature* indicates the sites of literary activity on the street map of central Vienna in the early twentieth century. Shown on the map are the location of the houses of famous figures (Freud in the Berggasse; Stefan Zweig in the Kochstrasse), as well their favorite meeting places: the Café Central, frequented by Robert Musil and Leon Trotsky; or the Café Griersteidl, frequented by Hermann Bahr, Arthur Schnitzel, Hugo von Hoffmansthal, Siegmund Freud, and Karl Kraus.[4]

Geographic location of plots: One map in Moretti's atlas traces the itineraries of the protagonists of sixteenth-century picaresque novels, such as *Don*

---

3. Print narratives differ from each other in the thickness of the book, but this dimension cannot be represented in a classical map view since it flattens the z axis. It would take an elevation view (horizontal) to show that *War and Peace* is thicker than *The Death of Ivan Ilyich,* for example.

4. There is a large body of literature focusing on the sites of literary activity. Hendrix (2008) and Trubek (2011) focus, for example, on the writers' homes. There are hundreds of guides to literary life in particular cities, regions, and countries. Morgan (2003) and Powell (2006) are examples focusing, respectively, on New York City and Paris. For some publishers like The Little Bookroom (http://littlebookroom.com/guidebooks.html), guidebooks of this sort make up a major part of their lists.

Quixote, Lazarillo de Tormes, and *La Picara Justina.* The locations identified on the map are all real-world towns: Madrid, Toledo, Seville, and the route of pilgrimages to Santiago de Compostela. Another of Moretti's diagrams locates the beginnings and endings of the plots of several of Jane Austen's novels on the map of England. This type of map represents both the fictional world and the real world; but the focus is on the intertextual space of several novels, rather than on any particular storyworld. The absence of place names specific to the novels suggests that the primary goal of the cartographer is to show how Spanish or English geography inspired literary works, rather than to illustrate how Spanish or English geography is integrated into storyworlds.

Another type of map that falls into the category of spatial context is a map that shows where the text is located as a physical object. When the text is contained in a single volume, this could be a map of where this volume can be found in a library. With the advent of digital technology, GPS, and mobile computing, the activity of locating texts in real space has been developed into games and artistic events. In a game of "geocaching," where the "treasure" is a fragment of a story that the players try to put together, a map maintained by the designers could indicate where the fragments are hidden. An example of a project that uses a map of spatial context is the cell phone-based locative narrative [murmur], to be discussed in chapter 5.

For the fans of a certain novel whose plot is set in the real world (or more precisely in a fictional world that contains counterparts of real-world locations), following the movements of the hero is a way to relive the pleasure taken in the novel, while retracing the life of the author in real space is a way to participate in a literary cult. The phenomenon of literary tourism (Bulson 2006) can combine both of these experiences. For instance, a literary tour that one of us took in St. Petersburg visited various landmarks in the life of Dostoevsky and also followed the itinerary of Raskolnikoff, the hero of *Crime and Punishment,* from his miserable dwelling (now situated in an affluent district) to the courtyard of the house in which he killed the old lady. Similarly, a visit to the childhood home of Laura Ingalls Wilder, author of the popular series *Little House on the Prairie,* immerses the visitor both in the environment in which the author grew up and in the storyworld she created. Her books are so precise in describing the details of her childhood home—now a museum—that quotes from them are used as interpretive captions for visitors. The maps of these literary tours would be another example of spatial context mapping.

Maps of Spatial Form

A map of spatial form is not a geographic map, but rather a diagram of formal relations between narrative elements. These maps capture structures of signification that only reveal themselves to the mind when it contemplates the text from a time-transcending, totalizing perspective. The spatial form approach was particularly popular among scholars of the structuralist school because of the movement's indebtedness to Saussure's view of language as a system that must be described synchronically rather than diachronically. Through its arrangement of the themes of the text into a geometrical shape, Greimas's semiotic square (1966) is a classical example of a map of spatial form, even though its corners represent different moments in the narrative time line. It may thus be seen as a spatialization of time.

A common model for maps of spatial form is the Venn diagram, which is borrowed from set theory. For instance, Franco Moretti proposes a diagram of social relations in Flaubert's *L'Education sentimentale* in which characters are grouped in different but overlapping sets, depending on who invites whom for dinner. (Figure 3.1 is our own redrawing of Moretti's diagram.) Characters situated at the intersection of several sets are the most socially mobile, since they frequent many circles of society. The hero, Frédéric Moreau, has access to all the sets but the virtual one he dreams of: a circle centered on him and the woman he loves, Mme Arnoux. The novel tells the story of Frédéric's repeated, and always unsuccessful, efforts to conquer this forbidden territory, but the diagram shows no trace of these attempts, since it is limited to a synchronic apprehension. On Moretti's diagram, the sets are defined on the basis of the total number of dinner invitations that take place in the novel. Yet who gets invited where evolves during the time span covered by the plot. The cartographer represents this evolution by redrawing the borders of one of the sets, the Dambreuse circle, to represent its state before and after 1848. (The Dambreuse circle after 1848 includes the pre-1848 circle.) This modest attempt to introduce a temporal dimension into a map of spatial form points to a larger domain of narrative cartography, a domain no longer limited by the representation of spatial phenomena: the diagramming of plot (which falls outside the scope of this chapter), because it involves time and the minds of characters. (For a fuller diagramming of plot, see Ryan 2007.)[5]

Another type of map that can be regarded as a representation of spatial form is the database map that underlies digital narratives organized

---

5. Herman (2012) and Moretti (2005) also propose diagrams relevant to the analysis of narrative, but they do not focus on plot.

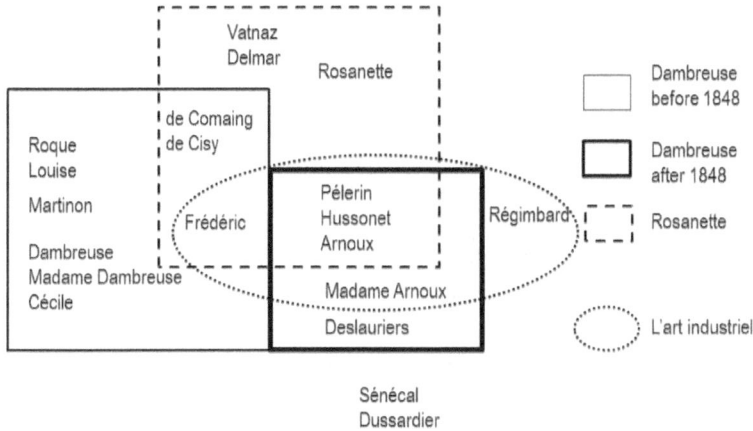

FIGURE 3.1. A map of spatial form: Franco Moretti's analysis of character relations in Flaubert's *L'Education sentimentale* (redrawn by authors from Moretti's *Atlas of the European Novel*)

according to the protocol known as hypertext, a term that designates a network of fragments connected by links. These maps can take various shapes, depending on the organization of the nodes and links (Ryan 2006, chapter 5): a network containing loops (preferred in postmodern hypertexts for its ability to represent the experience of being lost in a maze), a tree with branches issuing from a single root node (the structure typical of *Choose Your Own Adventures* stories), a wheel (preferred in informational web sites for its ability to control the reader's itinerary), and a vector with side-branches (preferred in children's stories for making it possible to follow a linear plot while looking at "roadside attractions" such as animations). The space represented by hypertext maps is a purely metaphorical space since it bears no relation to the physical space of the storyworld. And while the maps are represented as two-dimensional diagrams, they stand for something that has no spatial extension, or at best one dimension, since links consist of a "go to" instruction targeting a certain address in computer memory. A text mapped as a two-dimensional network exists in computer memory as a one-dimensional string of zeros and ones.[6] Textual space, in the sense given by hypertext theorists (Bolter 1991), does not really exist at all: it is entirely a creation of the mapping algorithm.

---

6. Turing machines, which can compute anything computable, operate on a long string, or tape, of binary data.

Maps of Narrative Space, or Storyworld: Gulliver's Travels *and* Treasure Island

From a narratological point of view, maps of narrative space can be classified into two categories: extradiegetic (i.e., external to the storyworld) and intradiegetic (internal to it). A good example of extradiegetic mapping of the storyworld is the maps that illustrate *Gulliver's Travels* (2001 [1726; amended in 1735]), Jonathan Swift's classic satire of human societies and eighteenth-century travel writing (figure 3.2). Gulliver, a ship's doctor, embarks on four trips, during which his ship is taken off course by storms, pirate attacks, or mutinies. He lands on previously unknown islands and discovers societies of supernatural creatures—the diminutive Lilliputians, the giant Brobdingnagians, the arts-and-science-worshipping but unpractical Laputians, the savage human-like Yahoos, and the reason-despising, tolerant but righteous, horse-like Houyhnhms—which, for all their strangeness, either mimic or offer an inverted image of some aspect of human nature. At the end of each adventure Gulliver is rescued by another ship and returned to England. The world of *Gulliver's Travels* thus combines fabulous countries with actual places: Lilliput lies off the shore of Sumatra, Brobdingnag is a peninsula jutting out of California, Gulliver reaches Laputa after being blown from somewhere near Tonquin in Indochina, and the land of the Houyhnhms is near Tasmania (Moore 1941, 221–23). The integration of the imaginary countries within real-world geography is reinforced by frequent references to latitude and longitude (even though, at the time of writing, the technology for precise measurements of longitude had not yet been developed): "About an Hour before we saw the Pirates, I had taken an Observation and found we were in the Latitude of 46 N. and of Longitude 183" (Swift 145). These measurements are complemented by precise indications of the miles traveled or of the size of the various islands. But all these notations come to nothing for future travelers, because Gulliver fails to say whether the longitude is E or W!

Travel writing and atlases were in high demand in the early eighteenth century. "Popular taste demanded maps in books of voyages," writes Frederick Bracher (1944, 70), "and [Swift] would give them maps." Why are the maps extradiegetic rather than intradiegetic? Since Gulliver discovers the various islands, they could not have been a part of the atlas of the known world when he departed for his journeys. Nor could they be part of a revised atlas created on the basis of the information provided by Gulliver after his return to England, because, as he tells us, the leading cartographer of the time, Herman Moll, refused to take his tales into consideration:

MAPS AND NARRATIVE • 51

FIGURE 3.2. Maps from Jonathan Swift's *Gulliver's Travels*: Lilliput and Blefuscu off the coast of Sumatra (left); Bobdingnag as peninsula on California's coast (right)

I lay all Night in my Canoe; and repeating my Voyage early in the Morning, I arrived in seven Hours to the *South-East* Point of *New Holland*. This confirmed me in the opinion I have long entertained, that the *Maps* and *Charts* place this Country at least three Degrees more to the *East* than it really is; which Thought I communicated many Years ago to my worthy Friend Mr. *Herman Moll*, and gave him my Reasons for it, although he hath rather chosen to follow other Authors. (Swift 260–61)

Herman Moll, a historical figure, produced a world atlas whose title, "New and Correct Map of the Whole World," seems to have been expressly devised for the purpose of justifying the postmodern critique of maps as authoritarian claims to truth. Moll's atlas relied in part on the reports of William Dampier, a sometimes pirate in the service of the British crown who circumnavigated the world several times. Through the wealth of its measurements, Gulliver's narrative could have fulfilled the same kind of cartographic function as Dampier's reports, but to no avail, since the fictional Moll chose to follow other authors. (If he had believed Gulliver, his atlas could have filled the blank spaces with creatures no less fantastic than one-eyed people, three-legged men, or monstrous hybrids of man and animal, all of which medieval cartographers placed on the frontiers of the known world, basing their maps on the unverifiable yarns of travelers.)[7]

While the fictional Moll disregards Gulliver's information, the maps inserted in the novel are doubly indebted to the atlas of the real-life Moll: they not only imitate its graphic style, they literally copy from it the contour of the actual coast lines (Bracher 1944, 63), such as the coast of California on the map of Brobdingnag. The inclusion of maps that look like real-world documents reinforces the fake claims to truth performed by the novel. It could be argued that all texts of classical fiction involve a denial of their own fictionality (by "classical," I mean striving toward immersive illusion rather than reflecting on their own textuality), but this denial is particularly prominent in the eighteenth century's predilection for narrative modes that imitate a genre of documentary discourse, be it a diary, autobiography, personal letter, editorial preface—or travel writing. In addition to this fake claim of truth, which extends to the reader an invitation to make-believe, the maps also make a genuine truth claim for the text as a whole, since by combining imaginary and real-world locations, they vouch for the real-world relevance of the satire.

While they strengthen the reality effect of the text, the maps of *Gulliver's Travels* provide little help to the reader in following the plot. Since each map focuses on one of the islands visited by Gulliver (or on several when they are grouped into an archipelago), none of them can show the itinerary of the sea journey in its totality. As for the islands, they are represented on too small a scale for the maps to be able to trace the movements of Gulliver within their territory. But following these movements exactly is not particularly important to the reader, since the geography of the islands does not really play a strategic role in the plot: the focus of the text is more on the description of the culture of the islands than on the adventures of Gulliver. The shape of the islands is therefore largely arbitrary.

Another reason for the failure of the maps to facilitate the mental simulation of the plot is their many discrepancies with respect to the text. The literary geographers Frederick Bracher and John Robert Moore have produced a long list of their infidelities: they contain numerous misspellings; they situate some towns on the wrong island; they blatantly ignore the text by locating

---

7. Swift satirizes the survival of this medieval habit in the eighteenth century in the following quatrain:

> So Geographers in *Afric*-Maps
> With Savage-Pictures fill their gaps;
> And o'er unhabitable Downs
> Place Elephants foe want of Towns.
> (Swift, "On Poetry: A Rhapsody," ll. 177–80)

landmarks in the west of an island when the text situates them in the southeast; and so on. Some of these errors can be attributed to the engraver, who might have misread the annotations on the drawings. But if the maps are inconsistent with respect to the text, it is mainly because Gulliver's narration is itself inconsistent and impossible to map. Here are three examples noted by John Robert Moore:

- Luggnagg is located at 29 degrees N. and 140 degrees E., and Balnirabi at 46 degrees N. and 177 degrees W. Yet the two islands are only separated by 150 miles—something impossible on a globe of the size of the Earth. Moore (226) concludes that Luggnagg is both northwest and southwest of Balnirabi.
- Gulliver's first shipwreck, according to the latitude and longitude indications, happens in the middle of Australia (221).
- The length given for Brobdingnag, 6000 miles, combined with its latitude, approximately 50 degrees N., means that the peninsula would wraps around the earth, reaching from California to Northern Europe, since the distance between meridians gets smaller toward the poles. This leads Moore to ask: "Was Swift so little in the habit of consulting a globe that he could not visualize the corrections needed for a map on Mercator's projection?" (219).

There are three possible explanations for the absurdity of Gulliver's geographic observations: (1) Swift's ignorance of geography; (2) the unreliability of Gulliver's narration; and (3) the configuration of the storyworld itself. In case (1), Swift wanted to create a consistent storyworld that adds a few imaginary places to real-world geography, and he wanted this world to be mappable on the basis of the narrator's declarations, but he failed in his project; in case (2), the storyworld is consistent, but Gulliver's measurements are false; therefore, the mapmaker should be entitled to ignore them; in case (3), the measurements are accurate, but the storyworld is an impossible space. Moore and Bracher, both writing in the 1940s, tend toward (1). But there are many indications that Gulliver is not to be completely trusted: among them are his pomposity, his righteousness, his failure to learn from experiences, and his occasional naivety, demonstrated in his advice for cleaning travel writing of lies and exaggerations. Since when would taking an oath prevent people from lying?

> I could heartily wish a Law were enacted, that every Traveller before he were permitted to publish his Voyages, should be obliged to make Oath before the *Lord High Chancellor* that all he intended to print was absolutely true to the

best of his Knowledge; for then the World would no longer be deceived as it usually is, while some Writers, to make their Works pass the better upon the Public, impose the grossest Falsities on the unweary Reader. (Swift 267)

I would tend, however, toward interpretation (3), because it is the most consistent with the tall-tale quality of the text and with its play with scale. Why should we expect geographic consistency in a world where anthropomorphic creatures can be as small as Lilliputians and as big as the inhabitants of Brobdingnag? The huge size of Brobdingnag reflects perfectly the size of its inhabitants, while the contradictory locations of Luggnagg and Balnirabi could be viewed as a satire of the cult of Reason that reigns in the neighboring island of Laputa. If Swift, who notoriously despised both the science of cartography and the genre of travel writing, allowed the inclusion of maps frequently unfaithful to the text, it could very well be *because of,* rather than *in spite of,* their shortcomings, since these shortcomings reinforce the satirical tone of the novel. As Ricardo Padrón put it, the maps of *Gulliver's Travels* "should be understood as traps" (2007, 271).

In stark contrast to the cartographic skepticism of Swift is the fascination for maps that inspired Robert Louis Stevenson's *Treasure Island.* As the author tells us in "My First Book," a text written some twelve years after the publication of the now classic pirate story, "I am told there are people who do not care for maps, and I find it hard to believe" (190). *Treasure Island* started as a painting that the author created to entertain himself during a rainy summer in Scotland, at a time when the story hadn't yet started to take shape in his mind. Stevenson explains that the map does not illustrate the novel, rather, it is the novel that grew out of the map:

> The shape of [the island] took my fancy beyond expression; it contained harbours that pleased me like sonnets; and with the unconsciousness of the predestined, I ticketed my performance "Treasure Island." . . . Somewhat in this way, as I pored upon my map of "Treasure Island," the future characters of the book began to appear there visibly among imaginary woods. . . . The next thing I knew, I had some paper before me and was writing a list of chapters. (190)

Stevenson praises the map for protecting him from embarrassing inconsistencies during the writing of the novel—such as making the sun set in the east—but the role of the map in the creative process extends far beyond the preservation of coherence. Some episodes in the plot are directly inspired by the features of the painting. It was, for instance, because he had called an islet

"Skeleton Island" that, in order to justify that name, Stevenson "broke into the gallery of Mr Poe" (193) by having the corpse of a pirate stretched out in such a way that its head and feet fell in a line connecting Skeleton Island to the location of the treasure. And it was "because I had made two harbours that the *Hispaniola* was sent on her wandering with Israel Hands (193). As Stevenson concludes: "The tale has a root [in the map], it grows in that soil; it has a spine of its own behind the words" (194).

The map that accompanies the novel (figure 3.3) looks like an authentic eighteenth-century map. An elaborate cartouche decorated with two mermaids indicates the scale, the empty spots on the sea, *pace* Swift (cf. note 8), are filled with galleons, and an elegant compass rose shows the orientation. But the map is not simply one of the many copies of a large-run edition: the handwriting designates it as a particular copy given by a certain J. F. [Captain Flint] to Mr. W. Bones in Savannah, Georgia, on the twentieth of July 1754. This status of individuated objects within the storyworld classifies the map as intradiegetic (or simply diegetic, to adopt the terminology of film studies). Yet the map we see in the book is not, literally, the one that inspired the tale. When Stevenson received the proofs, there was no map. He had to redraw it, fitting it to the narrative data, so that every allusion and place name contained in the text would be recorded on the chart. Just as travelers of old embarked on voyages to faraway places on the basis of maps, and returned with information that led to new mappings, so Stevenson's text is both the product and the source of a map. But as Stevenson writes, the authentic-looking map of the book, copied in black-and-white by professional engravers who made it to look like a eighteenth-century document, and then annotated by his father, who forged the handwriting of Bill Bones and Captain Flint, "somehow . . . was never 'Treasure Island' to me" (193). Only the spontaneous painting, most likely done in color, captured the *genius loci* of the island, because this genius lies in the creative outburst that made characters "[appear] visibly out of imaginary woods" (190) and live the plot of the novel.

The story that mediates between the two maps begins when an old and drunken former pirate, Bill Bones, wanders into the inn run by the parents of the narrator, an adolescent named Jim Hawkins. Bill Bones dies of a stroke after finding out he is being pursued by former shipmates. Jim manages to get hold of a piece of paper held in the dead man's sea chest and gives it to two local gentlemen, Squire Trelawney and Dr. Livesey. The piece of paper turns out to be a map:

> The doctor opened the seal with great care, and there fell out the map of an island, with latitude and longitude, soundings, names of hills, and bays

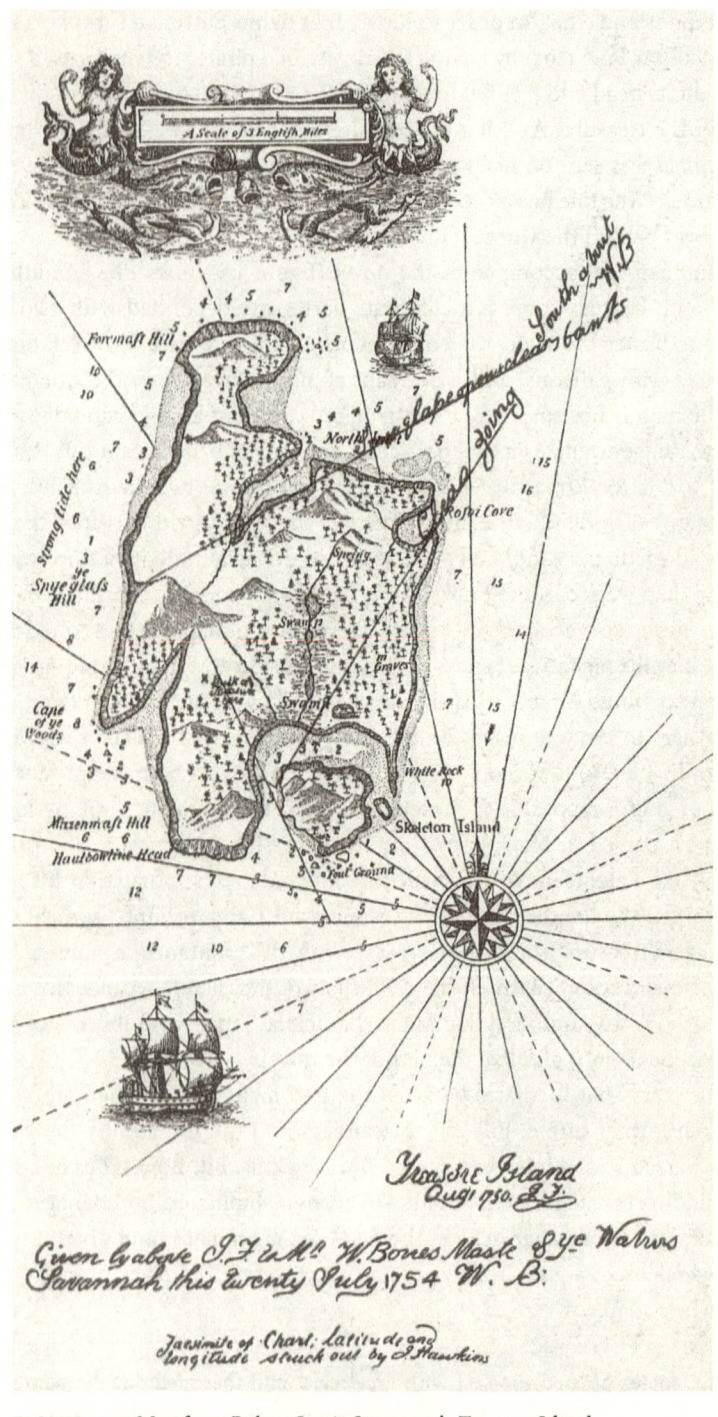

FIGURE 3.3. Map from Robert Louis Stevenson's *Treasure Island*

and inlets, and every particular that would be needed to bring a ship to a safe anchorage upon its shores. It was about nine miles long and five across, shaped, you might say, like a fat dragon standing up, and had two fine landlocked harbours, and a hill in the centre part marked "The Spyglass." There were several additions of a later date; but, above all, three crosses of red ink— two on the north part of the island, one in the southwest, and, beside this last, in the same red ink, and in a small, neat hand, very different from the captain's tottery characters, these words:—Bulk of treasure here. (32)

Squire Trelawney organizes an expedition to retrieve the treasure, which was buried on the island by the notorious, now deceased, pirate Captain Flint. Unbeknownst to the leaders, a large part of the crew consists of former pirates, led by the one-legged John Silver, a former shipmaster of Captain Flint. As soon as they reach the island, the pirates organize a mutiny, hoping to get the treasure and sail away. After many bloody episodes, during which the map ends up in the hands of John Silver, the pirates, who hold Jim hostage, locate the spot marked on the map, but the treasure is gone: it has been hauled away by Ben Gunn, a castaway who has been marooned on the island after an unsuccessful attempt to find the booty. In the end, Silver switches sides, the loyal members of the crew overcome the mutineers, get hold of the treasure, and sail away, leaving the surviving pirates on the island. The treasure is distributed among the loyal men (even Silver getting his share), who spend it wisely or foolishly, according to their temperament.

When the imagination engages in world-creation, it tends to favor islands. There are several reasons this insularity appeals to the creative mind. First, islands constitute a microcosm of the real world: they contain mountains, valleys, harbors, beaches, rugged coasts, and sometimes even their own islands. The more sinuous their coastline, the more diversified their geography. Second, islands satisfy the mind because their limited size makes them knowable and mappable. "Unlike a continent, with its vast spaces, islands can be taken in at a glance, giving us the impression that we can know them completely" (Padrón 2007, 265). Third, islands can be explored and settled, thus combining the freedom of movement characteristic of space with the intimacy of place. And last, the ocean that separates islands from the continents provides an allegory of the ontological difference that separates fictional worlds from the real world. Creating an island is creating a world, it reproduces, on a scale small enough for humans to achieve, God's act of creation.

Treasure Island satisfies most, but not all of these conditions. As a fictional entity, it is separated from the real world by the ocean of the imagination. From the height of Spyglass Hill, the entire island can be contemplated.

Its complicated shape offers a wide variety of landscape features and climate zones concentrated in a small area, and it presents an interesting shape to the eye. This shape is not only decorative, it also plays a strategic role in the plot: the South harbor is the site of a battle between the pirates and the loyal members of the crew, the North harbor allows the *Hispaniola* to anchor away from the pirate-occupied South harbor, and, as already noted, Skeleton Island serves as a landmark to locate the treasure.

Yet unlike many imaginary islands, Treasure Island does not offer a sense of place to its visitors, at least not if one associates place with security and a desire to settle down. As soon as the narrator catches a glimpse of its shores, he writes "I hated the very thought of Treasure Island" (70). And when he leaves, he notes: "To my inexpressible joy, the highest rock of Treasure Island had sunk into the blue round of sea" (185). While the map depicts an inviting landscape, promises safe landing, and offers clear guidelines for the conquest of the treasure, the island turns out to be shrouded in fog, mysterious and unfriendly. The quest for the treasure, far from being the easy conquest anticipated by the leaders, will exact a heavy cost of life. Moreover, in spite of its spatial accuracy, the chart fails to help locate the treasure, because territories evolve but maps can only represent a certain stage in this evolution. As for the location of the treasure, it might be a special place marked by an "X" on the map, but this place only matters because it is believed to hold something that will be taken away. The same can be said of the island as a whole: it never achieves the emotional status of place, because like so many areas in the real world that contain natural resources, it only exists for the characters—good guys and bad guys alike—to be plundered and left behind. Once the island is robbed of the treasure, there is no reason to go back: Jim Hawkins makes sure that nobody will be tempted to travel to the island by writing on the map, "latitude and longitude struck out by J. Hawkins." Through this symbolic gesture, he erases not only the island from the face of the earth but also the traumatic memories of the expedition from his mind.

But thanks to the text and the map, future travelers will return to Treasure Island, and experience it as a site of pleasure. These future travelers are the readers who want a good yarn rather than a fictional treasure. The map that lures the characters into a bloody adventure helps readers immerse themselves in the storyworld. Visual modeling of the setting is an important factor of narrative immersion, yet the individual descriptions that serve as blueprints for visualization tend to slip away in the reader's mind. The map enhances memory of the text by letting readers attach individual descriptive statements to specific areas or landmarks of the island, thereby gaining a global view of insular geography. This view makes it possible to follow the movements of the characters and to reach a better understanding of the strategic role of the terrain in the battles between the pirates and the loyal crew. In a narrative as centered on fighting, ambushes, escapes, and hostage-taking as *Treasure Island*, visualizing the lay of the land is an essential part of the mental simulation that leads to narrative comprehension.

GENEALOGICAL RELATIONS BETWEEN MAPS AND NARRATIVES

The German critic Robert Stockhammer (2007, 63) distinguishes several types of genetic relations between maps and literary texts:

1. Map precedes the text.
2. Author draws maps during writing.
3. Publisher puts a map in second or third edition.
4. Map is drawn by readers and critics.

We have already covered the first case with the discussion of *Treasure Island*. Here the relation between map and text is almost coincidental: when Stevenson started painting the island, he had no idea that a novel that would grow out of it. This particular scenario is probably unique in the annals of literary creation.

Much more common are situations where drawing a map is the first step in a deliberate act of world creation. In this case, the boundary between categories 1 and 2 becomes fuzzy, because the map can be altered in the process of writing. A good example of world-creation that starts with the drawing of a map is the phenomenon of the micronation. An offshoot of the literary genre of the utopia, a micronation is an independent "state" created by individuals who design its geography, define its form of government, write its laws, describe its customs, and invent its history. While some micronations exist in real space, by the will of a founder who declares the independence of a certain territory (a phenomenon documented by the 2006 *Lonely Planet* guide to micronations), most of these fictional countries reside on the Internet, where they can be reached by cyber tourists and prospective citizens through a click of the mouse. They are named Bergonia and Talossa, Uteged and Reuniao, Lizbekistan and Aerica, Freedonia and Aristasia, the Feminine Empire. The reasons for building micronations are as varied as their landscapes, customs, and political systems: fulfilling childhood dreams of inhabiting secret kingdoms, satisfying adolescent needs to revolt against a world ruled by grown-ups, exercising royal power, articulating social visions, simulating processes of self-government, but above all, the pure pleasure of writing the encyclopedia of an imaginary country. An indispensable feature of all micronations is a map that defines identity, for drawing a map is not merely adding a document to the encyclopedia that describes the country, it is a performative act that brings it into being. For the founder of Bergonia, the creation of his micronation is a declaration of love to maps and mapmaking:

> I had no purpose at all, only the joy of playing and inventing. . . . I'm sure that the discovery of my parents' grand atlas was the immediate hook. Drawing the first maps and dreaming up weird names was entirely a matter of play. I drew lots of maps when I was a kid, and Bergonia was then just one of many on-going projects. Over the years the work (play) of contriving a continent & nation has massively challenged me—a great expenditure and demonstration of imagination that wound up serving a multitude of incidental uses. The job has given me a vehicle and a focus for all my interests in geography & meteorology, anthropology & history, religion & mythology, and philosophy & psychology. (http://www.bergonia.org/why.htm)

As Mark J. P. Wolf (2012) has argued, building imaginary worlds involves the creation of three main components: space, or setting; time, or events; and existents, or characters. To each of these components corresponds a design tool that helps authors maintain coherence and helps readers—when the tools are made available to them—remember the relations between individual narrative elements: maps for setting, timelines for events, and genealogies for characters. The maps correspond to Stockhammer's second category. When authors such as J. R. R. Tolkien and William Faulkner draw maps as part of the writing process, they do not do so to create a multimodal work—for it is the verbal act of narration that brought their worlds into being—but rather to monitor the act of creation and ensure the spatial consistency of the storyworld. Such maps are particularly useful when authors are not just creating individual narratives but rather large imaginary worlds that contain numerous stories. For instance, Faulkner's map of Yoknapatawpha county helps situate his various novels with respect to each other, while Tolkien's elaborate maps of Middle Earth prepare the storyworld for the future episodes of a complex narrative full of subplots and parallel branches. When a novel is situated in a real-world location, authors can base their writing on existing geographic maps rather than drawing their own: James Joyce, for instance, who lived in a self-imposed exile from Ireland, used British Ordnance Survey Maps of Dublin to write *Ulysses* (Bulson 2007, 77–83). Joyce's expressed intent was "to give a picture of Dublin so complete that if the city one day disappeared from the earth it could be reconstructed from my book" (qtd. in Bulson 68).

While the maps drawn by Tolkien and Faulkner were handmade private sketches not meant to be published (though they are in some editions)[8], and the documents used by Joyce do not appear in the novel, many narratives include professionally drawn maps based on blueprints created by the author or reproductions of the geographical maps that guided the writing. These cases, which include Jean Auel's neolithic saga *Earth Children*, Georges Perec's *La Vie mode d'emploi (Life as a User's Manual)*, and Amitav Ghosh's *The Glass Palace*, can be seen as an extension of category 2.

Category 3, by contrast, consists of professional-looking external maps that become, by the force of habit or by popular demand, integrated into the text.[9] An example of category 3 is the maps of Dante's *Divine Comedy* that are included in some editions. From the Renaissance on, starting with Botticelli's map-like painting of the Inferno, the work of Dante has inspired a rich tradition of literary cartography.[10] When these maps are included in the text, they become for the reader authoritative guides to the storyworld, and they function as what Kendall Walton (1990) would call a "prop in a game of make-believe." What makes the world of Dante so appealing to literary cartographers is the explicitly symbolic character of its geography. Margaret Wertheim wittily compares Dante's cosmological scheme to "a great metaphysical onion" (1999, 54). Hell, Purgatory, and Paradise are all structured as a series of concentric circles, labeled with specific sins or virtues, and leading deeper into depravity or higher into grace. The vertical organization of Dante's world means that its mapping must abandon its traditional focus on the plane delimited by the x and y axes, and adopt a perspective that shows the z axis.

Through their coupling of topographical areas with allegorical meaning, the maps of the *Divine Comedy* perpetuate the medieval tradition of mystical mapmaking. The most eloquent visual expression of this mystical intent is the so-called T-O pattern of medieval maps, in which the Earth is depicted as a perfect circle (O) centered on Jerusalem and surrounded by the world ocean. The Mediterranean Sea (the base of the T, which lies sideways) cuts east to west across the map, dividing Europe from Africa. The cap of the T stretching

---

8. Faulkner reportedly included his map of Yoknapawpha County in *Absalom, Absalom*, but the editions I have consulted have no map.

9. Halfway between these two categories is the case of the maps of *Gulliver's Travels*, which were drawn by a professional cartographer on the basis of the text, yet probably not on the basis of maps drawn by the author. These maps appeared from the first edition on.

10. A Google image search on Dante's *Divine Comedy* or Dante's *Inferno* will reveal many of these maps.

north along the Don River and south along the Nile, divides Asia from Africa and Europe. Similarly, the maps of the cosmos included in some editions of the *Divine Comedy* (for instance the Oxford University Press edition of 1993) represent a view of the universe to which Copernicus and Galileo would deal a mortal blow: the cosmos is centered on the earth, which is itself centered on Jerusalem and on the Cross.

READERS' MAPS

Readers' maps constitute the fourth category of the genealogical relationships listed in the previous section, but since we discuss them in more detail than the other categories, we place them in a separate section. They are the maps sketched during the reading process that allow people to deepen their understanding of the plot, to develop personal interpretation, and when the text focuses on a mystery to solve—as in detective stories, pen-and-paper role-playing games, and the digital genre of interactive fiction—to work toward the solution. The kind of textual space that inspires spontaneous mapmaking activity is overwhelmingly what we have called strategic space, because maps can show better than text how geographical features and relations between objects affect the formation and pursuit of the characters' goals. Emotional space is much less in need of mapping because it consists mainly of memories, stories, and sensorial experiences attached to individual objects, rather than of possibilities of action. Here we will discuss two examples of spontaneous readers' maps.

The first is a map of *The Great Gatsby* of unknown origin (it was found as a piece of paper blowing in the wind), probably drawn by a high school student in preparation for a paper or an oral presentation (figure 3.4). The sketch reveals an approximate knowledge of the geography of Long Island, where the novel takes place, but its point is to capture the symbolism of the spatial relationship between the two main characters, Gatsby and Daisy. Their residence on opposite ends of a bay, West Egg and East Egg, stands for the separating effect of their social status: Daisy is a rich girl who marries old money, Gatsby is a *nouveau riche* whose wealth comes from suspect sources. From his waterfront mansion, Gatsby can observe Daisy across the bay, an activity which bridges space and expresses his passion for her. In contrast to Gatsby and Daisy, the narrator, Nick Carraway, occupies an unspecified location on the open sea that reflects his nomadic role as mediator between Daisy (his cousin) and Gatsby (his friend). The sketch is as interesting for what it ignores as for what it shows: by focusing on the Daisy-Gatsby relationship on Long Island,

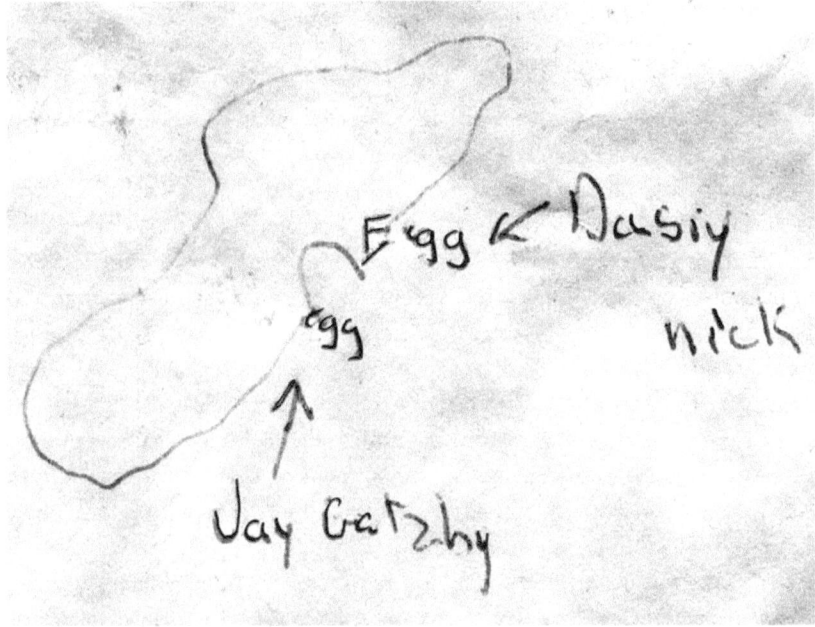

FIGURE 3.4. Spontaneous reader's map: Francis Scott Fitzgerald's *The Great Gatsby*

rather than on the Myrtle-Tom affair in New York City, or on the characters' movements between Long Island and New York, it highlights what the reader perceives as the main theme of the novel.

The school of criticism known as reader response (Iser 1980) conceives the act of reading as an activity of filling in the blanks in the text. But this activity is never complete nor systematic: the "texture" of the text, as Lubomír Doležel (1998) has shown, and its degree of informational saturation orient the activity of filling in toward certain areas to the detriment of others. Moreover, some readers are "visualizers," and they will imagine settings, objects, and characters in great detail, while others are satisfied with schematic mental images (Esrock 1994; Nell 1988). We may thus picture Gatsby's house or Gatsby's clothes without picturing Gatsby's face; and we may picture Gatsby's house and its spatial location with respect to Daisy's without locating this image on a specific shore of Long Island. As we put our mental representations on paper, however, we are forced to draw a more explicit picture, since drawings share the intolerance of movies for unspecified visual features (though, of course, to a lesser degree): just as cinematic shots do not permit characters without a face, drawings do not allow free-floating objects. Everything has to be situated *somewhere* on the sheet of paper, even when the text locates objects only within a broad zone. But it is reasonable to assume that the act of drawing figure 3.4 will fix the location of the Eggs in the reader's mind and produces a new mental model—what we may call a cognitive map—of the world of the novel.

Our second example of a spontaneous reader's map comes from Vladimir Nabokov, a passionate literary cartographer who could not separate the act of reading from the act of drawing. His private notebooks sketch whatever is sketchable in literary texts: the wanderings of Leopold Bloom and Stephen Daedalus through the streets of Dublin in James Joyce's *Ulysses,* the location of the novels of Jane Austen and Charles Dickens on the map of England, and the exact layout of the apartment of Gregor Samsa in Kafka's *The Metamorphosis* (figure 3.5). Kafka's novella involves space in a strategic role—a role to which Nabokov, as a chess player, was particularly sensitive—for at least three reasons. First, the transformation of the hero, Gregor Samsa, into an insect renders his human sense of embodiment obsolete and forces him to renegotiate his relation to space. As Gregor's mind slowly adapts to his new body, the objects in his room acquire new functions and afford new activities: for instance, the ceiling and walls, useless to Gregor's human shape, become a space for crawling, an exercise that represents his only form of pleasure. Second, since the metamorphosis has turned Gregor into an object of horror, especially for his mother, he must keep his new body hidden out of consideration for his family. The arrangement of furniture in his room, the location of doors, the direction in which they open, and more generally the floor plan of the apartment organize space into safe hiding places and forbidden open areas where Gregor could be seen. And third, the apartment must be reorganized to adapt to the new family situation created by the metamorphosis: since Gregor can no longer support his parents and sister financially, they are forced to take in lodgers, and the function of the rooms is changed. All of these possibilities of action are carefully recorded on Nabokov's map, either through the graphic representation of the floor plan and of the arrangement of furniture within the rooms or through textual annotations that indicate the changes in the use of the rooms. Spatial relations are so important and so precise in Kafka's text that we came up with a map very similar to Nabokov's during our own reading, without consulting Nabokov's. The main differences are that we were unable to situate the parents' room within the apartment, and we placed the staircase closer to the living room on the basis of a scene where the lodgers are expelled from the apartment; we also put the lodgers in the sister's room. These differences and similarities demonstrate the interplay of precisely located and floating objects in the text's representation of space. We will come back to this issue in the next chapter.

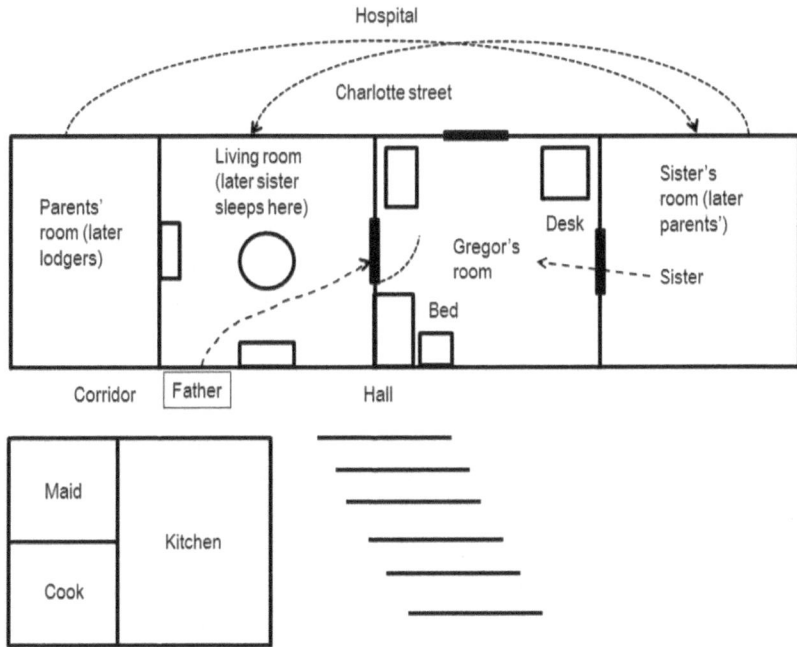

FIGURE 3.5. Vladimir Nabokov's map for Franz Kafka's *The Metamorphosis* (redrawn by authors from *Lectures on Literature*)

STORYTELLING THROUGH MAPS

Whether intra- or extradiegetic, the narrative maps discussed so far have all been instances of storytelling *with* maps. Now we are turning to a much more problematic question: is it possible to tell stories *through* maps? Or to put it differently: are maps able to tell stories? This is an issue that cartographers and geographers have only recently begun to address.[11] Denis Cosgrove and

---

11. The "narrative turn" that swept the humanities, medicine, law, and even musicology in the late 1980s and 1990s did not miss geography. It found one of its earliest expressions in a 1987 article by the cartography scholar Denis Wood (1987), in which he plays with the idea that maps, or more specifically atlases, could be considered a narrative form. This focus on atlases is easily explained by the fact that atlases, as collections of maps bound at the spine in a fixed order, present the sequential organization that constitutes one of the defining features of narrative. Yet even if one reduces narrativity to sequentiality, the narrativity of the use to which people put atlases is questionable, because atlases are often organized according to some purely random principle, such as the alphabetical order of the names of countries. This type of organization does not invite users to read atlases sequentially, as we read stories, but rather facilitates the consultation of individual maps by making them easy to find. What then is the

Veronica della Dora (2005) were among the first to do so in their study of the work of cartographer Charles Owen. Working during World War II, Owen drafted remarkable maps showing battles of the Pacific Theater for the *Los Angeles Times*. Denis Wood (2010) has also published some of the maps he developed, beginning in the 1970s, to portray life in the Boylan Heights neighborhood of Raleigh, North Carolina. Others have suggested that the concept of geo-narrative is a useful way of linking qualitative data to the quantitative structure of maps and geographic information systems (Kwan and Ding 2008). Indeed, the idea of "storytelling with maps" has recently become popularized by Esri (2012), one of the major software firms in the industry.

While narratologists ask the question, "How can maps enhance storytelling?" the geographer Margaret Wicken Pearce (2008) asks the reverse question: how can narrative enhance cartography? Maps are very good at representing space as a container for geographical objects (towns, roads, etc.) and as a system of relations between these objects, but their vertical perspective, which does not correspond to the perception of an embodied mind, prevents them from conveying a sense of place. Paintings and photographs are much better at capturing *genius loci*. When maps represent travel, the subject matter of many stories, they reduce the experience of the traveler to a one-dimensional line. But as Pearce observes, "Traveling is not a linear sensation but a sense of enclosure by a moving landscape" (25). As people

---

point of Wood's attempt to read atlases as narratives, if sequential reading goes against standard usage? His conception of the narrativity of atlases (or of maps in general) can receive several different interpretations. The first one challenges any practical use of maps: just as most people take pleasure in the reading of narrative fiction, Wood confesses to reading maps and atlases not for the sake of gathering information about the world, for he has no use for much of this information, but for purely aesthetic reasons. In the second interpretation, narrativity is a property of well-designed atlases. Wood praises some atlases for telling a coherent story while he rejects others for being structured like a list of unconnected elements, similar to the images in a children's book that presents first a picture of a sock, then a picture of a shoe, then a picture of a bib, then a picture of a cup, and so on. To understand a third, much more general conception of cartographic narrativity, the article must be placed in its proper historical and scholarly context—the attempt to develop a critical reading of maps inspired by deconstruction and the discourse of so-called "critical theory." Wood's work in general, and this article in particular, played a pioneering role in the development of a postmodern, literary-criticism-inspired approach to cartography. Narrativity, in such an approach, is largely synonymous with textuality. By reading maps as narratives (i.e., as the result of encoding decisions that serve particular human interests), critical cartography fights an alleged tendency to regard maps, if not as the territory itself (for nobody is naïve enough to confuse a piece of paper with a stretch of land), at least as something like a photographic image or a mirror reflection of the world untainted by human subjectivity. The narrative reading advocated by proponents of critical cartography is a metareading, which stands in sharp contrast to what we commonly understand as "reading a map": that is, consulting the map for some kind of practical purpose that makes the user dependent on some degree of accuracy with respect to external reality.

move through space, they take in the landscape that surrounds them, so for the mapping of a journey to be faithful to the experience of the traveler, it should represent the journey as a broad horizon, a strip corresponding to an evolving landscape. Looking at a map, we can see distances and landmarks, but only experienced map users can reconstruct what the landscape looks like from cartographic information (such as contour lines, the direction of rivers, or the density of named features). Even so, the map does not *show* the landscape to the eye, it only provides guidelines for its mental construction, just as a text-based narrative provides directions for imagining characters, setting, and events. It is only in combination of images taken from a horizontal perspective and textual annotations that maps can tell the story of a trip as a lived experience.

The page of the *River Guide to the Grand Canyon* shown in figure 3.6 gives an example of how this can be done, even though the guide does not focus on a particular journey. While the map view traces the itinerary common to all raft trips down the Colorado, signaling rapids and side-canyons, photographic inserts capture the look of the most notorious "places" (i.e., attractions) encountered on the way, and narrative annotations bring former expeditions to life, especially the first trip down the canyon by the Powell expedition of 1869 but also later trips that remain in the folklore of the river. The map of figure 3.6 commemorates Bert Loper, who made his second trip down the Colorado in 1949 at age 79, and collapsed and died while running a rapid. Looking at the map is like taking a trip through both space and history.[12]

Pearce's own solution to the problem of enabling maps to capture place and lived experience is very similar to the river guide, through it does not include pictures because she wants to stay as close as possible to what she calls the "cartographic language." The result is "The Intricacy of These Turns and Windings: A Voyageur's Map" (see http://www.journeycake.com/detail.pdf), a map inspired by the diary of an eighteenth-century voyageur, John Macdonell, that depicts his journey from Montreal to Grand Portage in the Canadian interior. The map is very large (25" × 76") and divided into frames corresponding to each day's progress—a small frame for a short distance (perhaps a portage around a rapid), a large frame for a large distance (on open water). The map is so large that it is hard to view all at once. Pearce seems have chosen

---

12. This type of guide, whose pedigree in the Western tradition dates back centuries or, arguably, millennia (some of the earliest guides concerned Roman roads and Christian pilgrimage routes), has received renewed attention beginning in the nineteenth century. Notable in this regard are Wordsworth's *Guide to the Lakes* (1835) and Henry Taunt's cartographic and photographic guide to the Thames River. Contemporary writers continuing this tradition include John McPhee, Annie Dillard, Frances Mayes, Barry Lopez, and many others.

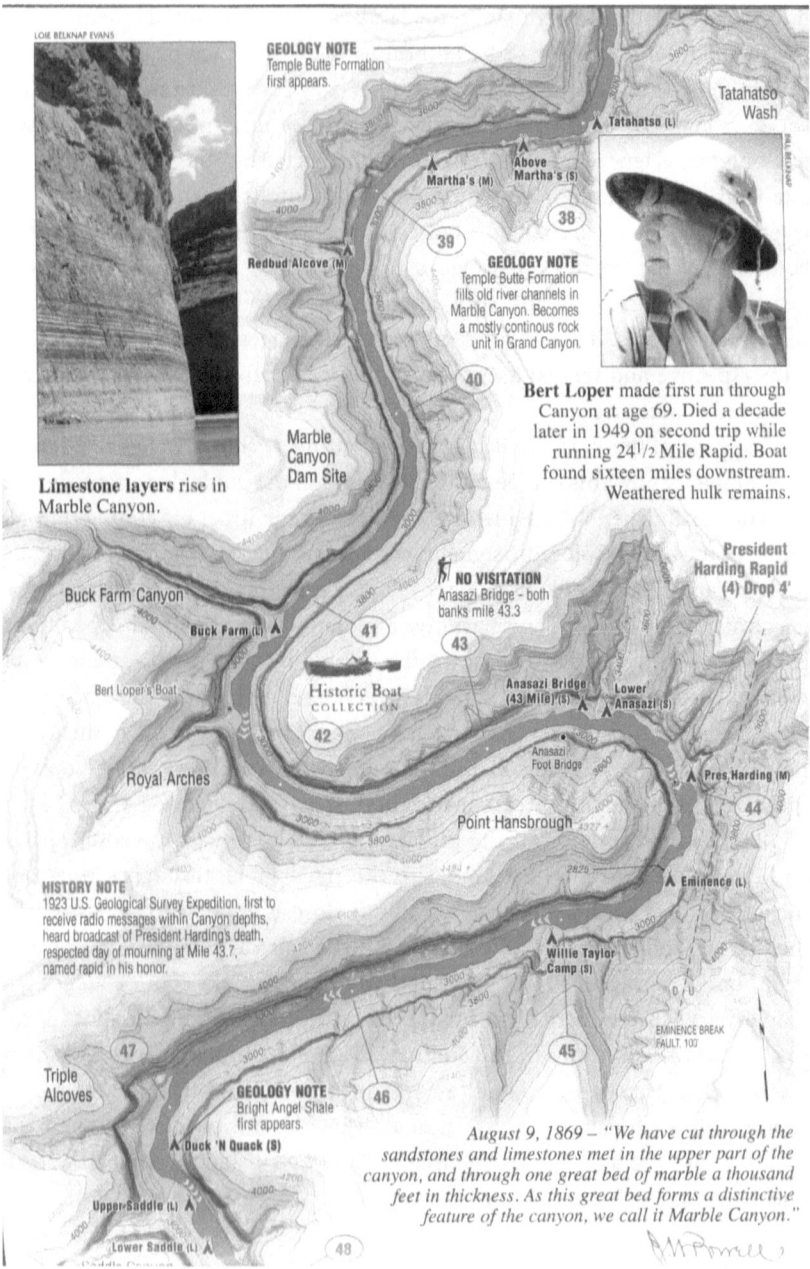

FIGURE 3.6. Page from *River Guide to the Grand Canyon*. Used with the permission of Westwater Books.

this epic size to give a sense of the vast distances Macdonell covered but also a sense of the intimacy of his experiences with place. Viewers have to choose whether to move in close to read excerpts from Macdonell's diary or stand back to see the entire map. In Pearce's map, viewers can't do both at once. The map is notably empty—except for the details Macdonell could see and record as he paddled west—giving a visible impression of how little early explorers knew about the great territories that stretched out from the river channel. A particularly innovative element of the narrative is Pearce's use of color and shading in each frame to depict Macdonell's emotional state, day by day, as he faced the struggles of his journey.

Purists would argue that truly "narrative" maps should be able to tell a story through visual means exclusively, rather than through extensive textual annotations. On the map shown in figure 3.7, language is limited to its standard cartographic usage: titles, captions, legends, and names. This map, a celebrated achievement in the art of narrative cartography, is Charles Joseph Minard's map diagram of Napoleon's Russian campaign of 1812. The tragedy of Napoleon's campaign is represented through six variables: the itinerary of the *Grande Armée* in a two-dimensional space (latitude and longitude count as two variables), the direction of movement (grey for the advance toward Moscow, black for the retreat), the size of the army, the rate of progression (marked through dates), and the temperature for each date. Taken together, these variables tell the story of an army decimated by desertion (the branch above Wilna that rejoins the army on its way back) and then by the sheer length of the journey. According to the width of the line, the battle of Borodino (a site slightly west of Moscow on the way in but not marked on the map) seems to have had a relatively minor effect on the size of the army, compared to the bitter cold that sets in during the retreat from Moscow, though historians generally agree that Borodino involved a huge loss of life. The reunion of the stray companies with the main group near Studianka temporarily boosts the strength of the army, but the crossing of the Berezina represents the final blow. Only 10,000 troops out of the 422,000 who started the campaign will cross the Niemen again. It takes a narrative based on a steady progression through space to lend itself to this type of spatio-temporal representation. Maps can tell in their broad lines stories of military campaigns, patterns of migration, the advance and control of fires, and picaresque wanderings, but they can no more represent the particular episodes and the abrupt changes of state that punctuate these processes than a diagram of the itinerary of the Tour de France can give an idea of the drama of the race.

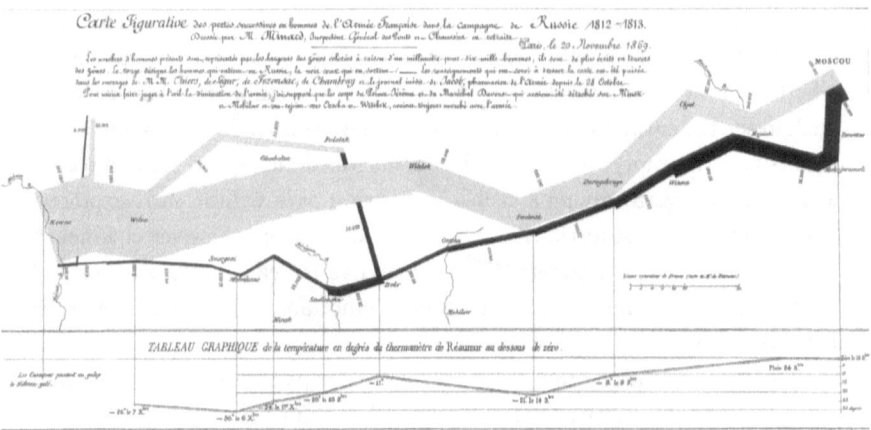

FIGURE 3.7. Charles Joseph Minard's map of Napoleon's Russian campaign of 1812

The storytelling power of maps relates to, but also differs from, the storytelling power of images. The question of pictorial narrativity is a large and complex issue that cannot be covered in this chapter; but it will be useful to point out some similarities and differences between maps and pictures with regard to storytelling. (By "pictures," we mean reasonably realistic images representing a roughly horizontal perspective.) Both maps and pictures are spatial, rather than temporal media, which means that their parts exist simultaneously for the viewer. This makes it difficult for them to suggest temporal sequence, a constitutive feature of narrativity, but they can overcome the limitation inherent to their medium through clues that guide the eye on a certain path, such as lines and arrows on a map (as in figure 3.7) or the depiction of roads and rivers on a painting. When a story consists of multiple episodes taking place in different locations, maps have a clear advantage over pictures because their bird's-eye perspective enables them to show multiple areas simultaneously, while the horizontal perspective of pictures hides distant locations behind close ones. Early Renaissance painting deals with this narrative challenge through a perspective-defying organization of space that divides the canvas into distinct areas—often separating them with architectural features—where different scenes can be represented (Steiner 2004), while friezes, comic strips, cartoon maps, and series of paintings (such as William Hogarth's "Marriage à la Mode") represent chronological sequence through multiple, discrete frames (Wolf 2002). On the other hand, pictures can show individual events better than maps because their horizontal perspective makes objects more easily recognizable (try to draw two lovers kissing on a bench as seen from an airplane!)[13]

As an example of a compromise between a map view and a picture view, consider figure 3.8, a German etching created around 1603 to celebrate the failed attack by the Duke of Savoy, a Catholic monarch, on the Protestant city-state of Geneva during the night of December 11 to 12, 1602. (This battle is known today as the Escalade, and it is commemorated every year through a celebration that combines a certain Calvinist austerity with the spirit of the Carnival.) The lake and the course of the two rivers that flow together in Geneva[14] are clearly shown in map view, while the city itself is represented from an elevated southern perspective (the oblique view favored in maps of ski resorts). The various episodes of the battle are represented iconically, but their location on the map is indexical, since it reflects where they took place in the city. We see the arrival of the enemy troops (1), the climbing of the city walls with ladders (2), and the infiltration of the sleeping city by enemy soldiers (3). Then the citizens of Geneva wake up, descend onto the streets, and repel the invasion (4). Enemies tumble down from the wall to the left of the ladders (5). While most of the battle scenes are represented from an oblique perspective similar to the view of the city, the last episode in the battle, the hanging of the prisoners (6), is depicted in a pure picture view, arguably because this is a spectacle meant to be seen from the ground. (The numbers are an addition.) The map is more than an illustration, because the German text at the bottom is subordinated to it (as a caption) rather than the other way around; but it is less than a story, because the spectator unfamiliar with the historical circumstances would be unable to reconstitute with certainty the chronology of the events; one could, for instance, imagine that the troops of Savoy (recognizable by the flags) attacked Geneva in retaliation for the hanging of compatriots. Still, this hybrid of map and picture goes a long way toward narrating without language. As the eye of the spectator familiar with the story moves from scene to scene, the mind simulates the unfolding of the events. For Genevans,

---

13. Similar issues also arise in recent research on "data narratives," "visual explanations," and "data visualization." Segel and Heer (2010) see the challenges of developing narratives in maps and graphics in very similar terms. At the same time, they also point to examples in which the spatiality of graphics can be used to portray nonspatial and temporal information. In some respects, Segel and Heer build on the earlier work of Tufte (1997). Other examples of parallel work include Klanten et al. (2008, 2011).

14. The course of the river at the bottom, the Arve, is wrong: rather than wrapping around the city, it should leave the map toward the south near the bridge at the bottom of the picture. Its course is obviously dictated by aesthetic rather than geographic considerations. The other geographic details are reasonably accurate.

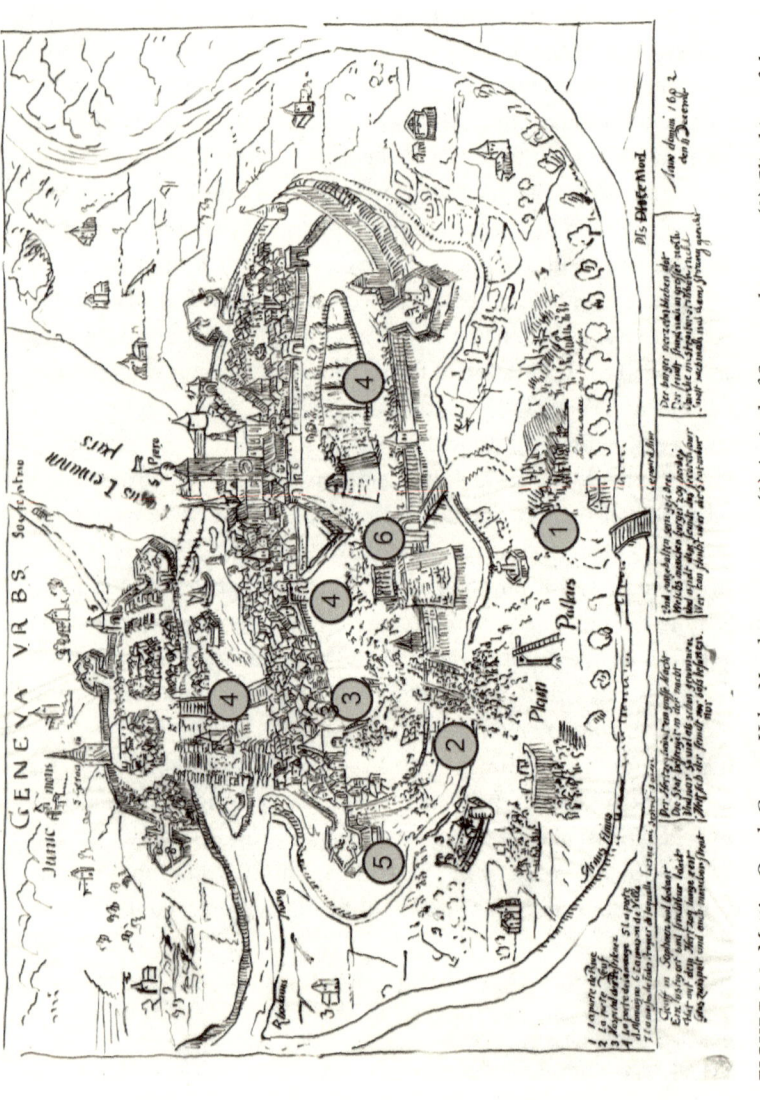

FIGURE 3.8. Mattias Quad, *Geneva Urbs*. Numbers represent: (1) Arrival of Savoyard troops. (2) Climbing of the city walls by the Savoyards. (3) Enemy soldiers invade city (in several places). (4) Genevans repel attack (could be in several places). (5) Enemies thrown down the city walls. (6) Prisoners are hanged. Used with permission of the Bibliothèque Publique Universitaire de Genève.

proud of their city, this map belies the claim that maps cannot convey a sense of place: it celebrates an event that has become a symbol of Genevan identity, and it captures a view of the city very similar to the one that can be seen from Mt. Salève, a popular destination of weekend outings. The map, admittedly, does not create a sense of place, but it certainly reinforces it in the minds of the people who have already developed an emotional attachment to Geneva.

Our last example of narrative map reverts to the case of an image dependent on language. In contrast to most of the preceding examples, the map of figure 3.9 does not tell a story about travel, but a story about . . . mapping. The accompanying text gives us the basic narrative theme: "People who find their neighbors tiresome can move to another neighborhood, while countries can't. But suppose they can." On this facetious map, published by *The Economist* in 2010, the countries of Europe have been rearranged according to where they belong, based on their political and economic tendencies. The direction of the move is toward like-minded countries that will make good neighbors. England has moved south, in the vicinity of near-bankrupt countries such as Spain and Portugal, because after its general election of 2010, it will need to confront "its dire public finances." Belgium, often described by *The Economist* as a country that should not exist, has managed to survive the reshuffling by moving to central Europe, where it can participate in the endemic strife of the region's ethnic minorities. Its spot has been taken by the Czech Republic, a "stolid, well-organized" country that "will get on splendidly with its new Dutch neighbors." Meanwhile, Switzerland has moved close to Sweden, because it is often confused with it. In its new Scandinavian location, Switzerland will be able to snuggle with Norway, its fellow refusenik of the European Union. Notice also that the reshuffling makes room for some purely fictional countries, such as the central European countries of Syldavia and Borduria of the Tintin comic books. One may wonder why quite a few countries—France, Germany, Spain, and the Nordic countries—have maintained their place: is it because they are bastions of stability or because they consider themselves to be the cornerstones of European identity? The answer is as much graphical as it is political. If some countries did not retain their place, the general shape of Europe would become unrecognizable, and the map would look like a random scramble of elements, rather than like a story of political tendencies.

Where, to conclude, does the difference reside between storytelling *with* maps and storytelling *through* maps? Whether it uses intra- or extradiegetic documents, storytelling with maps can fulfil a variety of functions—promoting immersion, facilitating the understanding of the plot, revealing the strategic or symbolic configuration of the setting, or commenting ironically on the

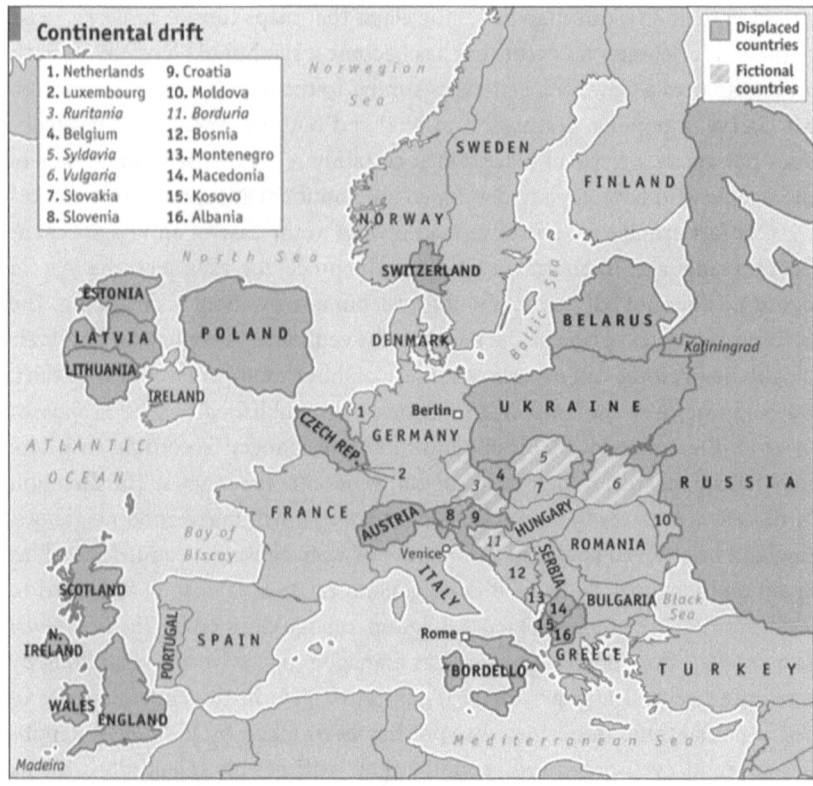

FIGURE 3.9. Redrawing the map of Europe. Used with the permission of *The Economist*.

discipline of cartography, as in *Gulliver's Travels*—but they remain subordinated to the text. The function of these maps is similar to the role of illustrations in those children's books where text bears the weight of narration. (It is, in fact, no coincidence that at least until recently, maps appeared mainly in narratives for young readers.) In storytelling through maps, by contrast, the relation map-text is similar to the relation image-text in comic strips, graphic novels, and some children's books, such as Maurice Sendak's: visual and linguistic signs are either inextricably involved in the production of meaning, or articulated language becomes altogether dispensable. Yet, in moving into digital media as we do in chapter 5, these distinctions may blur somewhat. As McCloud (2000, 200–240) has written in his *Reinventing Comics*, the "infinite canvas" offered by digital media may make it possible to tell stories *with* and *through* maps in very different ways.

CHAPTER 4

From Cognitive to Graphic Maps

THIS CHAPTER WILL FOCUS ON THREE QUESTIONS: (1) What elements of narrative lead to the construction of a mental model, or cognitive map, of a storyworld? (2) Through what representational, or cartographic, strategies do readers turn these mental models into graphic maps? and (3) How important is it to build a cognitive map as part of the reading process?[1]

These questions will be approached through an informal experiment for which we make no claim of scientific rigor. A group of high school students was asked to draw maps of the world of *Chronicle of a Death Foretold* by Gabriel García Márquez.[2] The students, all college-bound seniors participating in an advanced literature course, had read the novel during the preceding summer. They discussed it with their teacher for about three weeks in December 2000 and January 2001. They were tested in January, before the class moved on to the next text. Some of the students might have reread the book and some others might not, but the class discussion should have refreshed the plot for all of them. In contrast to the reader-maps discussed in

---

  1. An earlier version of this chapter, entitled "Cognitive Maps and the Construction of Narrative Space," appeared in Herman (2003, 214–42). Used with permission of the Center for the Study of Language and Information.
  2. We would like to thank Darren Marshall and his twelfth-grade students in the International Baccalaureate program at Poudre High School in Fort Collins, Colorado, for their participation.

the preceding chapter, these student maps are not spontaneously created artifacts; still, by emphasizing some elements and ignoring others, they provide an inside glimpse into the process of constructing mental models of narrative space. This process is particularly important in *Chronicle of a Death Foretold*, because the spatial configuration of the storyworld has a strategic impact over the development of the plot. Before turning to the text, let's first situate the notion of cognitive map within psychology and literary theory.

COGNITIVE MAPS AND LITERARY TEXTS

The concept of cognitive map means different things to different people. It was introduced in 1948 by the psychologist Edward Tolman to describe the navigational skills that enable rats in a maze to reach a food box when the familiar path has been blocked. In more recent years, the term has been applied to people's memorizations of graphic maps (as we will call what we commonly regard as "geographic" maps: road maps, topographical maps, world maps); to mental images of complex spatial environments, such as a city (Lynch 1960); to the knowledge that enables people to draw freehand images of city streets, countries, or continents (Tuan 1975); and to private representations of geographical entities that ascribe personal values to different areas: dangerous, safe, desirable, vacation spot, good place to live, and so on (Gould and White 1974). Tuan (1975, 210–11) further proposes five functions for mental maps: (1) They make it possible to give directions to strangers. (2) They enable people to "rehearse spatial behavior" (as does a rider who goes mentally over an obstacle course before a jumping competition). (3) They are used as mnemonic devices (the *loci* technique of memorization). (4) They are means to structure and store knowledge. (5) They serve as "fields of dreams" to the imagination (for instance, dreaming of Bora Bora).

Research on cognitive mapping has moved in many directions since the pioneering work of the 1960s and 1970s mentioned above. From the standpoint of our argument, one of the most important steps was Richard Bjornson's proposal to extend the term to the cognitive processing of literature. Relying principally on Lynch's idea that "the observer [of an environment] selects, organizes, and endows with meaning what he sees" (1981, 53), Bjornson uses the term of cognitive map to denote a global mental representation of the literary text that involves not just spatial relations but any type of meaning and formal organization. Drawing a broad analogy between graphic maps and mental representations of texts, and echoing (or perhaps even anticipating) the claims of critical cartography, Bjornson writes that cognitive maps "are necessarily incomplete and schematized; they can never achieve exact correspondence with the territory they represent, and any claim that they embody absolute truth deserves to be regarded with skepticism" (55). It took the adoption of the term by a scholar as prominent as Fredric Jameson to put "cognitive mapping" on the literary-critical map. Also claiming inspiration from Lynch's *Image of the City*, Jameson (1988) proposed to extend the concept from the purely spatial to the social domain. To draw a "cognitive map" of social phenomena, in Jameson's sense, is to study these phenomena not in isolation but as part of a world-spanning network. The "phenomenological experience" of somebody living in London might for instance be bound up to "the whole colonial system of the British Empire," as this system "determines the very quality of the individual's subjective life" (Jameson 1988, 349). Geographers and cognitive psychologists might have a hard time associating Jameson's cognitive mapping with their own use of the term, especially since his conception of cognitive maps evolved throughout his career (Tally 2013, 67–74), but Jameson's adoption of the phrase paved the way toward cultural and globalization studies, and it opened the floodgates to a proliferation of map and mapping metaphors in literary theory.

Here we will work from a much narrower and literal definition. A cognitive map is a mental model of *spatial* relations. But this definition presents sufficient versatility to reach into narrative territory. The space represented by the map can indeed be real or imaginary. The mental model can be based on embodied experience (moving through space, seeing, hearing, smelling the world) or on the reading of texts. The text can be a graphic map or a verbal evocation. The verbal evocation can be narrowly focused on space (directions, descriptions, travel guides) or treat space as a stage for narrative events. The focus here will be on the second of each alternative.

CHRONICLE OF A DEATH FORETOLD AS TUTOR TEXT

For our investigation of the reader's construction of narrative space we have chosen *Chronicle of a Death Foretold* by Gabriel García Márquez. This text recommends itself for the study of mental maps through its meticulous attention to spatial configuration. It tells about the death of Santiago Nasar, a twenty-year-old member of an Arab minority in a Caribbean town. Presented as the investigation of a crime by a narrator-witness, *Chronicle of a Death Foretold* is a murder mystery without suspense. Readers know from page one that Nasar will be murdered, and they learn the identity of the killers on page 16. If there is any mystery in this pseudo-detective novel, it concerns the identity of the man for whom Nasar vicariously dies: for Nasar is killed by the brothers of a bride (Angela Vicario) who was returned to her mother on her wedding night because she was no longer a virgin. When Angela denounces Nasar as the perpetrator, her twin brothers Pedro and Pablo restore the family's honor by slaughtering the alleged culprit. But the unconcerned attitude of Nasar, as he walks to his death, makes it amply clear that Angela was covering up for somebody else. We never learn the identity of her secret lover, though Gonzalo Díaz-Migoyo (1988) has ingeniously argued that he must have been the narrator himself. But Nasar does not die for Angela's lover only. He becomes the scapegoat whose expulsion reaffirms the unwritten law that defines the institution of marriage in this society, a law that preserves the proprietary rights of husbands over wives by limiting male sexual activity to wives, servants, and prostitutes so as to leave untouched the wives or future wives of other men, and by forbidding expressions of female desire, an interdiction that Angela violates since there is no suggestion that she acted against her will. The ritualistic dimension of Nasar's death explains the ambivalence of the townspeople *vis-à-vis* the murder. Everybody is aware of the killers' intent, and many people make discreet attempts to warn the future victim, but nobody is willing or able to stand up and stop the unfolding of a sacrifice that both upholds the values of the community and repulses its members when taken individually.

As in most detective stories, the topographical layout of the setting fulfills a strategic function of utmost importance. It is common for investigators to draw a map of the crime scene and to plot on this map the movements of victim and suspects. In García Márquez's novel, this map is implicitly drawn by the narrator's minute-by-minute reconstruction of the events that led up to the murder of Nasar. The first section relates Santiago Nasar's actions on the morning of his death up to half an hour before the murder (which takes place at 7:05 a.m.). Nasar gets up at 5:45 in the morning after one hour's sleep—hung over from the wedding celebration of the previous day and a visit to the local madam—to greet the bishop who is visiting the town on a river boat. The whole town is there to honor the bishop, but he merely gives a blessing from his boat and sails on. After the departure of the bishop, Nasar is invited by the narrator's sister to have breakfast at their house further down on the river, but he decides to first change clothes, and he heads back toward his house with a friend, Cristo Bedoya.

The second section narrates in a flashback the courtship and wedding of Bajardo San Román and Angela Vicario. The third retraces the events following the end of the wedding celebration: the bride being returned to her mother; her brothers learning about her shame; the preparations for the murder; the brothers' waiting for Nasar at the milk shop (which doubles as a bar) across the square from Nasar's house; and Nasar, after visiting the brothel on this way home from the wedding, getting into his house safely through the back door to catch a few hours of sleep before the bishop's visit. The fourth section narrates the aftermath of the crime: the autopsy, the trial, and Bajardo San Román returning to Angela twenty years later. The last section picks up the chronicle of the last hour of Nasar's life where it had left off earlier in the narrative: Nasar gets separated from Bedoya when an Arab shopkeeper tries to warn Bedoya of Nasar's impending fate; he visits his fiancée's house; and finally returns home, to be butchered like a pig by the front door of his house, which his mother had inadvertently closed a few minutes earlier. The last scene shows Nasar staggering through the neighbor's house to get to the back of his own house. He sees the narrator's aunt on the other side of the river, answers her question, "What has happened to you?" with a laconic, "They've killed me, Wene child" (García Márquez 1982, 143), enters his house through the open back door, and falls dead in the kitchen.

RECONSTRUCTING THE MASTER MAP OF THE STORYWORLD

It takes a special agenda to attempt the systematic reconstruction of the "textually correct" map of a storyworld. It was only on a third reading of *Chronicle of a Death Foretold* that a reasonably complete and accurate representation of the novel's topography could be produced. The first reading of a literary narrative is typically a reading for the plot, and it needs to take so much information into consideration—characters, setting, events, and the stylistic quality of the writing—that it cannot focus on certain features at the expense of others. This first pass over a text typically leaves readers with a vivid, though spotty visualization of the setting: something like those reconstructed Cretan frescoes made of pictorial fragments separated by blank areas. Subsequent readings are more specialized, since it is mostly "professional" readers with a specific purpose who have the luxury to reread a text. In the present case, the second reading was concerned with whether or not the text was a good choice for an experiment in narrative mapping. During this second pass, a preliminary map was sketched, but the process needed a lot of erasing, and it is only through a third reading, during which all nonspatial information was bracketed out, that the map could be systematically checked against the text. We present the results of that third pass (figure 4.1) not as the mental image that any "good" reader should reach but as the representation of a mythical "model reader" or "super-reader" with whom no real reader will identify, because this model

80 • CHAPTER 4

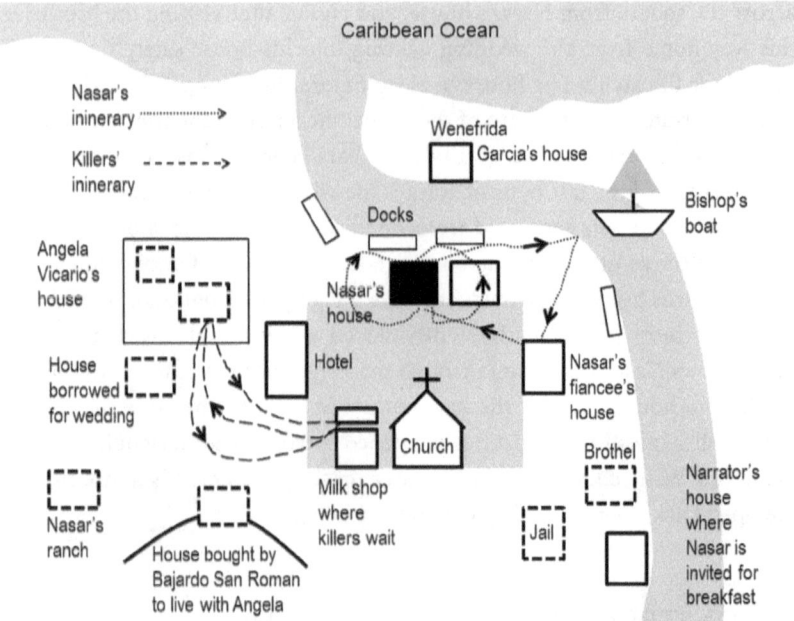

FIGURE 4.1. Master Map of *Chronicle of a Death Foretold*. Note: Nasar's itinerary starts at 5:45 a.m. on the day of his death; it does not include his earlier return from the wedding.

reader has near perfect recall and reads purely for the map. The purpose of this exercise is to build a standard of comparison for the drawings and reading acts of the flesh-and-blood informants.

We have seen in chapter 2 that the presentation of space in narrative can take two major forms: the "map," also called the survey and the "tour," also called the route. Another variable parameter is the timing of the disclosure of spatial information. The text can either disclose this information all at once to set the stage for the action or distribute it throughout the narrative. With its neat gathering of information, the all-at-once approach facilitates the task of the investigator who reads for the map, but it taxes the memory and attention span of those who read for the plot: how many of us can honestly say that we never skip descriptions? As we have seen in chapter 3, some narratives bypass this difficulty by presenting a graphic map of the setting. But the most widely practiced alternative to the setting the stage all at once is to unfold the representation of space gradually by linking the disclosure of spatial information to the actions of characters or by interleaving short descriptions with the report of narrative events. This is indeed the mapping strategy of *Chronicle of a Death Foretold*. Whereas the information tied to the moving bodies of characters creates mini-tours, the short descriptions outline mini-maps. To gain a panoramic view of narrative space the reader must be able to synthesize this information through a bottom-up process of construction.

Here is a sample of the variety of statements from which cartographic data can be derived (all page references are from García Márquez 1982):

Direct description:

> [Santiago Nasar's] house was a former warehouse, with two stories, walls of rough planks, and a peaked tin roof. (10)

> *Mapping action*: Give two stories to the house. (On a map with a pure vertical perspective this information cannot be used.)

Implication from report of events:

> By the time Ibrahim Nasar arrived with the last Arabs at the end of the civil wars, seagoing ships no longer came here because of shifts in the river, and the warehouse was in disuse. (10)

> *Mapping action*: Put Nasar's house reasonably close to an arm of the river; put the town at some distance from the ocean (on a delta or estuary).

Narrativized description[3]:

> Ibrahim Nasar bought [the warehouse] at a cheap price in order to set up an import store that he never did establish, and only when he was going to be married did he convert it into a house to live in. On the ground floor he opened up a parlor that served for everything, and in back he built a stable for our animals, the servant's quarters, and a country kitchen with windows opening onto the dock. (10)

> *Mapping action*: The entire floor plan of the house can be drawn from the narration of Ibrahim Nasar's remodeling.

Object movement:

> One morning when a servant girl had shaken the case to get the pillow out ... the pistol went off as it hit the floor and the bullet wrecked the cupboard

---

3. Term proposed by Harold Mosher (1991).

in the room, went through the living room wall, passed through the dining room of the house next door with the thunder of war, and turned a life-size saint on the main altar of the church on the opposite side of the square to plaster dust. (4)

Mapping action: Put Nasar's house on the town square. Next to it put another house. On the opposite side of the square put a church.

Character movement:

It was through [the front door] that [Santiago Nasar] went out to receive the bishop, despite the fact that he would have to walk completely around the house in order to reach the docks. (11)

Mapping action: Place the front door on the square side, away from the docks. This passage also reinforces the location of the back side of Nasar's house near the docks and the river.

Explicit specification of character position:

The only place open on the square was a milk shop on one side of the church, where the two men were who were waiting for Santiago Nasar in order to kill him. (16)

Mapping action: Place the milk shop next to the church and at a short distance from Nasar's house. Since these two buildings are on the side opposite to Nasar's house, and since Nasar's house can be observed from the milk shop, make the square fairly small.

Backgrounded specification of character location (a), character report (b), and character act of perception (c):

The landlady of the (a) bachelor's boarding house where Bayardo San Román lived told (b) of how he'd been napping in a rocking chair in the parlor toward the end of September, when Angela Vicario and her mother crossed the square carrying two baskets of artificial flowers. Bajardo San Román awoke, (c) saw the two women . . . and asked who the younger was. (30–31)

Mapping action: From (a) infer the existence of bachelor's boarding house in the town; from (b) and (c) locate it on the square.

Disembodied act of perception: [About the house of the widower Xius, which Bayardo San Román has bought to live with his future wife, Angela Vicario]

> It was on a windswept hill, and from the terrace you could see the limitless paradise of the marshes covered with purple anemones, and on a clear summer day you could make out the neat horizon of the Caribbean and the tourist ships from Cartagena de Indias. (39)

> *Mapping action*: Place the house on a hill at a distance from the town square; place the town in the vicinity of the ocean; situate the town in a simulacrum of real-world geography.

Omniscient representation of what characters do and do not perceive:

> From the place were [Plácida Linero, Nasar's mother] was standing she could see [the killers] but she could not see her son, who was running toward the door from a different angle. (138)

> *Mapping action*: Since at this point we know that the killers are coming from the milk shop, and Nasar from his fiancée's house, place the milk shop and fiancée's house on different sides of the square.

Figure 4.1 shows the map that results from these actions. We present the diagram not as *the* map but as one of the possible maps of the textual world. Just as texts project many possible worlds—one for every imaginative concretization—they project many topographies. The famed incompleteness of texts and the need to fill in informational gaps to reach a coherent interpretation is particularly acute when one tries to translate textual information into mental models of space, and these mental models into visual representations. A graphic map is not a cognitive map, but only the more or less faithful image of a cognitive map. Whereas the reader's mental image of textual worlds can leave the location of objects unspecified, graphic maps must situate every feature somewhere on the page.

What figure 4.1 does not properly show, then, is the degree of precision of the textual mapping. The world of *Chronicle of a Death Foretold* is organized into four zones of decreasing sharpness and resolution. The inner circle is constituted by the house of Nasar, the beginning and ending of the journey of both his day and his life. The text facilitates the drawing of the floor plan by chronicling Ibrahim Nasar's remodeling of the former warehouse. This strategy, which builds the house before the reader's inner eyes, follows the eighteenth-century thinker Gotthold Ephraim Lessing's recommendation that the temporal medium of poetry turn static descriptions into narrative action, as when Homer describes Juno's chariot by chronicling how Hebe puts it together piece by piece (1984 [1766], 80).

The middle circle, which encompasses the square and the docks by the river, is the scene of the last hour in Nasar's life. The location of landmarks in this area is of great heuristic importance, since it enables the reader-investigator to trace the movements of the victim and of the killers, but the strategy of space presentation adopted by García Márquez allows only a partial and relative situation of objects. This strategy falls into a no-man's-land between the various systems of representing space distinguished by discourse analysis: viewer-relative, absolute, and object-relative (Tversky 1996). A viewer-relative description (which can take the perspective of either character or narrator) presents objects as being left, right, in front of, or in back of the observer. An absolute description uses the coordinates south, north, east, and west. An object-relative description will locate an object as being "in front" of another, from this other object's "point-of-view"; thus a bench can be described as being in front of the church, because a church is an asymmetrical building with an implicit front (the entrance) and back. García Márquez's text occasionally uses the object-relative system (i.e., the front and back door of Nasar's house), but the vast majority of spatial notations do not belong to a particular system: for instance, the information that the milk shop is "next" to the church can be used in all three approaches. The absence in the text of what Ferguson and Hegarty (1994) call "anchors" does not facilitate the reconstruction of a spatial relations within the second circle. An anchor is a landmark that serves as point of reference for the location of other items; for instance "square" in this made-up description: "In the middle of the square is a fountain; on its south side, a church and a bar. The other three sides are lined with houses and shops. A narrow street takes off from the northwest corner of the square and leads past the jail and brothel to the river docks." Though the square forms the strategic center of the plot, it is not used in García Márquez's text as an orienteering tool; it is only through relatively complex deductions that the reader can place some landmarks around it (e.g., the description of the bullet flight quoted above).

The third strategic zone in the novel encompasses the outskirts of the town. This is the scene of the events that lead up to the murder: the courtship, the wedding, and the activities of characters between the end of the wedding and the visit of the bishop on the next morning. Here buildings are mentioned, but we only know that they lie at some distance from the square. The arbitrary location of a building on the map is indicated by broken lines.

The last zone, not sketched on the map, is the liminal area from which characters emerge (for instance, Bajardo San Román arriving one day on the weekly boat) or into which they disappear: the killers sent to jail in Riohacha, or Angela Vicario exiling herself to a village in the interior. In this broadest circle, the storyworld blends with real geography (Riohacha, Cartagena), but real-world locations lie far away on the horizon, leaving the town and its surroundings a free-floating area on the map of Colombia.

THE EXPERIMENT

Whereas the scientific approach to narrative cognition decontextualizes the act of reading, presents readers with texts specially designed for the occasion (texts usually so bland that nobody would have reasons to read them in real life), and evaluates mental processes in strictly quantitative terms (usually the time taken to perform specific tasks), the informal approach taken here, whose representatives include Victor Nell (1988) and Richard Gerrig (1993), attempts to penetrate into the mind of readers by inviting them to talk freely about their experience of "real" narrative texts—texts worth reading on their own merit. It is as a visual form of self-expression that the students were asked to draw pictures of the topographical layout of *Chronicle of a Death Foretold*. They were encouraged to use their imagination when their memory failed, and it was made clear to them that we were not conducting a test of how well they had read the text.

Sixty students participated in the experiment, but five of them limited their pictures to the floor plan of Nasar's house, and one returned a blank map. The floor plans were in general much more accurate than the larger maps, but the task was easier because the configuration of the house is described very clearly in the passage narrating Ibrahim Nasar's remodeling, and also because it is reinforced by several episodes that take place indoors. In the discussion below, we will ignore the floor plans and concentrate on the far more complex task of drawing a map of the whole town.

As an expression of the reader's mental representation of a storyworld, the maps can be evaluated in terms of three criteria: inventory, spatial relations, and mapping style.

Inventory

Examining maps in terms of inventory means paying attention to what kind of objects readers include on their drawing, where these objects come from—the text, or other sources—and what the selection tells us about the mapmaker's conceptualization of the plot. Table 4.1 lists the most frequently mentioned

TABLE 4.1. The most often mentioned items on the maps

Feature (* = Not Mentioned in Text)	Mentions (out of 55)	Percentage (rounded)
Santiago Nasar's house	54	98
River	43	78
Square	37	67
Docks	32	58
Angela Vicario's house	31	56
Church (cathedral)	30	54
Widower Xius's/newlyweds' house	27	49
*Fountain on square	25	45
Milk store/bar/saloon	23	41
Bishop on boat	22	40
Butcher (*butcher shop)	22	40
Front door of Nasar's house	18	32
Brothel	12	21

features in descending order. Not surprisingly, the most prominent landmark is the house of Nasar. This suggests that the drawings are plot-centered, which means that the mapmakers retrieve from memory the salient features of the storyworld by mentally replaying the fate of the hero. The plot can be replayed in terms of two parameters: the spatial movements of Nasar on the morning of his death, and the network of interpersonal relations that cause his murder. The spatial system explains the importance of the river, square, bishop's boat, front door of Nasar's house, and narrator's house, while the interpersonal system produces the buildings associated with the wedding (Angela Vicario's house, the widower Xius's house, Bajardo San Román's hotel), as well as those directly involved with the killers' actions (milk shop, knife shop, butcher shop).[4] Of the items at the top of the list, the least connected to the characters and to the logic of the plot are the church and the fountain. The church is the object of several textual references, but it is most strongly called to mind by the cover of the book, which shows a plaza with an imposing Baroque cathedral. The fountain is harder to explain, since it is not mentioned in the text nor depicted in an illustration. The students must have used standard cultural images of what a town square or a Latin American plaza looks like.

4. Literally speaking, there is no butcher shop in the text. The brothers raise and slaughter pigs, and keep knives in their workshop. They sell the meat at the meat market. Applying the cultural schema of the town square as shopping center, the readers who mentioned these locations turned the workshop into a knife store and the meat market into a butcher shop. They also added a coffee shop, though it is at Pablo Vicario's fiancée's house that the killers drink coffee.

The bottom of the list (i.e., the features mentioned only once or twice) was divided between landscape elements of purely atmosphere-creating importance (fields, mango grove, flower pots, dogs, chicken coops, hills), houses of minor characters (Divina Flor, Pablo Vicario's fiancée, Yamil Shaiun), and nontextual items brought into the picture by cultural schemata, personal experience, or (one suspects) by the pure pleasure of letting the imagination loose: cemetery, cactus, school, cow pen near the milk shop, restaurant, drugstore, coffee shop, ghetto, trailer park, beach, and even a road sign pointing to the United States. The maps were just as revealing of their authors' conceptualizations of the plot for what they omitted as for what they included or added. In general, the landmarks mentioned in the early episodes were much better represented than the features of the later ones. The scene of the bishop's visit on a riverboat, told in the first section, had a strong impact on the readers imagination (78 percent drew the river, 40 percent drew the bishop), while the dramatic last scene, in which the mortally wounded Nasar staggers through the neighbor's house and sees the narrator's aunt across the river, left minimal cartographic traces: only four maps (7 percent) mentioned the neighbor's house, and none included the house of Wene García. This suggests that in reading matters, as in other domains of experience, the first impression is the strongest: the representation of textual worlds gels early on, providing the imagination with a playfield for the moves of characters, and it expands from a core of information that remains vividly inscribed in memory.

Spatial Relations

The evaluation of spatial relations is much more difficult than the analysis of the inventory, because it deals with scalar rather than binary categories. While an item is or isn't on the map (the only doubt here is what the reader meant with the label), it can be located at variable distances from another item. How close, for instance, does a house have to be from the river to be scored as "on the river"? The criterion used here is that an item is next to another when there is no other item in between. Once one decides on criteria, the diagramming of spatial relations can be scored in a more rigorous way than the mapping of what is there. Inventories are more or less complete but never totally wrong, since the presence of nontextual items can be attributed to the imaginative need to flesh out the textual world. But in their representations of spatial relations, the sketches can be shown to be accurate or inaccurate on the basis of solid textual evidence. Since the maps differ widely in what objects they include, the evaluation of the correctness of spatial relations was based

TABLE 4.2. Representation of spatial relations. Relevant field indicates the number of maps that include all the locations named in the relation: for instance, number of maps that have both Nasar's house and a square for the relation "Nasar house on square."

Name of Relation (*Textually Inaccurate)	Number of Maps Showing Relation	Relevant Field*	Percentage of Relevant Field
Nasar's house on square	19	37	51
Nasar's house near river	15	43	34
Nasar's house on square and near river	6	34	17
*Nasar's house not on square nor river	14	34	41
Church on square	19	20	95
Milk shop on square	11	17	64
Milk shop next to church	4	9	44
Milk shop on square opposite Nasar's house	3	12	25
Church opposite Nasar's house	12	20	60
Angela's house away from square	16	21	76
Xius's/San Roman's house away from square	27	27	100
Butcher away from square	6	15	40
Brothel away from square	2	7	29

on the subset of the maps that show the relevant objects; for instance, thirty-seven of the fifty-five maps show both Nasar's house and the square; of these thirty-seven, nineteen place Nasar's house directly on the square; the accuracy of the spatial relation "Nasar house vs. square" is therefore nineteen out of thirty-seven, or 51 percent (see table 4.2).

Most of the maps select the square as anchor point, a decision justified by its thematic and strategic prominence. The highest percentage of accuracy concerns the placement of the church (95 percent) and of the widower Xius's house (100 percent). The location of the church on the square is enforced by textual description, cultural schemata, and the illustration on the book's cover. As for the widower Xius's house, it is the subject matter of a memorable episode, during which the text makes it very clear that it is situated on a hill at a distance from the town center. The items that fall in the middle range of accuracy (60–80 percent) display a tendency to bring strategically important characters or locations from the periphery toward the center. For instance, 76 percent of the maps correctly place Angela's house away from the square, but the 24 percent that place the house on the square most likely do so because she is a main character and must therefore be located in the heart of the action. Similarly 60 percent of the maps that represent the knife "shop" (see note 1) move it erroneously to the square, not only because of its connection to the killers, themselves important characters, but also as part of the commercial zone that surrounds the plaza. The misplacing of the brothel (29 percent accuracy) further suggests a tendency to allocate a central location to all the buildings that belong to the cultural image of a town, even though brothels are usually hidden in the outskirts. If we discount the placement of some items too rarely mentioned to be statistically significant, the largest proportion of errors concerns the location of Nasar's house between the square and the river: only 17 percent of the maps that had Nasar's house, the square, and the river correctly placed the house between the other two items. These misplacements can be explained by the lack of explicit information regarding spatial relations. The actions of characters imply that Nasar's house is close to the river, as well as that it is on the square, but the text never presents these hints in the same passage, nor does it explicitly mention that the square is close to the river—a mandatory inference, if Nasar's house borders on both.

But the factors that determine the placement of buildings are not necessarily textual. In their mapping of the textual world, many students seem to have started with the two most important landscape features, the river and the square. Other objects could have been added according to one or the other of two drawing strategies: either cluster objects around the two anchors; or try to fill the empty space between the square and the river, so as to produce a well-balanced picture. Students might also have been reluctant to erase a false start that left no room for proper location. Purely graphic considerations might thus explain why a large percentage of those students who had both a river and a square on their map placed Nasar's house at a distance from both of these landmarks. This graphic consideration leads us to the next mode of evaluation.

Mapping Strategies

While a map is an abstract model of space drawn from a (usually) vertical perspective, a picture is an iconic representation drawn from a horizontal point of view that corresponds to the visual perception of an observer. These two basic modes of spatial representation allow various degrees of compromise: maps can contain iconic symbols or adopt an oblique perspective that gives the spectator an idea of what the world looks like to an embodied observer located on the ground, while pictures can represent a landscape from a slightly elevated viewpoint, acquiring a map-like quality. Table 4.3 shows the distribution of the maps of our corpus along this continuum. "Pure plan" (figure 4.2)

90 • CHAPTER 4

TABLE 4.3. Map styles

Map Style	Number (out of 55)	Percentage (truncated)
Pure plan	20	36
Iconic plan (subset of Pure plan)	2	3
Mixed plan-picture	26	47
Predominantly pictorial representation	6	10
Pure picture	3	5

either avoids elevation-style elements or tolerates them only for the sake of differentiation; for instance, a church icon may allow the viewer to distinguish two types of buildings, churches and houses. "Iconic plans" (figure 4.3) are consistently represented from a vertical perspective, but the icons reproduce visual perception. This trend is even more dominant in "mixed plan-picture" (figure 4.4), which represents a wide variety of objects in elevation view. "Predominantly pictorial representation" (figure 4.5) selects an elevated point of view, and while it shows spatial relations, it attempts to convey a sense of the appearance of the buildings or landscape. These map types are not clear-cut; they rather form a continuum.

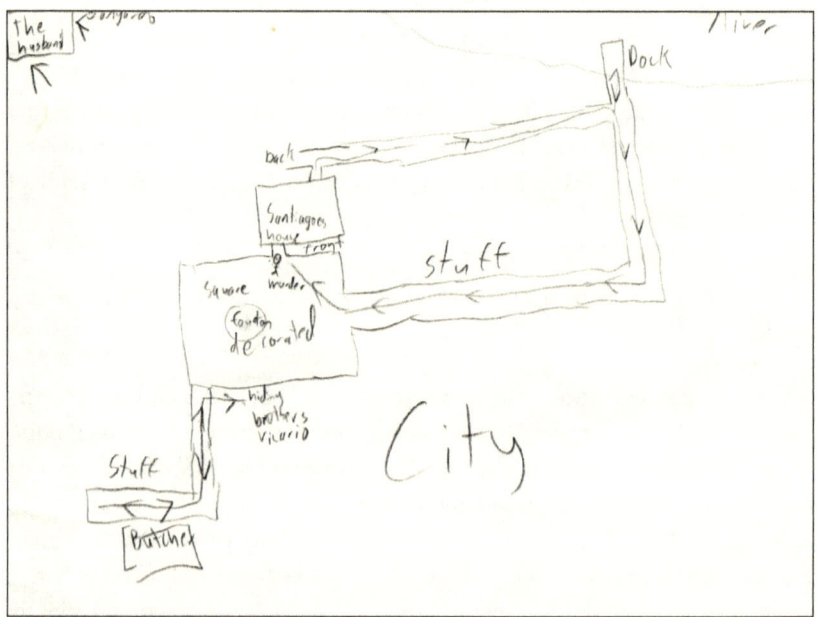

FIGURE 4.2. Itinerary map: Pure plan

FIGURE 4.3. Symbolic map: Iconic plan

In addition to occupying various points on the continuum running from pure plan to pure picture, the maps of our corpus illustrate the following pairs of opposite mapping strategies:

- Bringing every item important to plot to the center (as many maps not reproduced here do) versus drawing the town square according to cultural models).[5]
- Trying to be accurate with respect to the plot (figure 4.2) versus trying to draw a pretty picture that fills the page nicely (figures 4.3 and 4.4)
- Limiting the map to plot-significant items (figure 4.2) versus situating plot-significant items within a broader representation of a town (figure 4.4)

Let's now discuss briefly the mapping strategies and narrative emphasis of three of the sketches. The examples were selected for their diversity, as well as for their (obviously relative) accuracy in terms of either inventory or representation of spatial relations.

---

5. For reason of space the maps in the database that represents this strategy are not shown.

92 • CHAPTER 4

FIGURE 4.4. Storyspace map: Mixed picture-plan

Map of Character Movement (Figure 4.2)

This map could have been produced by a detective investigating the case. Consistently drawn from the vertical perspective of a city plan, it combines time and space by representing the respective itineraries of Nasar and the killers. It is one of the few sketches that places Nasar's house both on the square and close to the docks. The line of the river meanders away from Nasar's back door, but this is consistent with the text, since the river is said to have changed its course from when Ibrahim Nasar acquired the warehouse. The two-directional arrow for the murderers' itinerary from their

FIGURE 4.5. Predominantly pictorial representation

slaughtering shop to the milk store indicates their back-and-forth movement, itself a symptom of their hesitations: they take knives from their shop, go to the milk store, return home, get new knives, and go back to the milk store. The map, drawn by a male student, conceptualizes the plot as the interaction of three parties, all represented by male characters: the ex-future husband, Nasar, and the killers. Visual details are generally omitted, which makes it all the more surprising to find a fountain on the square. Though the fountain is not a textual element, it helps differentiate the town square from the other square shapes on the map.

Symbolic Map (Figure 4.3)

With its drawing of the town square as the intersections of the two arms of a gigantic cross, this map privileges graphic design and symbolic meaning over the logic of the plot. Was the mapmaker (female) influenced, perhaps subconsciously, by the religious theme of the novel and by the crossings of the square performed by Nasar and Angela? (Nasar, the innocent who dies for another, is a Christ-figure who ends up literally crucified on the front door of his house.) The dominant episode here is the wedding of Angela and Bajardo; no explicit mention is made of the murder. But the map alludes to the waiting of the killers by situating the milk shop catercorner from Nasar's house with nothing in between to block the view of the brothers. Another diagonal runs from the brothel to the wedding house, suggesting the contrast of marriage and prostitution, while a symbolic triangle links the Vicario house to the church and to the wedding house, bypassing the brothel: the triangle of socially approved marital love.

Storyspace Map (Figure 4.4)

Many of the maps suggest that the assignment was a chore for the cartographer. This reader (whose gender was left unspecified) took it as an opportunity to let the imagination embroider new tales on the canvas of the storyworld. On the borderline between map (vertical perspective of the spatial layout) and illustration (frontal perspective of the individual objects), this drawing might not meet the highest standards of accuracy in the area of textual topography, but it captures beautifully the verve, tall-tale exaggerations, and gossip quality of García Márquez's narrative style—a style deeply influenced by oral storytelling. With the Halloween motif in the foreground, the beach and sea monsters in the background, and the shopping mall lining Main Street, the map turns the South American town into a hybrid of amusement park and U.S. city. But the thematics of the novel are not entirely forgotten. By making the church (on the left) and the brothel (on the right) the two salient features of the landscape, the drawing suggests the ambiguous opposition that dominates the life of the townspeople: should we read it as good versus evil (as would the official ideology), or as the repression versus the liberation of sexual energies? Sacrificing textual accuracy to symbolic meaning, the drawing underscores the public nature of the murder and the complicity of the whole town by moving the death of Nasar from the doorsteps of his house to the center of the plaza.

COGNITIVE MAPS AND THE READING PROCESS

From Cognitive Maps to Graphic Maps

What can we learn from this experiment about the importance of cognitive mapping, or mental models of space for narrative comprehension? It is important to avoid confusing the students' sketches with their purely mental models of narrative space. The drawings are in a sense the exact opposite of a cognitive map. Whereas cognitive maps internalize an experience of space that is usually based on visual cues (studying a graphic map; walking through a city; reading a text[6]), the sketches drawn by the students are graphic transpositions of mental images. Even though the experiment was conducted informally rather than staged in the controlled environment thought to be necessary to scientific rigor, it cannot avoid the fundamental ambiguity of scientific observation, an ambiguity known in the social sciences as the Hawthorne effect. This effect arises when subjects change or improve aspects of their behavior when being observed simply because they know they are being studied, rather than in response to any particular experimental modification of their work environment. A graphic map is a heuristic tool that feeds back into the reader's mental image, shaping it through the very process of representing it.

By asking the students to draw a map rather than a picture, we implicitly imposed a certain visual form on the graphic transposition of their mental image. But as the preceding section shows, many of the students resisted this suggestion by choosing a compromise between the map and the picture. Most students regarded the experiment as an opportunity to develop, rather than mirror, a vision of the storyworld, but at least one of them took the assignment as a literal invitation to reproduce a preexisting mental image. This student declined to draw a map, justifying his or her decision with the comment "never gave any thought at all to trying to place locations in relationship to one another or map them while reading the text."

The fact that the students represented their view of the storyworld in map or semi-map form does not necessarily mean that mental models of space constructed on the basis of narrative texts resemble graphic maps—as does, for instance, our internal representation of the map of the world. The issue of the resemblance between graphic and mental maps and of the importance of visualization for the construction of spatial models has received considerable

---

6. As the case of blind people forming a representation of the arrangement of their house suggests, mental maps can also be built on the basis of nonvisual experience.

attention in cognitive science. In work dating back to the 1960s, the cognitive psychologist Allan Paivio (1986) suggested that information can be stored in either pictorial or propositional, quasiverbal form, depending on the mind-style of the subject (some people are "visualizers" while others are not) and on the nature of the data. Some types of information—for instance the meaning of a sentence like "the cat chased the dog"—can be stored in both forms while other types ("I think therefore I am") can only be stored as a proposition. This is known in cognitive psychology as the "dual-coding" theory (Esrock 1994, 96–104). A mental model of a storyworld clearly belongs to the type of information that can be represented both ways.

Experimental research on the nature and functioning of mental models of space associated with texts has taken two directions. The first (Bower and Morrow 1990; Morrow, Bower, and Greenspan 1989) consists of asking subjects to memorize a graphic map before reading a story that takes place in the represented setting. These authors have argued that readers perform the same types of operations on such models as they would on a graphic map. The travel of characters is simulated by locating them on the mental map, moving them from spot to spot, and visualizing the objects that surround them at every stop. It takes a longer time for subjects to imagine travel that covers a long distance on the internalized map than to mentally move characters between close locations, and objects located near the character's current coordinates are more easily retrieved from memory than objects located away from the character. While this research demonstrates the possibility of map-like mental models of space, its relevance to the processing of literary narratives is, at best, limited to the case of novels that include a graphic map.

The second type of research (Ferguson and Hegarty 1994; Tversky 1991, 1996) addresses the issue of the construction of mental maps from a purely textual input. But it tends to deal with short descriptive texts that foreground the representation of space. For instance, Ferguson and Hegarty (1994) asked informants to draw a sketch map on the basis of this passage:

> The little town of Crestview is an old mining town. To reach Crestview by car, drive north along the highway. Crestview begins when you cross the Green River. The river flows out of some low hills that lie on your left. Just after you drive across, you can see Crestview High School, which lies on the back to your left at the base of the hills. The small curvy Frontier Road begins on your left and provides the connection to the high school from the highway. On your right, directly across from the entrance to Frontier Road, you pass a gas station. The gas station is on the river bank, and fishing bait and tackle can be purchased there. (472)

This type of data is not particularly useful for the investigation of the importance of cognitive maps for the processing of semantically complex literary texts that treat space as a stage for narrative action. It should come as no surprise that the sketch maps obtained by Ferguson and Hegarty were infinitely more faithful to the text than the drawings of our informants.

The maps we collected seem far too incomplete, the salient features too randomly distributed on the page, and the representation of spatial relations too inaccurate to suggest that their authors followed the narrative by moving the image of Nasar on the mental equivalent of a comprehensive plan of the town, as one moves a pawn on a game board. This does not mean that readers do not form vivid mental pictures of the hero at various points in his itinerary. Even the authors of the sloppiest drawings might have been be able to visualize Nasar leaving his house, waiting for the bishop by the river, heading home through the streets, turning the corner to the square, being attacked by his front door, or entering the kitchen to die. But these individual visualizations are too ephemeral to be assembled into a global representation comparable to the master map of figure 4.1.

Cognitive Maps and Memory

To understand the disparity and relative inaccuracy of the students' sketches we must take into consideration the full complexity of the reading process. As cognitive scientists Marschark and Cornoldi (1991, 165) observe, text processing occurs simultaneously at several different levels, corresponding to words, sentences, paragraphs, and passages. To this list one may add the level of the global meaning, or narrative macro-structure. Reading also involves two levels of memory. Whereas the global representation is stored in long-term memory, smaller textual units affect primarily what has been called the sketch pad of short-term memory. It is on this sketch pad that readers form their most detailed visualizations. It seems safe to assume that these visualizations are picture-like representations that encompass both the characters and the characters' fields of vision. We see the characters, but we also see with them, and we share their horizontal point of view.[7]

---

7. The cognitive psychologist Barbara Tversky (1996) has argued that mental models of space constructed on the basis of texts are neither map-like nor tour-like in nature, but manipulable images that do not come with a fixed perspective. Adopting different points of view on their mental models, readers can answer map-like questions ("is a north or south of b") on the basis of tour-like descriptions, and tour-like questions ("what does a traveler see on the left after passing the lake") on the basis of map-like descriptions. Tversky's finding were, however, obtained on the basis of short texts exclusively focused on spatial relations, similar to the Ferguson and Hegarty (1994) passage quoted above.

The master map of figure 4.1 represents an attempt to retain the images of short-term memory, to turn them into cartographic symbols, and to situate them on the global map of long-term memory. But on the sketch pad of short-term memory, the visualizations generated by the individual scenes merely replace each other. The reader may thus be perfectly able to imagine the story's main episodes without precisely situating each events on a global map. Or if the reader does indeed situate events, the coordinates may be forgotten when the next event fills the screen of the mind. If spatial imagination proceeds piecemeal, the reader will situate site a with respect to site b; then site b with respect to site c when a character is shown moving between these points, but the reader will not necessarily situate c with respect to a on her mental model, unless the relation is crucial to the logic of the plot.

The act of reading has often been compared to "cinema in the mind." If the metaphor is accurate, we construct the story, scene by scene, as a series of camera shots or "fields of vision," as Gabriel Zoran (1984, 311) has called these discrete mental units. When we watch a movie, we see individual images of the strategic locations of the storyworld, but we are usually unable to locate these sites with respect to each other, even when the movie begins with an establishing shot that shows the setting from a bird's-eye perspective. The purpose of these shots is to capture the atmosphere of the setting, but since they quickly disappear from the screen, they cannot serve as a reliable orientation device. Novels are more conducive to the construction of plan-like models of space than movies because their readers set their own pace through the story, and also because the signs of language, which speak to the mind rather than to the senses, leave more room to the imagination. But the example of movies tells us that most plots can be followed with the help of very rudimentary sketches of global space. The role of mental maps is to provide a common background to the individual images (or "little movies") of short-term memory, allowing these individual images to cohere into a world and a story. But the background is not constructed by fitting together the images of short-term memory like the pieces of a puzzle, for this would mean that long-term memory collects everything that affects short-term memory, and also that comprehensive images of textual space cannot be fully formed before the end of the text. If mental maps help readers follow the plot, they are needed throughout the reading process. This means that readers must form from the very beginning some kind of global vision of the spatial configuration of the storyworld, no matter how full of gaps this vision might be.

The items most frequently included on the students' sketches give us a good idea of what permanent landmarks readers find indispensable to make themselves at home in the world of *Chronicle of a Death Foretold*: a town, a river, a public square, a church, and a house for the main character. These landmarks surround a drama that involves Nasar and the characters associated with the next few items on the frequency list: Angela and San Roman (linked to widower Xius's/the newlyweds' house) and the killers (linked to milk shop/bar). The students' sketches might not be transparent images of cognitive maps, but they provide a useful document of the selective work of long-term memory. In their emphasis on characters' houses they corroborate this observation by Ralf Schneider: "Readers focus their interest in the storyworld on the characters rather than, for instance, fictional time or space or narrative situations" (2001, 628). Mental models of narrative space are centered on the characters, and they grow out of them, in contrast to the stage setting of a play, which normally starts out as a fully furnished but unpopulated space and gradually fills up with characters.

The Construction of Mental Models of Narrative Space

We can only speculate about the dynamic formation of mental models of narrative, but it seems evident that it differs from the production of the master map and of geographic maps in general. To draw the master map, we started with a blank page, added spatial features, one by one, as we went through the text, and we relocated these features when their placement on the map turned out to conflict with later information. It took a lot of erasing, throwing away of faulty drafts, and starting over from scratch to create a map consistent with the text. The novel offered a far greater amount of spatial information than memory can hold, and the mapping activity would not have been possible without pen and paper.

In contrast to graphic maps, mental maps are drawn and used by the same individual, and the processes of surveying and consulting are conducted almost simultaneously. Readers need mental maps to follow the plot, but they construe these maps on the basis of the plot. Out of the movements of characters (what Zoran [1984, 313] calls chronotopic space), we construct a global vision (Zoran's topographic space) that enables us to situate events. While this global vision is constructed through a bottom-up activity, it provides top-down guidance to the explorer of the textual world. Since the reader's imagination needs a mental model of space to simulate the narrative action, it is important to achieve a holistic representation of the storyworld as quickly as possible. In table 4.2, the most frequently occurring elements are indeed all landscape features that appear in the first few pages of the novel. Once a rough sketch of the storyspace map has been mentally sketched, it will be relatively resistant to new input or modifications. When new information conflicts with the reader's mental model of space, it is easier to concentrate on the visualization of the current scene and ignore the discrepancy than to reorganize the whole map. This would explain the inaccuracies of the students' maps with respect to the letter of the text. If this hypothesis is correct, the relative stability of mental models of space contrasts with the dynamic character of character models (Schneider 2001, 628). Whereas space functions as a background, characters stand in the foreground of narrative interest; and whereas space mainly consists of permanent features, characters are evolving bodies and minds who continuously add events to their personal history. It seems reasonable to expect that the changing foreground will be the object of a more intense updating activity than the stable background.

While the readers' exploration of the storyworld is complicated by the necessity of constructing the map as they go along, the mapmaking activity is somewhat simplified by the fact that the map does not have to meet the needs of any other user. Geographic maps contain information for a wide variety of users, both travelers and dreamers; they must consequently include an equally wide variety of possible landmarks, destinations, and routes. But the mental map of a textual world is exclusively geared toward the mind that constructs it. Though one cannot speak of a specific destination in the case of narrative texts—here, the goal is a rich imaginative experience of the entire action and a reasonable understanding of narrative logic—the mental map of a narrative can fulfill its cognitive function of allowing the reader to mentally simulate the evolution of the storyworld without being complete, or narrowly faithful, to the text. As we observed above, people read for the plot and not for the map, unless they are literary cartographers. We construct mental models of narrative space only as far as we find a cognitive advantage in this activity—only as far as is needed to achieve immersion in the storyworld and understanding of the action.

CHAPTER 5

Space, Narrative, and Digital Media

IN 1997 (and again in 2011), Janet Murray identified spatiality as one of the four major distinctive properties of digital media, along with being procedural, participatory, and encyclopedic. This pronouncement, which falls in line with Fredric Jameson's (1991) claim that late twentieth-century culture is characterized by a "spatial turn," has been widely accepted by researchers. Yet the meaning of Murray's formula, "Digital media are spatial," can be conceived in many different ways, depending on what kind of space one focuses on.

Ever since the term "cyberspace" was borrowed from William Gibson's 1984 novel *Neuromancer* to refer to what we reach through computer networks, more particularly through the Internet, we have developed the habit of thinking of computers as machines that take us into a separate reality—a domain conceived in terms of spatial metaphors. There is nothing inherently spatial about a collection of documents stored on remote computers and made accessible to us through digital networks, except for the physical location of the computers. Nor does cyberspace present the basic properties of real-world geography, which might be why it is now associated with the clouds rather than with an imaginary country. Far from being physically limited, like the earth, it expands indefinitely, like the universe, as new pages are added to it, and people can homestead by building their own site without depriving others of the same opportunity. Rather than containing places and roads separated by more or less empty territories, cyberspace consists exclusively of places (the pages) and roads (the links), so that travelers cannot wander off the path: in cyberspace, you are either visiting a page or on your way to a new page. In physical space there are long and short roads, depending on the closeness of the places they connect, but in cyberspace all links have the same length, or rather no length at all. The speed of travel (read: of downloading) is not determined by the physical distance between your computer and the machine that hosts the data, but by the number of links to be traversed. If it weren't for delays and detours caused by traffic congestion and the amount of data to be downloaded, movement between linked places would not be travel, but teletransportation—a mode of access that denies the existence of separating distances. We move in physical space through a steady progression along a line, but we travel cyberspace in jumps, without experiencing a developing landscape, since there is nothing between our point of departure and our destination (Ryan 2004).

Despite these obvious differences between real and virtual geographies, the cyberspace metaphor invites us to think of the Internet as forming a parallel universe made of countless galaxies, planetary systems within these galaxies, worlds within these systems, and nations within these worlds. The technical jargon of Internet culture, with its "home" pages, suggests that cyberspace is experienced not only as an open space to be explored though a nomadic impulse but also as a collection of places to inhabit. The cyber-cartographers Dodge and Kitchin, relying on observations by P. Adam, observe that "cyberspace is replete with the vocabulary of place—nouns such as rooms, lobbies, highway, frontier, cafés; and verbs such as surf, inhabit, built, enter" (2001b, 56).

Far from being limited to the Internet as a whole, spatial metaphors have been used by scholars and developers to describe the specific organization and the mode of reading individual documents. On the Internet, information is structured as hypertext, which means as a network of data-containing nodes connected by links. Through their selection of links, users are said to "navigate" individual hypertexts (as well as the global hypertext of the World Wide Web), a conceptualization that combines nautical travel with the image of a road map. *Storyspace*, the name of the hypertext authoring system developed by Eastgate Systems in the late 1980s, reinforces the idea of the inherent spatiality of hypertext; so do other metaphors applied to hypertext, such as the labyrinth or the Borgesian image of a Garden of Forking Paths.

While the spatiality of hypertext exemplifies what we have called spatial form, digital media share with other modes of representation, such as print text, oral storytelling, still pictures, and movies, the ability to create worlds imagined as three-dimensional (or four with time). But it is only in digital media that a represented world offers the user the opportunity to travel and explore its space, because it is only in digital media that users are placed in an environment that can be dynamically reconfigured in response to their actions. As Janet Murray (1997, 82) observes, "The interactive process of navigation" is the distinctive feature of New Media spatiality.

Yet the spatiality of digital media, and of the experiences they make possible, is not limited to the spatial form of hypertexts nor to the virtual space of represented worlds: the development of mobile technology, global positioning systems (GPS), and augmented reality counters the tendency of computers to lure sedentary users into virtual worlds by replacing simulated environments with real-world settings and by sending users on a treasure hunt in physical space.

In this chapter, we will examine uses of digital technology that illustrate one or the other of these forms of spatiality and that offer new ways to experience the connections between space, place, and narrative:

1. Allowing active participation in story-rich virtual worlds.
2. Exploiting the properties of digital maps to create new forms of narrative.
3. Anchoring narrative in real space through mobile technology.

ACTIVE PARTICIPATION IN STORY-RICH VIRTUAL WORLDS

With the creation of interactive virtual worlds, whether online and multiplayer or single-player and located on the user's computer, digital technology has taken a major step toward a new form of entertainment: a form based on an unprecedented combination of narrative and games. Thanks to these worlds, the narrative experience is no longer limited to imagining the life of other people; recipients can be active agents whose decisions play a decisive role in determining what happens in the storyworld. Conversely, games are no longer sequences of formal moves prescribed by rigid rules and taking place on an abstract playfield, what Huizinga (1950, 10) called the magic circle; they simulate the types of action that the residents of the real world or the inhabitants of fantastic worlds perform in the pursuit of personal needs. In standard sports games or board games, the players' goals are only made desirable by the rules of the game; without these rules, players would have no reason to align three tokens on a line, as in *Tic-Tac-Toe,* or to kick a ball into a net, as in soccer. Computer games also started out as the pursuit of conventionally determined goals (think of *PacMan, Tetris,* or computer chess), but they quickly developed into a simulation of inherently desirable action, such as flying airplanes, rescuing princesses, or killing dragons. (These last two goals might seem rather conventional, but given the proper circumstances, who would not want to rescue a beautiful and wealthy princess and kill a threatening dragon?) By proposing practically, rather than conventionally, desirable goals to the players, and in many cases by projecting the player as an individuated character situated in a concrete world, video games present a built-in affinity with narrative.[1]

Yet the marriage of narrative and games is not without its own domestic problems, and the union has required significant concessions from each of the partners. Narrative had to sacrifice its thematic and formal diversity in order to make itself compatible with the modes of interaction afforded by the medium. It is easy for the computer to represent physical action, such as moving around the gameworld, picking up objects, and using these objects (primarily to fight enemies), but it would take very advanced artificial intelligence to simulate the major elements of complex literary narrative: verbal interaction, mental processes, or the emotional reactions of characters to events. This explains, in part, the dominance in games of the narrative pattern of adventures and quests (as described by Campbell 1973 [1949]; Propp 1968), which consist mainly of the performance of heroic deeds. Games, on the other hand, had to put limits on the agency of the player in order to satisfy the demands of narrative interest, which ask for compelling characters showing evidence of mental life, evolving networks of interpersonal relations, and moral dilemmas. It is mostly through noninteractive film-like cut scenes (Klevjer 2002), during which the player is reduced to the role of spectator, that most games develop the rich narrative background that motivates players to pursue the game goals.

Computer Games and Space

According to Espen Aarseth, the founding father of computer game studies, "What distinguishes the cultural genre of computer games from others such as novels and movies, in addition to its obvious cybernetic differences, is its

---

1. The ability to represent familiar objects also had a great advantage from a strategic point of view. When a game is played on an abstract playfield players must learn the rules before playing the game; but when it is played in a concrete world, they can bring in their life experience. For instance, if you see a car in *Grand Theft Auto* you know right away what you can do with it—you know its affordances.

preoccupation with space" (2001 [online], 161). Borrowing from French sociologist Henri Lefebvre the concept of "spatial practice," Aarseth observes that in computer games, this practice takes two forms: "As spatial practice, computer games are both representations of space (a formal system of relations) and representational spaces (symbolic imagery with primarily aesthetic purpose)" (163). The terms "representation of space" and "representational space," which are directly borrowed from the English translation of Lefebvre, are somewhat opaque, and we prefer to label the first type of spatial practice "strategic design" and the second "mimetic design," but this does not take anything away from the importance of the two concepts. As a formal system of relations, strategic design organizes the playing field into distinct zones where specific events can happen; as symbolic imagery, mimetic design is the representation of landscapes and objects familiar to the player, such as mountains, deserts, cities, castles, cars, airplanes, and swords. It is tempting to associate mimetic and strategic design with Deleuze and Guattari's (1987) notions of smooth and striated space: the mimetic design invites the player to adopt the attitude of a nomad traveling through game space for the pure pleasure of seeing the landscape evolve and making unexpected discoveries, while the strategic design subordinates travel to the points to be reached and the tasks to be performed in order to progress in the game.[2]

The difference between strategic space and mimetic space is illustrated by the contrast between figure 5.1, a screenshot from *Ms. PacMan,* and figure 5.2, a screenshot from *World of Warcraft. PacMan* is an early game (1980) with a largely abstract scenario: the player receives the goal of moving a shape through a maze and passing over all the dots that fill the pathways, without running into four other shapes that move unpredictably. The fact that both the player's shape and those controlled by the computer are individuated by names invites the player to narrativize gameplay as a good guy (or gal, in *Ms. PacMan*) being chased by evil monsters. But this narrative content is very thin, and the game takes place on a minimalist playfield rather than in a visually rich gameworld. The playfield is shown in map view, a projection that enables the player to contemplate it in its entirety and see clearly its strategic structure. This structure is that of a maze, with visible walls limiting the directions in which the player's character (or rather, token) can move. The dots that fill the paths have a strategic value, since they bring bonus points to the player once his token moves over them, but they

---

2. As Deleuze and Guattari (1987, 353) put it: "The smooth and the striated are distinguished first of all by an inverse relation between the point and the line (in the case of the striated the line is between two points, while in the smooth the point is between two lines)."

FIGURE 5.1. *Ms. PacMan*: Abstract playfield

are totally deprived of mimetic dimension. This is not to say that *Ms. Pac-Man* has no visual design; but this visual design is entirely motivated by its strategic configuration.

In figure 5.2, which shows a screenshot from the MMORPG[3] *World of Warcraft*, the abstract playfield has become a concrete world. This world, which is much larger than the landscape shown in the picture, is represented from the perspective of an embodied character who contemplates it from a horizontal point of view (or from a slightly elevated perspective, so that the player can see both his avatar and the surrounding world). The horizontal

---

3. Massively multiplayer online role-playing game. This is a type of game in which large numbers of players interact with one another within a virtual gameworld.

FIGURE 5.2. *World of Warcraft*: Playfield as world

perspective renders the strategic organization of game space invisible: all the player can see is a smooth landscape that gives the impression that her avatar could move in all directions, if it weren't for natural obstacles, such as rivers and mountains.[4] In this view, close objects hide remote objects, so that the avatar cannot see what dangers lurk ahead. But underlying this smooth mimetic representation of the gameworld is a strategic design that determines what the player's character can and cannot do. Within a concrete gameworld, some objects have "behaviors" (read: code) attached to them (i.e., they can be picked up and manipulated) and some others are inert stage setting (Juul 2014). Similarly, some regions contain possibilities of action (dragons to be slain, gold to be found; characters to be met), and some others are only there to be traversed on the way to other, more strategically significant places. The space of a gameworld is made, in other words, of both meaningful destinations and mere transit areas. Figure 5.3, a design document for the game *Zanzarah*, shows the strategic organization that underlies game spaces, the quests that the player has to perform in order to progress in the game, the sequence of the tasks to be performed, the areas to which the quests take the players, and the entities involved (represented by symbols).

---

4. Some games combine a horizontal representation with a tiny map view that allows the player to plan the journey of her character through the gameworld.

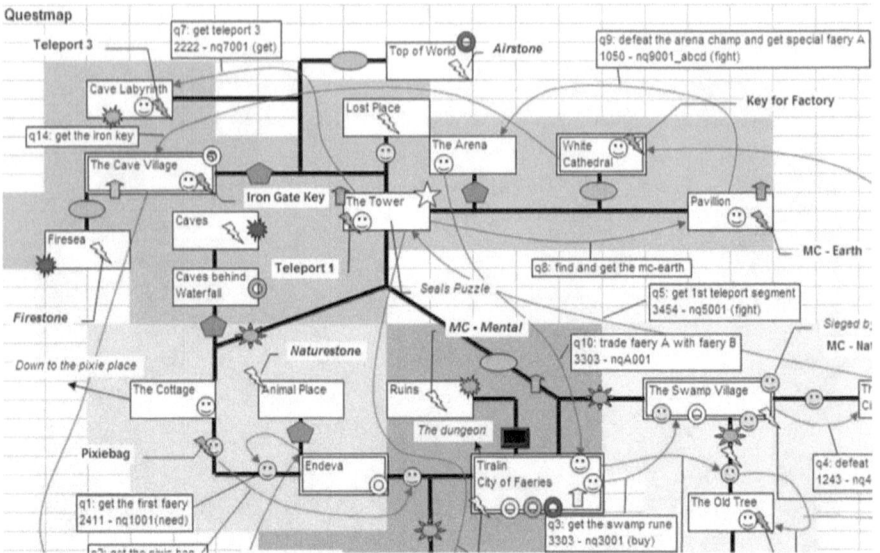

FIGURE 5.3. *Zanzarah*: Design document from Funatics. Used with permission of Michael Nitsche and reproduced from his book *Video Game Spaces: Image, Play and Structure in 3D Worlds*. Cambridge, MA: MIT Press, 2008.

Strategic Design of Gameworlds

The strategic design of gameworlds can be described on two levels: on a literally spatial level (i.e. the level on which areas of the gameworld (or of the display) support player action) and on the level of the thematic (i.e., narrative content that supports the spatial organization). Michael Nitsche (2008) has described several kinds of purely spatial design: tracks and rails, for games that restrict the player's activity to movement along a linear area of a certain width (such as racing games); labyrinths and mazes, for games in which the player must find the way to a goal, making choices among several possibilities; and arenas, where space is the fundamental condition of the actions that lead toward the fulfillment of the goal. These actions can be the movement of pieces on a game board or the gestures of the body in sports, such as fencing or wrestling. Games also differ from each other in how space is involved in the goal of the players. In some games, such as *Go, Monopoly,* or the video game *Civilization,* space is regarded as an inherently desirable commodity, and the winner is the player who manages to control the greatest area. When gameplay consists of transporting an object across a dangerous zone in order to put it in a safe place (bringing a ball over the goal line, circling bases to return home, moving a pawn along a maze to reach the exit), space is conceived as an obstacle, and it must be negated in order to score. In a game like *Tic-Tac-Toe*, where the players try to trace a figure on the board, as well as in online worlds focused on building things, such as *Second Life*, space functions as a medium, drawing board, blank page, or sandbox. When the purpose of the game is to win a battle or capture a certain object, space is a resource that must be properly managed, not in order to own it but in order to reach the strategic position from which the winning move can be performed. And finally, when the goal of the game is to find hidden objects, as in an Easter egg hunt, space functions as a container.

Turning to narrative design and relying on categories described by Henry Jenkins (2004)—without, however, adopting his taxonomy wholesale, because its constituents do not seem to belong to the same level of description[5]—we propose to distinguish the following configurations:

The *journey*, or *epic narrative*. This pattern focuses on the exploits of a solitary hero who travels across a world full of dangers to fulfill a mission. The story can be endlessly expanded by giving new tasks to the hero and by adding new episodes, which correspond to distinct levels or sequels. The player might have the impression of moving freely through the gameworld, but he progresses along a storyline that has been fully plotted by the designers, even when the plot presents multiple branches. After each level is completed, the branches come together, so as to place the gameworld in the same state for all players at the beginning of the next level. Jesper Juul (2005, 5) calls this structural type "games of progression" and observes that because of the strong top-down control of the designers, it is the most amenable to narrativization. Its most typical manifestation is the adventure game genre.

Embedded narratives. This type of structure is inspired by the epistemic plot of the detective or mystery story, a genre whose trademark is the superposition of two plot lines: one constituted by the events that took place in the past, and the other by the investigation that leads to their discovery. When the pattern is implemented in a game environment, it combines an authorially defined story—the events being investigated—with a variable story created in real time by the actions of the player, who plays the role of investigator.

---

5. Jenkins's categories are (1) evoked narratives—games relying on stories known to the user from other sources (this category does not seem to belong with the others because it is not a formal type); (2) enacted narratives—games in which "the story may be structured around the character's movements through space" (2004, 129) (since all first person games are enacted, regardless of their formal structure, I find the label misleading); (3) embedded narratives and (4) emergent narratives. In the present taxonomy I ignore (1), rename (2) "journey or epic narratives," and keep (3) and (4).

The search for the hidden story takes advantage of the visual resources of digital systems by sending the player on a search for clues hidden in the storyworld. While the order in which the clues are found and the embedded story is reconstituted can be constrained by relations of causality (before you open the chest where the will is kept, you must find the key), this order is much more flexible than the sequence of actions that need to be performed in the epic plot.

Emergent narrative. In this configuration, which, in contrast to the other two, does not originate in literature but is native to digital media, the predetermined plot line is replaced by a world full of existents (objects and characters) with built-in behaviors, or affordances. The player, who typically manipulates these characters from an external or "god" perspective rather than impersonating a member of the gameworld, creates a narrative by activating the behaviors of which the existents are capable. When the gameworld contains many existents capable of a variety of actions, most of which have side effects that affect other existents, the system becomes too complex to predict its behavior: in contrast to narratives of progression and embedded narratives, emergent systems cannot be diagrammed. To the extent that the player chooses events, she is the author of the story, but to the extent that events have surprising consequences, she is also the reader. The prototype of this type of structure is *The Sims*, a game in which the player creates a family and selects from a menu the actions performed by its various members (Ryan 2011). These actions have an impact on the mental state of characters and on the affective relations between the agent and the patient. For instance, if one character constantly irritates another, and then asks for her hand in marriage, it is likely—but not certain—that he will be rejected; if he is, he may sink into depression, lose his job, and have to sell his house. When the player selects an action, the system computes its consequences and updates the current state of the gameworld, opening up a new set of possible actions. The computer also plays the role of blind fate, by occasionally throwing in random events, such as a burglar stealing objects from the house, neighbors dropping by unexpectedly, or death claiming a character. Yet even when the computer takes a turn at implementing events, it does not operate on the basis of predetermined narrative templates. The game simulates the randomness of life, rather than the teleology of narrative.

Each of these configurations involves a different attitude toward space: in the epic narrative, space is a carefully designed obstacle course, and it exists only to be conquered (which means: traversed); in embedded narrative, space is there to be searched, since it contains the clues to the story that need to be retrieved; in emergent narrative, finally, space is a resource, a totality to be managed. This aspect is particularly prominent in *SimCity*, a game in which the player must govern a city as its mayor and keep its citizens satisfied (otherwise, she will be voted out of office), or in games in which the player must maintain the ecological balance of a microsystem. In *The Sims,* the player not only determines the day-to-day lives of the characters but also builds their living space and furnishes it with objects that keeps them happy; for the Sims's well-being relies not only on social relations, but also on the satisfaction of their needs for food, hygiene, rest, exercise, entertainment, self-esteem, and mental stimulation, all of which depend on material possessions.

While journey, embedded, and emergent narratives may exist in pure form, it is tempting to postulate a fourth structural type, "the world," and to define it as a combination of all of the others. Henry Jenkins calls it "environmental storytelling" (2004, 122) and compares this design to a theme park, because it is a space that offers a variety of activities. Players can freely wander around the gameworld, interact with other players in multiplayer environments, explore the landscape, or engage in quests in order to "level up" in the game. The geography of the gameworld is diversified into distinct regions that allow different activities: for instance, you can dig for gold in the mountains; you can fish in the stream; you can buy and sell items in the city, and you can fight ferocious beasts in the forest. In the world design, there is no overarching story but a variety of little stories that relate to the various regions of the world's geography. For instance, if you wander near a certain village, you will meet a NPC (nonplaying character) who will give you gossip about the villagers. Further down the road, another character will tell you about a serious problem that plagues the area and will give you the mission to solve it. You may or may not accept this mission. Every area of the gameworld has its own folklore, its own creatures, and its own opportunities for gaining experience and acquiring merit.

The world design is the standard design of multiplayer online games such as *World of Warcraft* or *EverQuest* because it solves a narrative problem inherent to this type of game. This narrative problem is created by the need to accommodate large numbers of players in a persistent environment—an environment that exists and in which other players are active even when your computer is turned off. If the actions of other players could have important consequences for the world as a whole, when a player returns to the gameworld after playing hooky in real life, he would find a transformed world, like Rip van Winkle awakening from a hundred-year sleep, and he would feel completely lost. His absence would make him unable to follow the story of the gameworld as a continuous evolution. To avoid this situation, the "world" design does not contain a global narrative arc but only little stories, or micronarratives, that do not create significant changes. These micronarratives are of two kinds. First, there is the embedded stories of the folklore, which includes gossip and backstories that recount the past of certain areas—just as the folklore of the real world tells the stories of specific locations. Second, there are the quests that are given to the player. The fixed script of the quests can be regarded as a potential story that passes from virtuality to actuality when it is performed by the player. But the future stories of the quests also connect to the past stories of the folklore, since it is past stories that explain the roots of the problem to be solved by the player. Here is an example from *World of Warcraft* that demonstrates the connections between the folklore and the quests:

> The ancient prophecy of Mosh'aru speaks of a way to contain the god Hakkar's essence. It was written on two tablets and taken to the troll city of Zul'farrak, west of Gadgetzan. Bring me the Mosh'aru tablets. The first tablet is held by the long dead troll Theka the Martyr. It is said his persecutors were cursed into scarabs and now scuttle from his shrine. The second is held by the hydromancer Velratha near the sacred pool of Gah'rzilla. When you have the tablets, bring them to me. (Krzywinska 2008, 129)

In a normal narrative world, when somebody performs an action, this action has durable consequences: if the hero kills a monster, the monster is dead and does not need to be killed again. But not in online worlds: the tasks that the player performs can be repeated over and over again by other players. For instance, if a player kills a certain dragon, the dragon will respawn a few minutes later, so that other players will also be able to kill it in order to earn merit points. In a multiplayer world, the only effect of the player's actions concern the player herself: they do not transform the world, but they promote the player to a higher status. Online worlds are ahistorical spaces full of players who live and make stories, but there is very little interaction between these individual stories.[6]

In addition to containing the scripted blueprints of the quests and the embedded narratives of gossip and folklore, the world structure is a fertile ground for the emergence of stories unforeseen by its developers. In a single-player world, emergence might be the discovery by a player of a "cheat" that offers a shortcut in a quest, or the design of a "mod" such as new "skins" (costumes) for the avatars or new mazes to run; in a multiplayer world, emergence is manifested by the scenarios spontaneously produced by the community of

---

6. Players may form alliances with other players in order to solve difficult problems such as killing a particularly powerful boss. If they succeed in this task, the world is changed for all of them, but the boss remains alive for the players who are not part of the alliance.

players (for instance: getting married in *Second Life*), or by ingenious ways to get around the code. A prime example of emergent behavior that game administrators would like to stamp out, but haven't managed to eliminate, is the practice of selling avatars and other objects created in an online world for real-world money (Castronova 2005).

Gameworlds as Objects of Emotional Attachment

A testament to the attachment of players to the virtual world of their favorite game is the widespread custom of displaying official maps of these worlds (figure 5.4), or of creating their own maps. Through their unique power to make visible that which we cannot experience directly, namely the shape of islands, countries, or continents, maps give a visual identity to large geographic entities and turns them into places. The shape of a country often functions as an object of emotional attachment. People feel connected to France as a hexagon or to Italy as a boot or to Britain as an island, and they would be very upset if a war took a bite from their country's territorial integrity. Now that nationalism is generally frowned upon, this attachment to the shape of one's country is often transferred to virtual countries, such as *EverQuest, Liberty City,* or *World of Warcraft*. The maps of these gameworlds are much more than tools that help

FIGURE 5.4. Map of *World of Warcraft*

players achieve high status in the game: they symbolize the pride that players take in being citizens of a virtual world.

Celia Pearce (2009), an ethnographer of digital media, provides an eloquent example of the sense of place that binds players to virtual worlds. This example concerns the world of *Myst,* one of the most popular games of all times and a landmark in video game history. *Myst* is a combination of journey structure and embedded narrative: in order to complete the game, players must travel through several worlds, and in order to move through these worlds or to pass from one world to another, they must solve puzzles, such as finding keys, locating secret codes, and launching rockets. The motivation for the quest is to find the pages of a book that tells the backstory of the gameworld. But the popularity of the game comes as much from the surreal beauty of the graphics—a beauty both realistic and dreamlike typical of computer-assisted graphics—as from the strategic gameplay or the narrative interest of the story being discovered. The aesthetic pleasure that the player takes in the landscape does not focus on specific objects at the expense of others, as does the strategic approach, it embraces the whole of the gameworld.

Pearce tells a story of exile and longing for a lost homeland that presents striking similarities with the diasporas of real-world communities. An online world based on *Myst* was created in 2003, called *Myst Online: Uru* (pronounced "you are you") *Live,* but in 2004 it was closed for lack of subscribers. Many of its members migrated to other worlds—among them *Second Life*—where they founded communities in exile. (The *Second Life Uru* community at the time of Pearce's writing had about 600 members.) In *Second Life,* the members of *Uru* used the building tools of the system to recreate the landscape of the lost world, and this landscape serves as the setting for regular gatherings of *Uru* ex-pats. The recreated world of *Uru*—a virtual world within a virtual world—is expanding with new islands full of puzzles and legends in the style of *Myst.* There is also a blog devoted to keeping the *Uru* community together until the Second Coming of *Myst Online* (which indeed happened in 2011). The many reincarnations of the *Uru/Myst* homeland demonstrate how integration in a community, memories of happy times, narrative tradition (i.e., the legends of the *Myst* games), and landscape aesthetics come together in creating a sense of place.

DIGITAL MAPS AS NARRATIVE GENERATORS

Compared to standard print maps, digital maps are distinguished by the following properties (Dodge and Kitchin 2001b):

- Easily updated
- Interactive: the user can alter the scale by zooming in and out, or pan across the map
- Dynamic: digital maps can be animated, like movies
- Responsive to live data: they can be updated in real time
- Customizable: users can produce their own maps by annotating existing maps

In the examples we discuss below, some of these properties are used as active generators of narrative. Thanks to these properties—which differ from example to example—the maps do not simply illustrate a preexisting narrative but take an *active part in the process of narration.*

Narrating through Annotations: Memory Maps

The Web site Memory Maps (2013), one of many projects of this type,[7] offers an opportunity for users to tell their own stories through a different mode of organization than the chronological order that is typical of autobiography: a spatial mode through which stories are associated with specific locations. The map serves here as a mnemonic device that activates personal memories, just as in the *loci* technique of memorization in which items to be remembered are attached to certain locations. Looking at (or thinking of) a place, Memory Maps narrators remember episodes from their childhood that took place in this precise location. These narratives create a sense of place that is unique to the writer. Yet other users can add notations to the map, turning it from a personal autobiography into a more collective representation of place. The annotations are limited by the space of the medium, just like Twitter messages are limited in their number of characters. This leads to a highly laconic

---

7. A much larger, and much more diversified, project of this kind is City of Memory (2013), funded by the Rockefeller foundation, which gathers stories told about New York City. The introductory text reads: "Welcome to this grand, new repository for all New York City's stories and experiences. Explore this interactive urban story map yourself to meet the city's greatest characters, visit its diverse communities, and enjoy the most amazing stories. Things that happened forty years ago or something that happened to you this morning—all are welcome in the City of Memory." The project stands halfway between Memory Maps and [murmur]: like Memory Maps, it situates stories on an interactive map (though it is much richer in its semiotic resources: it uses images, sound, and videos, and it offers themed tours such as "Haiti New York"), but like [murmur], it collects stories that describe a city in its human and architectural diversity, rather than focusing on the autobiography of a specific individual.

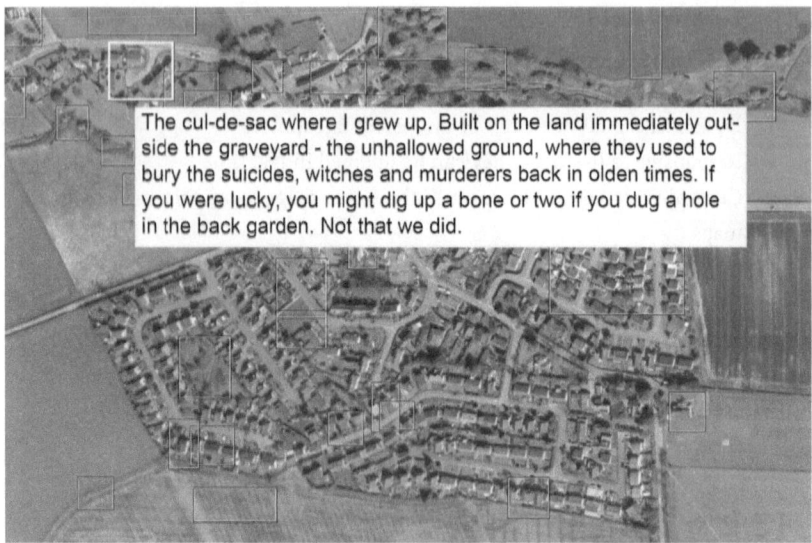

FIGURE 5.5. Memory Maps: Carnock, Scotland, annotated by Diarmid Mogg, "Map of important sites of interest in Carnock, Fife, Scotland, with an emphasis on the golden era of humankind (otherwise known as the mid to late 1970s)." Used with the permission of Diarmid Mogg, aka Angus McDiarmid.

narrative style in which the life of the narrator is captured though small stories contained in discrete vignettes.

Figure 5.5 shows a map that recounts the childhood of a narrator named Angus McDiarmid in the Scottish town of Carnock. While the Google Earth photo that serves as a map covers the area in its totality, impartially recording every feature visible from the air, the narrative map created by the annotations is highly selective in its choice of locations. Some areas are places, because memory associates them with a story, and others are empty nonplaces. Among the places worthy of annotation is a whole area of new buildings that the narrator designates as a *terra incognita*. Ironically, the lack of stories inspired by this area singles it out as a special place! Through their selectivity, the annotations perform on the photo the same interpretive work that graphic maps accomplish with respect to real space. Graphic maps also make a choice of items to be shown, rather than representing all the features visible from the air.

The map is brought to life by the kind of stories that Tom Sawyer would have told if he had been able to use digital technology: the annotations deal mainly with the mischief of the boys of the town. One annotation signals the place of the narrator's worst crime (so elusively told that it must be guessed), another marks the second-worst crime, a third commemorates the place where the boys of Carnock hid during wars with the boys of the next village. Horror plays a prominent role in these memories: among the places that are singled out is the house of the woman with a gun who shot at kids, the house of drug dealers, and the field where the boys found the corpse of a cow, hiding their discovery under great secrecy. The whole of the Memory Maps project can indeed be regarded as a secret geography created by the boys of the town as a challenge to the adult organization of space and its centers of authority: the school, site of "incessant humiliations" (but also a few triumphs) and the church, left "largely unvisited."

An important part of these childhood recollections consists of stories that reach much further back in time than personal memories. For instance, a field is said to be the site where suicides, witches, and those who died of the plague were buried in the Middle Ages; a tree marks the site where John Knox gave sermons; and stones in a field are said to be part of an extinct volcano. This kind of annotation suggests that our sense of place comes as much from folklore, tradition and secondhand information as from lived experience and genuine recollections.

A theme that runs through several Memory Maps is how space has changed since the youth of the writer. Many of the narrated events involve a use of space that is no longer available, because buildings have been destroyed, or public spaces have been turned into private ones. On another map, for instance, we are told that the golf course where kids used to go sledding has been replaced with a housing project. This nostalgia suggests the ephemeral nature of place, compared to the enduring nature of space. The location of the sledding can still be identified on the map though spatial coordinates, but what defined this point in space as a place was an activity that is no longer possible. The space is still there, but the place exists only in the narrator's memory. The prevailing mood of Memory Maps is nostalgia for a time when kids could roam freely in the neighborhood, invent their own games, spy on strange people, and build their own secret places in abandoned buildings, rather than live in a regimented world where leisure activities are supervised by adults, where these activities take place in officially designated spaces, and where possibilities of dangerous games have been eliminated.

Narrating through Animation: The 21 Steps

Our second example, *The 21 Steps* (figure 5.6) (Cumming 2008), also uses Google Earth photos as maps (though it also uses regular maps), but the role of these images and the conception of space that they convey are quite

FIGURE 5.6. Telling stories through Google maps: *The 21 Steps*, by Charles Cummins

different from Memory Maps. *The 21 Steps* is not a spontaneous creation of a fan, published on a Web site that collects documents from amateurs, but a narrative specially commissioned by a well-known publishing house, Penguin, to an established author of thrillers, Charles Cumming, as part of a publicity campaign called "We Tell Stories." The purposes of the campaign were (1) to advertise the other works of the author and (2) to promote a "classic" work published by Penguin, by asking the participants in the project to create a text inspired by this model. The classic in this case is *The 39 Steps* by John Buchan (2013 [1915]), a novel considered one of the founding texts of the genre thriller. In addition to these commercial purposes, the project also had an artistic ambition: namely "to tell stories in a way that can only be told online." Penguin hired a design team that came up with various ideas for online storytelling; in the case of *The 21 Steps*, the idea was to tell a story through Google maps. The problem was to find a type of story that would truly benefit from this kind of interface. The designing team came to the conclusion that what maps do best is represent movement, and that the genre most fitted to do so is the thriller:

> When we had the idea for a story based around Google Maps, we knew that it had to incorporate a lot of movement—otherwise what's the point of having a map? So one early idea was a travelogue—a little like *Around the World in 80 Days*. Another was a thriller, like *The 39 Steps*. We ended up taking the latter option, due to its frenetic pace, and we asked Charles Cumming, an acclaimed British spy thriller author, to write a story for us.

To begin with, we simply told Charles to "bake movement in" to the story. However, from early on, it became clear that this was rather trickier than any of [us] had thought; it wasn't enough to have the protagonist walking and driving and flying around the place, they had to do it all the time.

Early drafts of the story saw the protagonist having a very tense discussion for a couple of chapters—riveting stuff—but it was all in one room. Luckily we had a great relationship with Charles and we worked together to incorporate more movement, or references to other locations, in every chapter. (Mssv 2008)

The story begins when the narrator, an unemployed man named Rick, walks to London's St. Pancras station to kill time and accidentally witnesses a murder. Shortly before dying (actually, pretending to die), the victim gives Rick a clue that takes him to the National Gallery and, from there, to Heathrow Airport, where he is being asked to take the identity of the dead man in order to smuggle a bottle of liquid on a flight to Edinburgh, an action that blatantly violates the most familiar of airline security rules. In Scotland, he must penetrate into a closed room by retrieving the code, jump from a hotel window unto the glass roof of a station to avoid a hit man, escape the police in a boat, and so on. The same characters—for instance a man with a ponytail and an East European girl—seem to reappear rather strangely wherever he goes. In the end, Rick finds himself in the courtyard of Edinburgh Castle, where he learns that his adventures were planned as a test by a Greek millionaire who happens to be the father of a beautiful girl he has recently dated. In a fairy-tale ending, the millionaire is so impressed by Rick's ability to get out of the most dangerous situations that he hires him in his company and then takes him and his daughter to Brazil, where we assume they will live a glamorous life filled with amorous pleasures and profitable business deals. As one can see from this summary, *The 21 Steps* is a parody of the thriller genre.

Each of the chapters of *The 21 Steps* consists of text superposed on a Google Earth shot. The vertical perspective characteristic of maps is not conducive to the representation of a personal experience of space, because people see space from an embodied, largely frontal point of view, while maps present a disembodied isometric perspective. For instance, when the map of *The 21 Steps* shows St. Pancras railway station in London, few people will recognize this landmark, because our mental image of St. Pancras (if we have one) is what architects call an "elevation": a horizontal view of its façade. Moreover, when the narrator enters St. Pancras, the roof of the station prevents the map from showing what he is seeing: namely, "a flight of steps which brought me up under the vaulted roof. Now that was quite something, a brand new sky of steel and glass." On the map, we see the glass, but the "sky" becomes indistinguishable from the ground. An occasional green button allows the reader to look at things from a horizontal perspective, for instance at a statue within the station, but most of the time the reader's perspective is at odds with what the narrator sees. The maps, consequently, cannot be said to illustrate the text, nor to convey a sense of the presence of the setting. (The only time the map corresponds to what the hero sees is when it represents the flight from London to Edinburgh: we can imagine that it is one of those flight maps displayed on the entertainment screen.) But while maps suppress the appearance of things (except for the shape of the land), they are very good at showing what we cannot see, namely the trace of moving objects. The maps of *The 21 Steps* do this in two ways: through a panning motion that makes the map "move" across space; and through animated lines that show the trajectories of moving objects—in this case the body of the protagonist.

The purpose of these movements is not to reach desirable places, nor to explore the world, but to follow a trail of clues that has been set up by a higher power, the Greek millionaire, who can be seen as an allegory of the author who "emplots" the reader. The hero has no idea where the trail leads to, nor why it has been set up, but he never questions the tasks that are given to him. He is, in other words, a blind but fully willing participant in a conspiracy. The model for this conception of space is a game of Treasure Hunt. In a Treasure Hunt, players follow an itinerary carefully designed by a Game Master, in which every location to be visited contains a riddle pointing to another location. The last link in the chain corresponds to the site where the treasure will be found. In *The 21 Steps*, the treasure is the reward given to the hero by the Greek millionaire—a job and a modern-day princess—but from the point of view of the reader, the treasure is an event that Aristotle called *anagnoresis*: the revelation that dispels the mystery and makes every detail fall into place. For the literary critic eager to find self-reflexive elements, it is no coincidence that the *anagnoresis* presents the whole plot as a conspiracy, which means, quite literally, as a *plot*.

Through its game-like quality, the conception of space that emanates from *The 21 Steps* offer a particularly fitting example of strategic space. The vertical view provided by the maps resembles a game board on which players move their tokens from point to point. In order to connect the strategically important locations of the storyworld, the hero must overcome physical obstacles (such as closed doors and security checkpoints), take advantage in an imaginative way of the topography (jumping out of windows), or hop onto moving objects (cars, boats, planes, or the subway). Here, as in adventure games based on the principle of the journey, strategic space takes the shape of a vast obstacle course that tests the sagacity of the hero.

It is no coincidence that the team responsible for the cartographic interface of *The 21 Steps* specializes in the design of Alternate Reality Games (ARGs), a type of game to which we will return below. Not only does the plot of *The 21 Steps* resemble an ARG, the maps contain clues belonging to a "real" ARG that the reader can play. The Web site "We Tell Stories" contains links to six texts (of which *The 21 Steps* is one), but by clicking on green markers located on some of the maps, readers can find out how to retrieve parts of a seventh story titled *Alice in Storyland,* which is literally hidden under the six narratives that are accessible through visible tabs. Clicking on a green marker on one of the screens of *The 21 Steps,* for instance, will reveal a phone number to call to get parts of *Alice.*

Narrating though Real-Time Updating of the Map: Les Trucs

The third of our generative cartographic projects, Les Trucs (figure 5.7) (Collectif Microtruc 2013), is a French artistic experiment (or Web event) conceived by an artist collective called Microtruc and sponsored by the Jeu de Paume museum. It ran in real time between November 2010 and May 2011, but the documents produced by the project can still be accessed online (Herbet and Magnan 2011). The French word *truc,* which belongs to popular language, is commonly used to designate something to which one does not want to refer by its proper name. Among the translations that we have found are "stuff," "contraption," "gimmick," and "what d'yer call it." The mysterious, unnamed nature of the Truc is central to the project.

Les Trucs is a kind of game in which participants pass along an object like a hot potato. Four strange objects hidden in a bag were put into play every week by the members of the artist collective. They contained a tracking device that made it possible to localize them in space. The participants had to obey the following rules:

- The Truc must be given to another person within twenty-four hours.
- The Truc cannot be shown to anybody besides its temporary custodians (called "passeurs"). The person who receives a Truc must send an email explaining at what time the exchange took place, in what circumstances, and what the Truc suggests to them.

It was not necessary to specify the location of the exchange, since it was automatically recorded by the Truc, but the report of the circumstances often involved a description of the setting. The stories were published on the

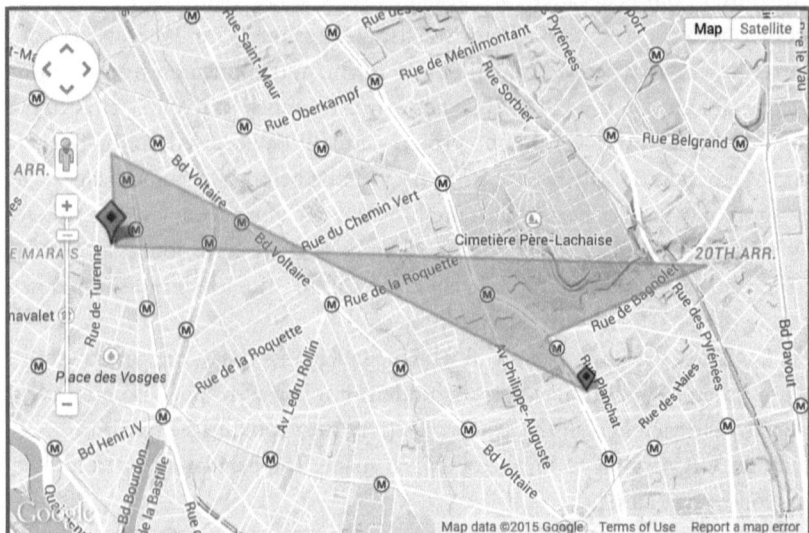

FIGURE 5.7. Itineraries from *Les Trucs*, by Microtrucs, showing moderate travel (top) and short travel (bottom). Used with the permission of the Microtrucs artist collective.

project's Web site as soon as they arrived, and the travels of the Trucs were monitored on a map, which was updated every hour.

The project creates two levels of narrativity, and it raises two types of curiosity. The first type concerns the itinerary of the object, and it focuses on the maps. During the actual run of the project, the maps created a modest form of narrative suspense by arousing in the spectator the desire to find out where the Truc would turn up next, but the hourly updates were far too spaced out to reward a continuous watching of the map. The project is more interesting when seen from a retrospective point of view that allows users to contemplate the entire weekly trajectories of the Trucs, together with the stories of the exchanges. These trajectories remind us of a type of novel or film in which an object passes from one owner to the next and creates a thread that links multiple lives across time and space.[8] The range of the travel of the Trucs—and for some people, the narrative interest of the project, as well—was limited by the fact that the Trucs ended their travel every week and were then put back in circulation, usually starting in Paris. Rather than traveling throughout Europe or even the world, the Truc performed a more condensed exploration, largely contained within the urban geography of Paris. (The Trucs occasionally ventured into the provinces but never left France.) The variable distance of the travel is reflected by the scale of the maps. When the distance is short and the scale is large (as shown on figure 5.7, bottom), the itinerary seems to cut across the walls of buildings, rather than following possible routes along the streets. This is due to the fact that the location of the Trucs is registered only every hour, and the system that draws the routes connects these points through straight lines.

The second level of narrativity manifests itself in the individual stories created by the passeurs. These stories display a wide variety of discourse strategies. Like the narratives of personal experience studied by Labov and Waletsky (1973), they range from minimal accounts of the transaction by rather reluctant narrators to exuberant writing performances by would-be poets and novelists. (Many of the storytellers seem to be artists, something easily explained by the fact that the first transmitter, every week, is a member of the artist collective Microtruc.) Here is the most minimalist account:

Hello
The Truc was given to me at my workplace at 16:45 by a very good friend.
Cordially
Lamia

---

8. This genre, known as It-Narrative or Circulation-Narrative, is represented by the novel *Accordion Crimes* by Annie Proulx (1996) and by the film *The Red Violin* (1999). Here is how Liz Bellamy describes the genre: "Novel of Circulation and It-Narrative are both terms coined to describe a particular sub-genre of fiction which developed in the eighteenth century, and has come under critical scrutiny in the last thirty years. These works recount the adventures of a non-human protagonist, such as a coin, a dog, a pin-cushion or a hackney coach, as it travels through society, encountering diverse characters and incidents." (http://www.litencyc.com/php/stopics.php?rec=true&UID=1535, accessed July 27, 2013.)

The would-be poets and novelists embroider on the fixed script of the exchange in many ways:

- By commenting on their relations to the transmitter, and describing the exchange as a meaningful human encounter: "My sweet darling, Floriane, gave me the Truc"
- By developing the circumstances: "It was to have tea and pastries, except that, instead of a nice sablé, I ended up with a rather strange Truc in my hands."
- By inserting dialogue: "When I saw the Truc come out of its bag, I fell in love with it right away. I showed it to Fred: 'It's freaky, right. It looks like something by Tim Burton or Cronenberg.' 'You think so? I like it, this Truc. It's cute, it reminds me of Annette Messager.'"
- By personalizing the Truc: "So I took Annette in my hands, I looked at her with her funny little eyes. 'Do you think I could give her a little mouth?' I introduced Annette to Merlin and Yoko, they sniffed her for a while, very curious—especially Merlin—but then they turned away, very busy with their nap."
- By treating the Truc as an erotic object: "I sucked on the Truc and fondled its seams: it was soft as a Doudou" (baby talk for blanket).

Above all, the most creative participants approach the assignment of describing the Truc as an opportunity to let their imagination loose. The incarnations of the Truc include: a hot potato (this is the most frequent comparison); the relationship between people, through a mystical process; a nurturing link in a human chain; pig meat with silky texture that reminds the narrator of a green valley full of dwarves; the bouillon of a Chinese soup; a failing organ, worn out by life; something organic and disgusting that contains all the microbes of the earth; a strange object that belongs to an old marabout whose purpose evades the narrator; a Voodoo doll (the narrator is tempted to pierce it with needles but is afraid of making somebody sick); the Holy Grail.

Yet many people feel that the Truc is hiding something suspicious: "I felt something hard inside, it gave me a strange impression"—and when they identify it correctly as a geolocating device, the reaction is usually chilly: "I have a hint it is a surveillance object," "I believe this thing is a spy," "Is there a GPS inside? Are we being tracked?" "It's a disturbing thing (at least the GPS trick, we got it right away), something we don't want to keep too long. Let's hurry to give it away."

The relation of these stories to the map is quite different from the two projects discussed earlier. While the annotations of the Memory Maps try to capture a sense of place deeply anchored in certain locations, here the "where" of the stories is quite accidental. What matters is the movement of the Trucs, the length of their itineraries, and not the particular aura of the sites where they are exchanged—usually rather anonymous cafés, workplaces, or apartments. On the other hand, Les Trucs differs from *The 21 Steps* in that the space though which objects travel is not a strategic space of problems to solve in order to reach specific places; it is as part of daily life that the participants receive and give away the Trucs, and the travels that the maps register is the trajectory of their normal activities. The fact that the itineraries do not follow straight lines between the sites of the exchanges demonstrates that the carriers pursue goals during the day besides transmitting the Trucs. The interest created by these movements of daily life within a familiar urban setting is part of a trend in contemporary art to provide a complete record of the trivial and ordinary; for instance, in *Soliloquy,* conceptual poet Kenneth Goldsmith transcribed everything he said in a week (Epstein 2012), and in *Tentative d'épuisement d'un lieu parisien,* novelist Georges Perec (1975) noted everything that he observed from an outdoor café on Place St. Sulpice in Paris. If it is cool for writers to turn themselves into recording machines, why not use real machines, such as a geopositioning system, to produce art?

Neither emotional nor strategic, but rather a canvas for the inscription of geometrical figures, the space of Les Trucs instantiates several of the ideas that were put on the intellectual market by leading figures of postmodernism. The participants' largely negative reactions to finding out that the Truc contains a tracking device might relate to recent concern about the growing prevalence of electronic surveillance or to the concept of the panopticon, an organization of prison space conceived by Jeremy Bentham that makes possible the constant surveillance of inmates, and that Michel Foucault developed into an allegory of contemporary society. The isometric or vertical perspective of the maps on which the movement of the Trucs are being monitored is symptomatic of the panoptic tendencies that Foucault detects in contemporary societies; from this perspective, the map represents the gaze of God, from which nobody can hide. The only way to escape from the cartographic field of vision would be to crawl underground, but with the invention of geotracking technologies, even this kind of escape becomes impossible.

By making visible the movements of the carriers, the project also literalizes a metaphor proposed by Michel de Certeau in an influential essay titled "Walking in a City" (1984). De Certeau wrote in the 1980s, at a time when the so-called "language turn" in the humanities inspired comparisons of virtually every meaningful phenomenon with texts and with language. It is therefore not surprising that for de Certeau, people walking through a city "write" an urban "text" "without being able to read it" (93), and that "the act of walking is to the urban space what the speech act is to language" (97). Just as the speaker of a language creates ever new utterances by applying the rules of grammar, the user of a city creates unique itineraries, full of detours and shortcuts, through the urban grid, actualizing "only a few of the possibilities fixed by the construction order" (98). The purpose of the Trucs, beside inspiring stories, is to catch the traffic habits of individual human lives, just as tracking systems catch the migrations of birds or help delimit the hunting range of predators. The project inscribes on the map a few patterns of use selected from an infinite set of possibilities offered by the city. Writing, however, is not simply a manual act of inscription: it is above all a mental act of sense-making through verbalization. While the individual stories told by the participants represent writing in the narrow sense of a deliberate shaping and emplotting of experience, the travels of the Trucs can only be called "writing" if by this term we understand a novel way to harness randomness, an exercise widely practiced in avant-garde movements from Surrealism to conceptual writing.

This idea of randomness leads to a third way to describe the space of Les Trucs: space as the theater of an aimless wandering akin to Charles Baudelaire's (1995) *flânerie*, or to Guy Debord's (1981) *dérive*. Both *flânerie* and *dérive* are characterized by their absence of a spatial goal, though they do not lack in purpose. This purpose is aesthetic in the case of Baudelaire, whose *flâneur* walks through the city in search, not of a precise object, but of serendipitous discoveries; and the purpose is social in the case of Debord, who was interested in studying the effects of geographic environments on the emotions and behavior of individuals. In Debord's *dérive,* people "drop their usual motives for movement or action, their relations, their work and leisure activities, and they let themselves be drawn by the attractions of the terrain and the encounters they find there." In Les Trucs, by contrast, the movements of the active participants are not motivated by a desire to make random encounters but at least in part by the need to get rid of the Truc. But as Debord observes, "The element of chance is less determinant than one may think" because cities have what he calls a "psychogeographic relief," a relief "which strongly discourage entry or exit into certain zones" (both these quotes and the lines above qtd. from Mitchell 2012, 119). In Les Trucs, the zones visited by the objects are determined by the fact that the carriers always give the objects to people they know—and they tend to know people of the same social group. It is a safe assumption that if the human chain had started not with artists, but with businessmen or with immigrants living in the infamous *banlieues* of Paris, the Trucs would wander into different areas. The trajectories of the Trucs mean therefore as much through the blanks they leave on the map as through the lines that they inscribe. If the maps of Les Trucs are readable as texts, it is because they speak of how people, though their use of space, create human geography.

CONNECTING STORIES TO REAL SPACE THROUGH DIGITAL TECHNOLOGY

Until digital technology came along, the main way to connect stories to the places where they actually happened was to put up a visible sign with a material inscription. This resulted not only in unattractive displays but also a limitation of the kind of stories that could be told, since the signs had to be approved by public authorities (see chapter 7). The stories, then, had to be part of an officially sanctioned version of history. All this changed with mobile technology. Thanks to GPS and other electronic positioning systems, it becomes possible to compose messages on mobile phones, attach them to particular geographic locations, and upload them onto the Internet. These messages, known as digital graffiti, are accessible only to people who happen to be in the proper location.

With positioning technology, everybody can upload messages and tell their own stories about places. This is both an advantage and a problem. The advantage lies in the fact that storytelling and history making become much more democratic. Rather than being limited to officially approved versions of history concerning famous people and important events, the digital graffiti lets everybody tell their own stories. But the democratization of storytelling also poses the problem of proliferation. If everybody is able to post stories, we risk being overwhelmed with the kind of trivial messages that one finds already in chat rooms, on blogs, or on Twitter and Facebook. If we don't find a way to filter out unwanted messages, we will walk in a reality augmented by the fleeting thoughts of every passerby.

Locative Narrative

An alternative to the uncontrolled proliferation of graffiti is the genre of locative narrative. An example is [murmur], a locative project that tries to reconcile the ideas of top-down design with spontaneous, bottom-up creation by the general public. The ambition of [murmur] is to capture the *genius loci* of a city by collecting stories told by ordinary people about various places and making them available in these very places through mobile technology. It was originally created in Toronto, but there were later versions in Vancouver, Montreal, and San Jose, California.

While the stories of [murmur] are told for an audience situated in the same location as the narrator—thereby realizing the rather rare communicative situation of same place, different time[9]—they are also collected in an ever-growing online archive, where the live environment is replaced by a picture of the site evoked in the story. As Ruth Page (2011) has observed, the experience of listening on-site vs. accessing the stories from the Web present significant differences. Whereas the on-site listener can turn around, following the directions of the narrator ("on your right"; "opposite this building,"), and apprehend space on a 360-degree basis, the online listener can only look at a narrowly framed picture. On the other hand, the temporal distance between narration and reception means that the on-site listener might be looking at a changed landscape, while the online listener is watching more or less faithful images of the landmarks that inspired the story (less, because the photo might have been taken at a different time of the day under different light and weather conditions).

The on-site users of [murmur] walk through the city of Toronto, equipped with a paper map that identifies the spots to which stories are linked. When the user gets to the spot, a green sign tells him that a message is available, and he dials a number on his cell phone to capture it. The experience lies halfway between a treasure hunt and *flânerie*—between a search for green markers and a stroll through the city open to serendipitous discoveries. The user of [murmur] aims for certain spots, but what he finds in these spots is not a concrete object but a new way to look at the environment. This new way has been compared to archeology because it allows the user to look beyond the surface of the present and to dig out artifacts from the narrative underground of the city. Just as legends from the past and tales about ancestors create a sense of place, the stories told by citizens about buildings and neighborhoods that are no longer there give a soul to the city. Here is how the designers describe this archeological spirit:

> Walking through Chinatown, it's clear these buildings and alleys are a storehouse of memory and emotion. Yet, as the city progresses and changes, and as people move in and out of the area, these memories are either neglected

---

9. The case of temporal and spatial proximity is represented by such forms of communication as conversation and live performance; temporal proximity combined with spatial distance by synchronous technologies such as telephone conversation and Internet chat; spatial and temporal distance, by books when the temporal distance is great, and by e-mail, the daily press, television, or SMS messages when the distance is short.

and undervalued, or kept inside of the heads of people. [murmur] wants to keep these stories alive and on the streets. Interesting things don't only happen at GM Place or Granville Island—the city is full of stories, and some of them happen in parking lots and bungalows, diners and front lawns. The smallest, greyest or most nondescript building can be transformed by the stories that live in it. Once heard, these stories can change the way people think about a place and the city at large. (Tinderbox 2010)

The phrase "small, grey, and nondescript" presents the project as the antithesis of a guide to tourist attractions: the user is not taken through the famous landmarks of the city, but rather through what most visitors would regard as nonplaces. Narrative, however, is not about the ordinary but about the extraordinary, and the storytellers of [murmur] face the difficult task of telling stories that are both tellable—that is, focused on exceptional events—and representative of everyday life.

As examples of the kind of stories that are collected in [murmur], we will focus on two narratives that relate to a public park in Toronto. We have chosen these two narratives because they embody quite contrastive voices, and yet they are both very representative of the spirit of [murmur].

The first story (archive document shown in figure 5.8) is told by a recent immigrant, a young woman of South Asian origin, and it is presented in both English and her native language. Here is the story:

> My name is Aixia. One day I was walking here in Grange Park. I saw a tall, very old woman. She must have had a lot of coffee because I saw a lot of coffee in her cart. She fell unto the meadow and her nose, face, and fingers were all covered with blood. She was sleeping there. It had started raining. It had started raining very hard and I didn't have a cell phone. I saw a man on a bicycle coming by. I went out and said "hello" and pointed out to his phone and said "phone." "Can you help?" I didn't speak English very well, but I said "can you help her?" The man stopped and called 911. The ambulance came and they carried the woman away. I went home. (Transcription of oral audio file on [murmur] Web site [Dong 2013])

This story gives the impression of being well-rehearsed and coherently put together. With a minimal amount of words, Aixia manages to represent a logically and fully consistent sequence of events. At every moment in the telling, the hearer is able to imagine the problems that face the characters: the old woman in need of help and the narrator, who wants to help but who lacks the resources to do so. Both characters are outsiders to society: the old woman is

130 • CHAPTER 5

FIGURE 5.8. [murmur] online archive

homeless, and the narrator is a new immigrant whose integration in the city is only partial. On one hand, she knows that 911 is the number to call for an emergency, on the other hand, she does not have a cell phone and she does not speak the language very well. The narrative could have been turned into a self-promoting tale of altruism or ingenious problem solving, but the narrator totally downplays her role in helping the homeless woman. If we compare this story to the patterns of oral storytelling described by Labov and Waletzky (1973), we are struck by the lack of evaluative devices—devices that emphasize the dramatic character of the situation and its emotional impact on the narrator. For instance, instead of telling us how she felt when she saw the old women fall, Aixia lets the facts speak for themselves. She describes the old woman lying on the ground, the blood all over her face, and the rain adding to her misery. Similarly, the last sentence of the story entirely lacks what one expects in a coda: a summary of the story, some kind of moral, or an evaluative statement, such as "It was so scary, but I am just glad that I was able to help, despite being a foreigner." What we get instead is "I went home," another way of saying "The End." Rather than building up the story as the recounting of a unique, extraordinary event, this ending presents the events as a routine experience: I went home—as I do every day. The story by itself has a lot of potential tellability, but this tellability is not developed.

While the story is told on-site, the storyteller does not exploit the particular resources made available by her spatial situation. The narration does not use any kind of verbal pointing, such as indexical expressions ("here," "over there"), and makes no attempt to situate the listener in a specific location. It could just as well have been told in a studio for a remote audience or be part of a written story. For this storyteller, space is not a lived environment—she only evokes the park as a transit area—but the stage of an event whose importance lies in its human significance. The point of the story is to suggest that Grange Park is not only a trendy public garden, a space of leisure and beauty where intellectuals meet to discuss art, but also a space that serves as shelter to the less privileged members of society. For some people, the park is a recreational space, an alternative to home, for others it is the only home they know, a space from which they cannot escape.

Our second story is very different in both the group it represents (the intelligentsia that haunts Grange Park) and in its use of narrative devices.

> This is Todd Harrison from *Spacing* Magazine and *you are* standing on the place where *Spacing* was born in 2002. . . . So, that magazine was born *here* and as soon as we started talking about it we started generating ideas left right and center you know and I learned from Journalism School that the more ideas you can come up with when you first propose a new magazine the better your magazine will likely be and it was clear from the outset that *Spacing* was a magazine whose time has come because we couldn't stop coming up with ideas and you cannot help wondering with the Art Gallery of Ontario just *to the North* there and the Ontario College of Art and Design just *to the East* and Queen street and the rich culture that it provides to the city and to our urban fabric just *to the South* there, all those things, you cannot help wonder if all those things are coalescing in Grange Park and resulted in this wellspring of ideas that made *Spacing* what it is *today* which is a magazine that is still going 5 years later which is something that we are very proud of and we are very fortunate that we had such an inauspicious but fruitful beginning on the lawn just south of the A. G. O. (Abridged transcription of oral audio file on [murmur] Web site [Harrison 2013], emphasis added)

This reads almost like advertising for *Spacing*, a magazine that represents the same philosophy of urban space as the [murmur] project: a philosophy dedicated to the creation of communities through the development of public areas, where people can meet and participate in a variety of cultural activities, as opposed to the strictly private, isolating spaces of the suburbs. Because of this ideological similarity, the story is almost self-referential. It is the story of the birth of the ideas that eventually lead to [murmur].

Todd Harrison's story differs from Aixia's in two principal ways. First, the narrator draws much attention to himself and peppers the story with evaluative comments, such as "we couldn't stop coming up with ideas" and "which is something we are very proud of." Second, he draws heavily on the particular resources of on-site storytelling. Through his use of spatial deictics ("here") and of direct address ("you are standing"), as well as through its reference to various buildings as being to the south, north, or east of where he is located, the narrator situates himself, and situates the listener, in a specific point in space, from where he directs attention in various directions (Page 2011). In addition to promoting a lived, immersive experience of space, the story attributes to Grange Park a symbolic dimension. When the narrator tells us, "You are standing here on the place where the magazine *Spacing* was born," he suggests that we are standing on sacred ground. What makes this site so special, however, is not so much the decision to start a magazine as the wellspring of ideas that burst out and made it possible for the magazine to thrive. This wellspring of ideas did not burst miraculously out of the ground (as in so many legends told about holy sites), it rather represents the coalescence of ideas that came from three of the four directions of the wind rose: north, with the Art Gallery of Ontario; east, with the Ontario College of Art and design; and south, with Queen Street and its rich culture. (Only west is not represented.) The sacred site where the magazine was born is not isolated from its surroundings, it is rather the center of the world, where ideas from all around converge and create something new. Through this image of convergence, the narrator is not only sketching a mythical representation of space, similar in spirit to those that have been described by ethnographers such as Mircea Eliade (1998), he also, very cleverly, directs the audience's attention to the actual landmarks of the city of Toronto. This is precisely what the magazine *Spacing* and the project [murmur] are supposed to do.

Alternate Reality Games

We turn now to a type of digitally assisted project that shares with location-based narratives an anchoring in real space, but it differs from them in two respects: the stories are blatantly fictional rather than testimonial, and the spatial experience of the participants is much more strategic than emotional.

In alternate reality games (ARGs), players reconstitute a fictional story, typically presented to them as a mystery to solve. The clues can take many forms and represent diverse media: for instance, messages hidden in a Web site that seems to have been created for other purposes, e-mails sent to the players, phone numbers to call, SMS messages on the player's portable phone, and conversations with live actors who have been planted in the real world by the designers/organizers (puppet masters, in the jargon). The playfield of ARGs thus includes both the physical space of the world and the virtual space of the Internet (Labitzke 2013).

As already noted, before the digital age, most games—from chess to football—took place in a specifically designated area of space, described by Huizinga (1950) as the magic circle. In ARGs, there is no magic circle, no formal boundary between the real world and the playfield. This means that as the players perform the tasks of everyday life, they must be constantly looking out for the possibility of an intrusion of the game into their life. While the game can be played twenty-four hours a day, there is a global time limit: the games last a few weeks, and they are played only once. As soon as one or more players solve the mystery, the game is over for everybody.

By solving riddles, and by communicating with other people, players are directed toward ever new sources of information that allow them to access more and more of the story. The riddles are usually so difficult that people cannot solve them on their own; in order to progress in the game, it is necessary to communicate with other players—in other words, to form communities. When they arrive at the end of the trail, the players have put together a coherent narrative, much in the same way a detective assembles piece by piece the story of a case. This story is not really told in any of the fragments; it develops mostly in the minds of the players. Jane McGonigal (2011), a leading designer of ARGs, calls this mode of presentation "chaotic storytelling." This chaotic mode makes it very difficult for scholars to research the plot of ARGs. At the end of the game, all that remains of the story are isolated Web sites or Wikis created by the players on which they exchange information. Quite often these Web sites and Wikis are no longer accessible after the game, and the only traces of the plot are the summaries provided in paratextual documents, such as Wikipedia articles, or the private design documents of the developers. ARG stories are truly ephemeral phenomena. When the game is over, the public inscription of the story vanishes.

ARGs operate under a convention that denies their status as games. It is known in the jargon as TINAG (this is not a game): the players pretend that the clues have not been planted by the designers but are part of reality. Many of the Web sites that provide information relevant to the game look indeed like ordinary commercial or informational Web sites. Theorists of ARG seem to believe that the TINAG convention is unique to the genre, but the principle operates in all forms of entertainment that rely on make-believe. When we read a novel, for instance, we know that the story was invented, but we pretend to believe that the storyworld exists independently of the text and that the characters are real human beings. Insofar as pretense is the trademark of fiction, the TINAG convention underscores the fundamentally fictional nature of ARGs.[10]

The creation of stories in ARGs is much more dynamic (some will call it emergent) than in standard computer games. Rather than being rigidly predefined, the plot to be discovered can be at least partly constructed in real time, that is, during the runtime of the game. Yet the design remains fully in the hands of the producers, and the players' influence on the plot is not of the creative but rather of the indirect kind. When the designers notice that the problems to solve are too difficult, they can throw in additional clues; when the players are progressing too fast toward the solution, the designers can complicate the plot with additional problems to solve. This flexibility is comparable to the relations of a Game Master (Caïra 2007) to players in tabletop role-playing games. Just as in role-playing games, the Game Master adapts a plot, usually taken from a rule book, to the particular behavior of the players; in ARGs the puppet masters configure the game in real time according to the players' ability to discover clues and solve problems. But in contrast to role-playing games, ARGs do not invite active impersonation of characters, because there are so many players that it would be impossible to assign to each of them the role of a distinct member of the fictional world.

While the story to be discovered is firmly in the hands of the designers, the players create another story through their activity: the story of the investigation. These two levels can be compared to the structure of a classic mystery story. From the point of view of the detective, the events leading up to the murder are fixed, "in the book" of history, while the events that lead to the solution of the case belong to an open future that remains to be written. It is on this second level that the players can be considered active participants in a developing story.

---

10. A literary manifestation of this denial is the presentation of a novel by an editor-character who claims to have found the text. This practice was particularly popular in the eighteenth-century novel, which often imitated a genre of nonfiction, such as autobiography or collection of letters. Another overt form of fictional self-denial is the claim by the narrator of Balzac's *Père Goriot*, "All is true" (Furst 1995, 1).

A comment that one often hears about ARGs is that they deconstruct the boundaries between games and reality, life and fiction, or the virtual and the real. This idea is very popular with postmodern theory, but it does not withstand closer scrutiny. Far from blurring the borderline between fiction and reality ARGs make players more acutely aware of this boundary. In order to play ARGs successfully, players must be able to isolate the information the puppet masters have planted in the real world from the mass of data that exists independently of the game. For instance, they must be able to tell if a certain Web site conveys information about reality or if it is part of the game. Rather than blurring the borderline between fiction and reality, ARGs construct tunnels between two very distinct ontological domains. These tunnels are called "rabbit holes," by reference to the portal that takes Lewis Carroll's Alice to the alternate world of Wonderland. In ARGs, the rabbit hole is the initial clue that sends the players in search of the story and launches the collective act of make-believe that makes the game possible. To say that in ARGs life itself becomes a game really means that the process of picking the signs of the game within the space of the real world is an integral part of the game.

Can one consider ARGs a form of locative narrative? The clues to the mystery can be situated either in the virtual space of the Internet or in physical space, though anchoring in a specific place leads to a considerable reduction of the potential number of players. (Some games, such as "The Lost Ring," which advertised the Beijing Olympic Games of 2008, solved this problem by staging real-space meetings for players throughout the world.) But even when the game uses real-world locations, the story that the players reconstruct takes place in a fictional world, and its relation to the real world is one of accessibility, not of representation. As the name of the genre aptly suggests, the clues scattered in the real world and on the Internet function as a springboard into an alternate reality. In contrast to location-based narrative projects such as [murmur] that truly focus attention on a physical environment, ARGs' only contribution to an appreciation of real space is that they occasionally take their players to real-world locations, but they rarely encourage the players to develop a relationship with these locations that would be worth calling a sense of place.

CONCLUSION

The contributions of digital technology to our experience of space and to our awareness of what Scott Ruston (2010, 119) calls "the basic place-making capacity of storytelling" are as varied as the applications of this technology.

When the development of the Internet turned personal computers into a truly indispensable tool of everyday life, the data made accessible by digital networks was initially conceived as an alternate (or virtual) reality, and computers were thought of as spaceships that transported us into the great elsewhere of cyberspace. In this ontology, developing a sense of place meant contributing to the building of a virtual world, exploring its backstory, being accepted as member of a virtual community, and exchanging new stories with other participants. With the development of mobile computing, mobile phones, satellite positioning systems like the American GPS, and various types of online maps, however, the centrifugal force that takes the users of digital technology toward alternate worlds has been counterbalanced by a centripetal force that replaces virtual reality with augmented reality. The common feature of the stories described in the second part of this chapter (Memory Maps, *The 21 Steps*, and Les Trucs) is their anchoring in the real world, even when the stories are themselves fictional, but this anchoring is a matter of reference and representation, and it does not involve the physical text. As written artifacts residing on the Web, the maps and the stories associated with them can be downloaded anywhere in the world. The connection between stories and real space becomes more exclusive in the locative narrative projects discussed in the final section of this chapter, since the stories are originally told for an audience situated on the same spot as the storyteller and able to look at the same environment. In order to establish a strong sense of place, truly location-specific texts sacrifice the mobility that written texts have enjoyed, at least since the invention of print, by letting themselves be downloaded and read or heard only in the *presence* of their referent. This situated telling, as our analysis has shown, might leave stronger or weaker marks of the act of narration. But while locative narratives have a bright future for tourism, museums, and events such as cemetery walks, they can alienate us from the world as much as they can provide valuable information. For those who resent the mediation of a technology that cannot avoid drawing attention to itself, location-based storytelling by means of wireless networks is more valuable as a metaphor of how story can turn space into place than as a way to capture the unique spirit of the place, because this spirit, even though it is nurtured by collective memories and by stories told by others, does not exist objectively, but is fashioned by each of us individually.

We have left untouched what is probably the most significant potential contributions of digital technology to the study of the connections between narrative, space, and place. The computer makes widely available a set of tools that enable ordinary people—as opposed to professional writers and artists—to link their own stories, videos, photos, and sound recordings to spatial coordinates, thereby inscribing them as places on their personal maps of the world. As Frédéric Kaplan (2009) has suggested for the autobiographical documents that we increasingly create with digital media, these customized maps, of which Memory Maps gives a rudimentary preview, will be conceived much more for the private use of their authors, or for being shared by a small group of people, than for a general audience.

But it does not take digital technology to connect stories to physical space. As the next three chapters will show, such connections have long been part of Western and other cultures, whether they take the form of street names, guided tours of memory sites, or museum exhibits. It took the recent interdisciplinary and transmedial extension of narratology to draw our attention to the narrativity inherent to these practices.

CHAPTER 6

Street Names as Story and History

AT THIS POINT, our argument changes direction. Chapters 2 through 5 focused especially on the role space plays in narrative. They concentrated on two of the four theoretical issues introduced in the first chapter: (1) the "storyworlds" of narrative space and the symbolic and functional perspectives space and place play in plot; and (2) the space that serves as context and occasionally as referent for the text. We argued that narratives not only describe space, they shape the apperception of storyworlds and serve to situate writers and readers in space.

In this chapter, we pivot so as to turn to the ways that stories are sometimes told in space—that is, the way text and narratives are positioned in the environment through street signs, plaques, inscriptions, and historical markers applied to everyday places. In relationship to the four theoretical topics identified in chapter 1, we focus here on the third and fourth: the space taken by the text itself; and, especially, by the spatial form of the text. However, to avoid confusion, we need to be clear from the start that our concern in this chapter and the next two is considerably different from the "spatial form of text" as has been generally pursued in narratological theory. Here we are working outside the printed page, video screen, and worlds of digital media to focus on how stories are sign-posted and draped across cities, historical sites, and everyday environments, including museum spaces (see chapter 8).

This approach is, we think, one of the key innovations of this book. Our suggestion is that narrative theory offers insight into how stories are told using very different techniques in spaces and places that have not traditionally been the focus of narratological interest. Our concern is thus both with the way that narratology can contribute to theory building in geography—to what we term "narrative geography"—as well as with how the exploration of novel storytelling venues serves to expand the scope of narrative theory beyond some of its traditional concerns.

In geography, as we noted in chapter 1, recent writings have highlighted the discursive suppositions of theory, method, and practice in contemporary geography. At the moment, the concept of narrative is applied quite loosely in geography and is not necessarily informed by recent writings in narrative theory. Our efforts in this and the next two chapters concentrate on sharpening this focus and exploring the potential of narrative geography to advance theory in both geography and narratology.

We also need to be clear from the start that we are concentrating on texts in the environment that have some sort of narrative structure. Words and text are commonplace elements of everyday spaces and places—such as advertising; road, warning, and directional signs; logos and marquees; posters; and store signage. Although these types of text are of interest to other disciplines, we are interested here only in signs, plaques, inscriptions, and text that attempt to tell stories, however loosely or tightly these stories might be structured.

Perhaps a useful distinction to make at this point is between "being a narrative" and "possessing narrativity" (Ryan 2004b). Broadly speaking, having narrativity consists of the ability to evoke known or new stories. An artifact or even an event in life can have narrativity (i.e., it suggests stories to the mind) without "being a narrative" (i.e., without being a set of signs—a discourse—intentionally composed to transmit a story). In contrast to literature, poetry, films, and music, works of "spatial art" such as paintings, sculptures, and photos lack the built-in sequential structure necessary to tell definite stories (Herrnstein Smith 1968, 36). Intended to be apprehended "in a moment of time, rather than as a sequence" (Frank 1945, 225), they can't narrate an entire story, but they can possess narrativity since they are able to represent and highlight "pregnant moments" in the action that encapsulate, embody, symbolize, and otherwise recall an entire plot (Lessing 1984 [1766], 23, 78).

To foreshadow one key element of our argument that will become even more important in chapters 7 and 8, we suggest that when stories are told in the worlds of everyday life as well as in museums and designated historic sites, space is often used as a surrogate for time. That is, as stories are taken off the page and placed on real places, space assumes a somewhat unexpected narrative capacity. Distances between text, directions in which people move, and the overall spatial pattern in which text is arranged all can serve to represent time and the temporal sequence of a narrative. This means that telling stories in space involves not only different media (street signs, plaques, inscriptions) but a different notion of how space and time are used in storytelling. The underlying issue, posed rhetorically by Gurnemanz in the first act of Richard Wagner's *Parsifal* is what happens when "time here becomes space."

But as we move into this topic, one further caveat is in order. That is, neither the terminology of narrative nor the vocabulary of geography are perfectly suited to the task at hand. The concepts of both disciplines are both a help and a hindrance in writing about the overlap between the two fields, since many terms have somewhat differing meanings in varying contexts. We have tried here and in the next two chapters to define unfamiliar terms and borrow carefully from the terminology of both disciplines.

PLACE NAMES IN CONTEXT

In this chapter, we begin with place names as a first step in exploring the spatiality of text and narrative. The narrativity of place names (toponyms) pertains to their semiotic capacity to weld together language and landscape. As elements of language, place names are obviously spoken but also rendered official when inscribed in gazetteers, maps, ordinances, and notably public signs. The primary function of place names is to signify and thereby differentiate between geographical features such as mountains, creeks, cities, or streets. In this capacity place names "conjure up a presence to the mind" (Ryan 2001, 128).

With its overwhelmingly linguistic orientation, the traditional European approach to the study of place names has been largely focused on taxonomy and etymology (Stewart 1975). Interestingly, within academic geography, studying place names was consigned to be on the margins of scholarship. In particular, academic geographers interested in social theory largely ignored the study of place names as not worthy of serious scholarship (Rose-Redwood, Alderman, and Azaryahu 2010). The resurgence of academic interest in the study of place names since the 1980s has largely been manifest in applying a critical approach. Underlying the critical approach is the insight that place names are not mere signifiers of objective reality but belong to structures of power and discourses of identity. One line of critical research has been focused on the critical reading of place names inscribed on maps as an aspect of deconstructing cartographic representations of the world (Harley 1989; Jacob 2006; Wood 1992). Another line of critical research has been focused on naming and renaming places as "strategies of power" (Raento and Watson 2000, 728). The critical approach to the study of place names draws attention to how place names reproduce discourses of ideology and identity (Berg and Vuolteenaho 2009; Rose-Redwood, Alderman, and Azaryahu 2010; Rose-Redwood and Alderman 2011). A number of studies have focused on renaming streets following power shifts (Azaryahu 1986, 1992, 1996a, 1997, 2011b, 2012a; Faraco and Murphy 1997; Foote et al. 2000; Gill 2005; Light 2004; Light and Young 2014; Palonen 2008; Yeoh 1996).

Within the growing literature on the politics of toponymic inscriptions, several studies have explored street naming as a strategy of public commemoration involving power relations and ideological concerns that shape commemorative naming priorities and practices (Alderman 2000, 2002a, 2002b, 2003; Azaryahu 1996a, 2012b; Berg and Vuolteenaho 2009; Rose-Redwood, Alderman, and Azaryahu 2010; Tretter 2011). As these studies show, since underlying the politics of commemorative street naming is the issue of eligibility for public commemoration, street names are aligned with and conform to official narratives of national and local history.

These studies amply demonstrate that commemorative street names have much to tell about ideology and power, identity politics, and political history of the cityscape (figure 6.1). However, the narrative qualities of place names in general and of commemorative street names in particular have hitherto largely evaded scholarly attention. We argue that the spatial textuality of commemorative street names and their being embedded in the experience of the city affords insights into what can and cannot be achieved regarding history telling in spatial media. Obviously, regardless of its fame and significance in the urban texture, a single street name inscribed on street signs or featured in a city map is not a narrative in any conventional sense of the term. Moreover, the spatial arrangement of street names in urban space is ostensibly devoid of any inherent sequential structure, let alone a built-in, coherent storyline. However, as this chapter shows, commemorative street names are rich in narrativity. Street names may be woven into other types of narrative, but in respect to history telling, the narrativity of commemorative street names is a function of their belonging to master narratives of history and, not less important, to their capacity to evoke the stories of historical events and persons (Alderman 2002b, 2003; Azaryahu 1996a, 1997, 2012b; Stump 1988).

The first section of this chapter expands on street names as commemoration and in particular on how commemorative toponymic inscriptions that belong to a system of urban orientation weave history telling into the cityscape and into ordinary experiences. The second section offers insights into the narrative structure of a synchronous spatial configuration of commemorative

FIGURE 6.1. Story St., Cambridge, Massachusetts. Photo by Maoz Azaryahu.

street names as a city-text of "toponymic history." The last three sections address different issues pertaining to the narrativity of street names: street names as news, as literature, and the "stories behind" street names which feature their ostensibly "hidden" history.

STREET NAMES AS COMMEMORATION

Street names belong to the urban geographies of everyday life. When administered by the authorities, they belong to a written system of official orientation. The existence of official street names does not exclude the possibility that nonofficial systems of urban orientation exist (Mounin 1980; Yeoh 1992). Inscribed in street signs and nameplates, they constitute a seemingly trivial aspect of streetscapes. Inscribed in maps, they are featured in traditional and digital cartographic representations of the city.

The use of place names for commemorative purposes is intended to interweave remembrance into the everyday language of the landscape. Underlying the cultural convention that invests the name with mnemonic function is the premise that speaking or reading the name actuates remembrance: "For as often as I speak of him, I do earnestly remember him still" (Jeremiah 31:19).

While belonging to master-narratives of national and local history, each commemorative street name is also a "title" of a story that stands for and encapsulates a life story of a person or an account of an event. In this capacity they weave history and memory into spatial and social practices of everyday life. The commemorative function assigned to street names predominates in the naming process, when eligibility for commemoration and the placing of the commemoration in urban space reign supreme. It also figures prominently if and when the legitimacy of a toponymic commemoration is later contested and debated. However, in the context of their common use for urban orientation, commemorative street names transform history into local geography. As toponymic namesakes, Bismarck in Berlin, Martin Luther King Jr. in the United States, Herzl in Tel Aviv, and Napoleon in Paris are integrated into ordinary experiences of the city in terms of "where it is" rather than "who is he/she" and the history he/she stands for.

The availability and use of street names to navigate through urban space and to address locations in the city makes them inherent to everyday urban experiences and stories. For Inspector Reginald Wexford, Ruth Rendell's protagonist, the reading of nameplates was not a hobby or any other eccentric behavior, but rather a simple, almost banal, attempt to find his way in London:

> Wexford could easily believe it, as she seemed knowledgeable and he hadn't the faintest idea where Finsbury Park might be. He asked her how he could find Shepherds Hill and she gave him complicated directions through Crouch End. He set off to walk, looking for street names he thought he might have a chance of recognizing. One of these, a street called Hornsey Lane, had its nameplate on the brick wall of a medical center. (Rendell 2012, 213)

Inspector Wexford, like most people most of the time, was not interested in the meaning of the street names he encountered. What mattered was that the names could be read and serve the purpose of spatial orientation. In rare cases, a visual encounter with a commemorative street name inscribed on a nameplate might invest the experience with symbolic meaning. André Malraux relates in his memoirs how, after meeting de Gaulle and while walking the streets of Paris, reflecting on the significance of priests and military orders, "[he] glanced up casually before crossing a street: rue Saint Dominique" (1970, 105). This experience, however, is an exception rather than the rule. In a debate in Berlin's municipal parliament in 1927, a member of the assembly noted: "When I hear the name Friedrichstraße (named after Friedrich I, King of Prussia 1657–1713) or similar street names, I don't think at all that the street is named after Friedrich I or anyone else" (Loewy 1927, 303).

Not only are most people unaware of the commemorative function of street names in the everyday contexts of their use, but even if they are aware of this function, for the most part, they are not familiar with the history associated with the names. The narrativity of commemorative street names is a function of their association with (possibly exemplary) biographies and (often dramatic) events. Yet for residents and visitors, the association of commemorative street names with history entails prior knowledge about the history they stand for. This is not different from remembrance: obviously, it is not possible to remember someone we do not know and have never met, and speaking or reading a person's name without knowing who she was does not amount to a meaningful remembrance. However, lack of knowledge does not exclude the possibility of an educated guess. Such is how Jack Reacher, Lee Child's protagonist, made sense of the street names of a small town in Nebraska when he visited it for the first time:

> There were three side streets on the right, and three on the left. They all had names that sounded like people. Maybe original Nebraska settlers, or famous football players, or coaches, or champion corn growers. (Child 2010, 208)

Notably, Jack Reacher did not assume that these were the names of politicians, scientists, or poets. Of course there is always the possibility of mistaken identities. In reference to streets named after Clinton and Gore in Toronto, the official Web site of the municipality of Toronto informs visitors that

> Clinton Street and Gore Street were not named after two famous Americans, but were likely named after Henry Clinton, Secretary for the Colonies (1852–1854) and Sir Francis Gore, Lieutenant Governor of Upper Canada (1806–1817). Clinton Street was named in 1853, Gore Street was named in 1881. (City of Toronto 2013)

While the association of commemorative street names with history entails prior knowledge, there is also the possibility that street names perform as "cues" that prompt one to learn about history. In this case, the association of a street name with history is constituted as an educational process. Following the decision of the Tel Aviv Municipality in 1934 to systematically name new streets in the rapidly developing city after historical figures, a journalist suggested that such a policy would inevitably motivate people to find out who were the people whose names were inscribed on street signs (Goralick 1934, 4). According to the official at the head of the municipal committee in charge of naming streets in Tel Aviv, the commemorative naming of streets was also intended to encourage the public to learn history: "It is permissible, and even agreeable, to believe that in the course of time civilized citizens will be ashamed not to know who are those whose names adorn the street signs of their city. . . . Through street names citizens will inevitably learn history" (Ben-Yishai 1952, 37).

Curiosity might prompt individuals to inquire about the history evoked by certain street names, but there is also the possibility to enhance the history-telling capacity of street signs. A relatively simple and conventional strategy employed by municipal authorities is to add historical information on the street signs themselves, as in Paris, Tel Aviv, and Bucharest, or in a separate plate appended to the street sign, as in Berlin, Vienna, and Heidelberg. Adding historical information to street signs augments the narrativity of the inscribed street names by explicitly associating them with history and biography. Whereas the street signs and the names inscribed on them locate the street in urban space, the information added to the signs locates the street name in history.

With historical information added to them, street signs also perform as entries in an "open-space" encyclopedia scattered all over the city. The inscriptions are by necessity concise, since scarcity of space on the signs is a constraint. Consequently, explanatory inscriptions consist of what is considered to be essential information only. Passersby on Hardenbergstraße in Berlin are informed by the small plate appended to the street sign that the street is named after a Prussian prime minister who lived between 1750 and 1822 (figure 6.2). The explanatory inscriptions added to street signs in Paris inform visitors that rue Bonaparte was named after "Napoléon Bonaparte," who lived between 1756 and 1821, while Danton was a "Conventionnel" (member of the National Convention during the French Revolution) who lived between 1759 and 1794. Shaped like those in Paris, street signs in Bucharest offer a one-word explanation. For instance, street signs in the Rumanian capital inform that Strada Duiliu Zamfirescu is named after a "scriitor" (writer), Strada Ion Mincu commemorates an "architect" (architect), and Strada Arthur Verona honors the memory of a "pictor" (painter).

STREET NAMES AS CITY-TEXT

The spatial configuration of street names in the cityscape and in city maps constitutes a particular city-text that belongs to the semiotic makeup of the city. Such a city-text includes a finite number of street names (words) inscribed on street signs throughout the city and depicted in city maps and

FIGURE 6.2. Street signs in Berlin and Paris. Photos by Maoz Azaryahu.

their indexes (figure 6.3). A city-text has many authors over time—such as successive municipal committees and councils in charge of naming streets but also chiefs of police and national authorities involved in approving names. The commemorative elements of a city-text and the "toponymic history" they constitute represent not only an officially approved vision of history but also the commemorative priorities of former administrations. Villains, of course, are excluded from toponymic histories, since they are not entitled to the honor bestowed by a public commemoration. Hitler, Petain, and Quisling are absent from contemporary German, French, and Norwegian city-texts, respectively,

FIGURE 6.3. Street names in central Tel Aviv. One layer of a geographic information system database without the underlying tracings of the streets themselves. From the Geographic Information Forum open-access database maintained by the Department of Interior.

in spite of their paramount significance in twentieth-century German, French, and Norwegian history.

A city-text is not intended to be read as an entirety, and its eventual reading as a text does not involve any obligation to any prescribed order. Not having a definite beginning or an end, a city-text offers multiple "reading paths." Most, delineated by individuals while walking, driving, or searching city maps for a route, are ephemeral. Some, like bus or subway routes, are shared among users of the city and are depicted in diagrams and maps delineating routes of bus and subway lines. In both cases, the sequence of street names along each path follows movement in urban space and the chronological progression it entails.

A fundamental property of a city-text is that it lacks a built-in time arrow. The commemorative elements of a city-text coexist simultaneously in the cityscape but with no distinction between "before" and "after" and no linear thread of a chronological sequence connecting them. The assumption is that a "toponymic history" is associated with and is concomitant with ideologically coherent national and local narratives of history. In some cases, thematically related commemorative names are grouped together, for instance, the Napoleonic victories near the Tuileries in Paris (Ferguson 1988, 392). In Berlin-Weißensee, a whole area comprises streets named after composers: Bizet, Meyerbeer, Chopin, Smetana, Gounod, and so on (Azaryahu 1986). Such a toponymic practice creates a "themed neighborhood." The common theme invests a spatial cluster of toponymic commemorations with a sense of narrative coherence that reflects on the neighborhood as a whole.

The spatial configuration of streets does not produce any significant linear order, and the intersection of streets does not necessarily imply any temporal or thematic relationship between their names. For Walter Benjamin, "The meeting of two different street names makes for the magic of the 'corner'" (qtd. in Regier 2010, 189). Intersections afford imaginary encounters: in Mexico City, Beethoven meets Bach, and in Tel Aviv, President Lincoln meets President Wilson. In Berlin, Leibnitz meets Kant (figure 6.4). Such imaginary encounters are sometimes weighed down with irony. For instance, the intersection of the Boulevard Voltaire with rue Saint Sébastien in Paris is ironic in light of the notorious anticlerical disposition of the eighteenth-century philosopher. In Selma, Alabama, Martin Luther King Jr. Street and Jefferson Davis Street intersect, thereby suggesting a contemporary meeting point between the martyred hero of the American civil rights movement and the president of the Confederacy.

Spatially fragmented and lacking in-built temporality, "toponymic history" is clearly devoid of a narrative structure and its underlying chronologies and causal linkages. Any attempt to transform a "toponymic history" into a

FIGURE 6.4. A corner where two philosophers meet, Berlin. Photo by Maoz Azaryahu.

conventional, chronologically progressive historical narrative means a breakup of the spatial order of a city-text and the rearrangement of its constituent elements into a new text, according to an organizing principle that is not to be found in the semiotic structure of the original city-text.

An illustration of such a procedure is the reorganization of Berlin's "toponymic history" into a conventional narrative of German national history attempted in 1934 in an article entitled "Unsere Helden und ihre Taten in den Straßennamen von Groß-Berlin" [Our heroes and their deeds in the street names of Greater Berlin] (Giese 1934). In this article, a contribution to the study of Berlin and its history written shortly after the political triumph of National Socialism, the author compiled a narrative account of German history based upon the historical commemorations inscribed on Berlin's street signs. This meant the weaving together of the commemorated heroes and events in a narrative form that entailed both temporal progression and causal interpretations. The various commemorations were reorganized according to their relative location on the historical time axis; the evaluation of the commemorated heroes and their "deeds" was in a National Socialist framework of interpretation.

The historical account begins with the name of Hermann (Arminius), the ancient German warrior who defeated three Roman legions in 9 CE. Next, it includes medieval emperors, for example Friedrich I (Barbarossa); Prussian electors and kings, for example Friedrich II ("the Great"); Otto von Bismarck, the architect of German unification; as well as Prussian generals and field marshals. The culmination of the narrative account is the "national rebirth" propagated by the Nazis and represented by Nazi leaders, most notably Adolf Hitler.

As an official register of toponymic commemorations, a city-text comprises an authorized index of a putative narrative of history—notwithstanding the absence of "villains." This is manifest in the index of street names attached to a city map, which is but a rearrangement of the city-text as it mentions all the names that appear on the map. The alphabetical order of this list of street names on a city map implies neither spatial nor temporal order nor indicates hierarchy of historical significance. Rather it provides a pragmatic indexing device to facilitate retrieval of spatial information—"where a street is"—which highlights street names as elements of an official system of urban orientation.

CHANGE THROUGH TIME

Continuously written and partly overwritten, a city-text is in principle a work in progress. Like the city itself, it is a palimpsest. In contrast to many a street name left unchanged since first registered in the official record, some streets have changed their names a few times. A case in point is the public square in front of the Reichstag building in Berlin, where currently the Federal Bundestag is housed. In 1864, the square was named Königsplatz [Kings' Square]. In 1926, the republican city government initiated the removal of a monarchic symbol at the political center of the capital, and the square was renamed Platz der Republik [Square of the Republic]. A few weeks after the Nazi seizure of power in 1933, the square regained its former name. In 1948, the republican name was restored (Azaryahu 2011b).

Changing names entails the exchange of street signs. Occasionally, the palimpsest comes apart. As is often the case, when street names are changed, the old sign, marked as deleted, is left in place together with the new sign for a certain amount of time (figure 6.5). The coexistence of the old and new signs represents an officially sanctioned stage of transition: the objective is to mitigate disorientation by letting people who are accustomed to the old name get used to the new name. The idea is that after a certain period the old street sign will be removed, and at least as judged by street signs, a new status quo will have been reached, wherein the old name is no more an element of the official system of orientation. Yet officially discarded street names survive among residents, at least for some time (Mounin 1980, 494). Though rare, there is an

FIGURE 6.5. Renaming a street after David Ben-Gurion, Israel's first Prime Minister in Ramat-Gan, Israel, 1986. Photo by Maoz Azaryahu.

option that the old name, though not inscribed in street signs, persists in folk-geography, while the new name fails to garner popular favor. A case in point is Manhattan's Sixth Avenue. Though officially renamed Avenue of the Americas in 1945, New Yorkers rarely use the new name to the effect that both names are in circulation (Rose-Redwood 2008a, 2008b). The same in Paris, where the Place de l'Étoile was officially renamed after Charles de Gaulle, but the new name is not commonly used.

In certain cases, material traces of former names are preserved in the local streetscape. The old street name might persist in nameplates affixed by residents to the building. It might also endure in the name of a local business that bore the former street name. A case in point is the former Belle-Alliance-Platz in Kreuzberg, Berlin. The name was given in 1814 by the Prussian state to commemorate the victory over Napoleon, won a year before by the Prussian and Russian armies in the Battle of Leipzig. The commemorative name was later attached to a pharmacy opened at the square: Belle-Alliance Apotheke [pharmacy] in July 1886. In April 1946, the communist-led city government of Berlin renamed the square after Franz Mehring, a left-wing historian of the German workers' movement. The name of the pharmacy, however, was not changed, thereby preserving the former place name in the streetscape (figure 6.6).

FIGURE 6.6. Belle-Alliance Apotheke, Mehringdamm, Berlin-Kreuzberg. Photo by Maoz Azaryahu.

TEXT AND SCALE

The urban structure of a toponymic city-text provides a built-in scale to evaluate the relative status of the commemorated events and heroes. The general rule is that the importance of a thoroughfare and the prestige of the associated commemoration are positively correlated; urban form and historical significance usually harmonize in this way. However, the fact that "toponymic history" is a product of a protracted historical process is a source of distortion when it comes to reading a city-text. The history of the text has a twofold effect. One is the possible reevaluation of the significance of historical figures and events, which is an indispensable element of a societal discourse of history. This process is independent of urban developments. The other is the effect of urban dynamics on the prestige of streets and neighborhoods in general, which is independent of the academic and political discourse of history.

Urban dynamics is a factor to be reckoned with whenever the relative status of commemorations is deduced from the significance of the thoroughfare in the urban fabric. When street names are transported from history to geography, they clearly become susceptible to sharing the fortunes of their location. When obscure streets gain in urban significance, their namesake "heroes" gain in prominence and fame. The opposite is also true, when famous heroes are associated with the reputation of notorious slums or derelict neighborhoods. For a journalist writing in 1940 on what he considered the problematic relationship in Tel Aviv between the urban prestige of streets and the historical significance of the people commemorated by their names, it was only natural that when a neighborhood becomes a city, "the most magnificent streets are named after people of lesser rank than those after whom the first streets were named." However, in his view, chance also plays a role: "There is a name of the third rank that is associated with a beautiful and well-kept street, and there is a magnificent name that is wasted on a shabby street. It is all a matter of luck" (Heftman 1940).

STREET NAMES AS NEWS STORIES

Being designations of locations in the city, it is not surprising that street names are constantly mentioned in news stories. Another issue altogether is when street names themselves are news stories. Though not exclusively, such news stories focus on and highlight the politics of street naming and its association with power and ideology. At times, a simple announcement of street renamings is in itself a potent narrative. A case in point is an announcement that appeared in the *Military Government Gazette*, the official publication of the American military government in Mannheim, in occupied Germany, July 21, 1945 (Stadtkreis Mannheim 1945, 1):

Until now:	In the future:
1. Adolf-Hitler-Ufer	Am weißen Sand
2. Adolf-Hitler-Platz	Friedensplatz
3. Horst-Wessel-Platz	Philosophenplatz
4. Platz des 30. Januar	Georg-Lechleiter-Platz
5. Reinhard-Heydrich-Platz	Gutenberg-Platz
6. Schlageter-Straße	August-Bebel-Straße
7. Dr. Todt-Straße	Schubert-Straße
8. Dietrich-Eckhart-Straße	Ludwig-Frank-Straße

9. Paul-Billet-Straße   Theodor-Kutzer-Straße
10. Adolf-Hitler-Schule   Goethe-Schule
11. Carin-Göring-Schule   Sickinger-Schule
12. Herbert-Norkus-Schule   Wald-Schule
13. Hans-Schemm-Schule   Schönau-Schule

The announcement pronounced changes in the names of streets, squares, and schools that commemorated the vanquished Nazi regime. On the left were the old, discarded names. On the right were their new and ideologically correct names. The emphasis on "before" and "after" told in unequivocal terms the story of the toponymic purge, and hence symbolic end, of the Nazi regime in Mannheim's cityscape. Erased from the official register of toponymic commemorations were the names of Nazi leaders, martyrs, and "prophets" of the Nazi revolution. Goethe, Gutenberg, and Schubert celebrated cultural heritage and humanistic tradition.

Stories about controversial names and conflicts regarding renamings are often about how contemporary sensibilities stimulate demands to delete names of discredited past heroes from the street signs. At the center of the political drama is a clash of interests between proponents and opponents of renaming, where historical reputations are debated and local reputations are at stake. A case in point is the features about Marshal Pétain and his controversial toponymic commemoration in the United States and France. The stories of Petain Avenue and rue Pétain were featured in two *New York Times* stories in 2010 and 2011, respectively (Applebome 2010; Tagliabue 2011). In both countries, Marshal Pétain, the venerated French hero of World War I, was honored by naming streets after him, usually together with other heroes of the war. However, during World War II, Pétain led the Vichy regime that collaborated with Nazi Germany. His tarnished reputation is the basis of demands to rename streets bearing his name.

Opponents of the naming of Petain Avenue, a tiny, side street in Milltown, New Jersey, pointed out that the Marshal's commemoration was morally inappropriate. A local resident opposed the change since the street name conjured local memories and sense of place: "Petain Avenue is not a person. [It] is my home, a part of my history and my family's history. We do not want our history changed." The local council voted against a change of the name.

The story about rue Pétain in Tremblois-lès-Carignan, a village in northeast France, is also a story about pressure exerted on a village to rid itself of a street named after Marshal Pétain. But in contrast to Milltown, the village in France yielded, and the single street sign with the name of Pétain was replaced with another with the inscription rue de la Belle-Croix, after a chapel located there. Though many residents were not disturbed by a street named after Pétain, the council voted to delete his name from the register to avoid the embarrassment. With the renaming in Tremblois-lès-Carignan, Pétain's name no longer adorns French street nameplates.

Controversial street names and conflicts around renaming are stories with special appeal. These are stories that involve political drama and reputational politics. These stories formulate ethical and ideological approaches to politics and divergent visions of history in everyday terms of ostensibly banal street names. Importantly, these are stories that address issues such as who is entitled to be honored in public—and who should be denied a place in public memory.

Stories about (re)naming streets are basically about symbolic entitlements and the allocation of symbolic capital in urban space. But occasionally, such stories suggest the possibility that the function of street names as elements of an urban system of orientation might be at odds with their commemorative function. In April 2011, the *New York Times* published a story entitled "After 3 Decades, a Bronx Historian Loses his Road" (Grynbaum 2011). The feature was about two name changes in New York City approved by Mayor Bloomberg. Whereas former Mayor Edward Koch received a namesake bridge, Theodor Kazimiroff, the founder of the Historical Society of the Bronx, lost a boulevard that had been his namesake since 1981. Officially, the latter change was portrayed as a matter of practicality: the official explanation for changing the name of the Dr. Theodore Kazimiroff Boulevard was that the commemorative function of the name undermined spatial orientation. The Theodore Kazimiroff Boulevard was the northern extension of Southern Boulevard, and the configuration of names proved confusing for many. A sign of the times, another complaint that was mentioned concerned GPS devices: the difficulty of spelling Kazimiroff accurately and the need to include "Dr. Theodore" while typing in an address.

STREET NAMES AS LITERATURE

In 1907, the English writer Gilbert Keith Chesterton complained that whereas in London only a few streets were named after writers, in Paris many streets were named after literary celebrities (Galbraith 1907). Priscilla Parkhurst Ferguson notes in her fascinating study of Paris's street names that the percentage of "literary" street names in the French capital is percentagewise considerably higher than in London, Berlin, Boston, and New York (1988, 388). In her interpretation, the proportionally high number of writers inscribed on the street signs of Paris is congruent with a culture that places much value on the written word, conflates language with national identity, and associates literature with national grandeur. Branded the "city of literature," Dublin chose its street names to honor Irish writers. The list of literary street names includes

Sean O'Casey Avenue, Clarence Mangan Road, James Joyce Street, Dean Swift Square, and Le Fanu Road (Dublin City of Literature 2013). Another example, "Literary Chicago" consists of streets named after Goethe, Schiller, Dante, Shakespeare, and Poe (Holden 2001, 282–84).

Naming streets after writers is an honorific measure, where greatness is rewarded by a permanent place in the city's "hall of fame," embedded into the rhetoric of the city and the experience of navigating its streets. Concurrently, streets named after writers not only commemorate literary figures but also have the potential to call to mind their literary work: the names of authors commemorated in street signs are, metaphorically speaking, "trailed" by stories and literary characters. Whether members of the public are familiar with the connoted stories and characters is a different issue; it should also be borne in mind that with the exception of a few famous names, most of the writers commemorated by their topographic namesakes are not necessarily household names.

In addition to authors, literary street names also commemorate fictional characters and literary works. John Galt Boulevard in Omaha, Nebraska, was named by the developer after a character in Ayn Rand's *Atlas Shrugged* (Frischbach 2011). Streets in the Village Home development in Davis, California, are named after characters and places in J. R. R. Tolkien's *The Hobbit* and *The Lord of the Rings* (Village Homes 2013). In Paris, a street is named after *The Count of Monte Cristo*, Alexander Dumas's famous novel. In 1833, a street in the Greenwich Village, New York, was named Waverley Place after Sir Walter Scott's Waverley novels. A century later the developer of a new suburb near Melbourne, Australia, also named it after the Waverley novels (Woodwards Mount Waverley 2013).

Streets are named after literary works, but literary works are also named after streets. The three novels of Naguib Mahfouz's *Cairo Trilogy* are named after real streets in the Egyptian metropolis. Both Alexanderplatz in Berlin and Washington Square in New York are commemorative namesakes of a Russian Czar and the founding father of the United States, respectively. Yet as titles of major works of fiction, the stories signified by these street names ignore their commemorative function. The use of street names as titles of works of literary and cinematic fiction as well builds on the idea that as urban designations, street names can be used as metonyms for action and complex experiences. *Berlin Alexanderplatz* (Döblin 2003 [1929]) is actually, as the subtitle makes clear, "[T]he story of Franz Biberkopf," the main protagonist of the novel. Washington Square, New York, is the fashionable address of Catherine Sloper and her father, Doctor Sloper (James 1880). As titles of novels, the narrativity of the street names is also a function of their association with and evocation of fully fledged literary narratives.

THE STORIES BEHIND

The "stories behind" street names are largely about the provenance of the names. Storytelling involves exposing or revealing these stories in books and Web sites. Such stories satisfy human curiosity about origins: who chose the names, when, and, arguably most important, why? But they are also about what the names stand for, which, in the case of commemorative names, means biographical stories and tales about local history, heritage, and nostalgia. Importantly, these afford insight into local culture and its evolution over time.

Myriad books as well as blogs dedicated to particular cities offer accessible venues to telling the stories behind local street names. Another example—and, in 2012, the first of its kind—was an exhibition at Singapore's national library entitled "Stories behind Singapore Streets." The objective was to showcase "the origins of local street names," highlight "stories about people, their lives and achievements," and trace "the history of Singapore through street naming conventions" (National Library Board Singapore 2012). On display were maps, photographs, and original street signs; the stories of Singapore's street names were also told in guided tours and public lectures.

Obviously, the display of street signs in a historical exhibition dedicated to street names directs attention to the stories behind the names. A different issue is when a street sign on display in an exhibition serves as a metonym for a historical period or an ideology. In its metonymic capacity, such a street sign does not signify a location. Either emblematic of a bygone period or associated with the ideology of a former political regime, street signs in an exhibition are visual illustrations of the exhibition's narrative. A case in point is the Museum of Communism in Prague. Focused on the totalitarian regime that was in power in Czechoslovakia from 1948 to the "Velvet Revolution" of 1989, the museum's theme is "Communism—the Dream, the Reality and the Nightmare" (Museum of Communism 2013). Among the authentic artifacts on display is a street sign bearing the commemorative name "Leninova" (figure 6.7). Introduced by the communist regime as an honorific gesture to the Soviet leader, as long as the street name belonged to the official nomenclature, it was emblematic of the Soviet-oriented regime. After the street was renamed, the discarded street sign was a symbol of a former period in the political geography of Prague and the political history of the Czechoslovak Republic; its display in the historical museum is a visual statement about the communist chapter in Prague's history as well as on the demise of the discredited communist regime.

The stories behind street names featured in the press and in popular books seem to be in stark contrast to the academic literature that, highlighting the "power-laden character of naming places" (Berg and Vuolteenaho 2009, 1),

FIGURE 6.7. Leninova: A nameplate on display in the Museum of Communism, Prague, Czech Republic. Photo by Maoz Azaryahu.

subscribes to the critical approach to the study of street names. The critical study of place names directs attention to the politics of naming practices and its impact on the choice of certain names and the rejection of others. In this, however, the critical study of street names also offers, albeit sophisticated and theory-informed, accounts of the origin and meaning of street names. Notably, such accounts tell the story behind street names as the political (hi)story of (re)naming.

CONCLUSION

Embedded in and evocative of stories of different kinds, street names are deeply imbued with narrativity, even though they rarely comprise complete narratives by themselves. As signifiers of location, they are woven into a myriad of ephemeral personal stories about daily experiences. They also call to mind culturally shared stories that associate the street with social milieus, leisure, commercial, protest, or illicit activities and, importantly, specific reputations. In their metonymic capacity, real street names and the urban locations they denote provide a sense of specificity and palpability to a set of diffuse urban experiences and to the stories through which they are conveyed and shared. In a similar vein, when used as titles of literary works, real place names associate fictional stories with the reputations and cultural meanings of actual places.

The narrativity of street names is substantially enhanced when they are invested with a commemorative function. As commemorations, street names are associated with the biographies of persons and the stories of events found worthy of public memorialization. Concurrently, commemorative street names belong to officially sanctioned narratives of municipal and national history. Notwithstanding the politics of commemoration, toponymic commemoration links places with stories that in most cases took place elsewhere. This is clearly the case with streets named after other places that are laden with historical meanings and memories, most prominently battlefields or historical sites such as Trafalgar Square in London or Masada Streets in Israel or the United States.

The advantage of toponymic commemoration is the result of the ostensible ordinariness of street names that allows them to effectively implicate remembrance into the practices of everyday life and ordinary urban experiences. The downside is that toponymic commemoration does not impart historical knowledge. Not only are most people unaware of the commemorative function of street names in the everyday contexts of their use but for most part they are also unfamiliar with the stories of and the history behind the names. Adding information to street signs is a simple method to achieve this, yet recent developments in mobile technology offer exciting possibilities to increases the narrativity of street signs. Using smartphones and other mobile devices, passersby can satisfy their curiosity by searching for stories on the Web. It is also possible to add scannable codes to street signs that provide instant links to stories via cell phones.

The spatial textuality of street names highlights the distinction between "being a narrative," which entails an underlying sequential structure, and possessing narrativity. While urban toponyms are rich in narrativity, the spatial configuration of street names in the city lacks a sequential structure and, therefore, it is devoid of a storyline. Nonetheless, as the case of landscape and museum narratives discussed in the next chapters show, a storyline becomes an option whenever a chronological or a thematic sequential structure is introduced into a spatial arrangement of coexistent elements in the form of routes and paths that direct movement in space.

CHAPTER 7

Landscape Narratives

THIS CHAPTER CONTINUES with the issues raised in the last: how texts and narratives are positioned in the environment to tell stories using signs, inscriptions, and historical markers. Chapter 6 began this discussion by concentrating on the narrative qualities of toponyms. In the current chapter, we turn to the related issue of how text is positioned on signs, plaques, and other displays to tell stories at historical and heritage sites. Whereas we argued that toponyms possess qualities of narrativity but are somewhat limited in their storytelling potential, the examples considered in this chapter are often designed quite explicitly to tell stories (Azaryahu and Foote 2008). The broader theoretical focus of the two chapters remains the same and will continue into chapter 8: the space occupied by the text itself, and, especially, the spatial form of the text, two of the four issues identified in chapter 1 as the core concerns of this book.

Again, to avoid any potential confusion, we need to be clear from the start that our approach in this chapter and as well as in chapters 6 and 8 is considerably different from the way the "space taken by the text" and "spatial form of text" has previously been approached in narratological theory. Here we are conceiving of stories written on signs and plaques that are positioned in the environment across areas both large and small. Although many of the examples we discuss in this chapter have also been the subject of conventional narrative forms, such as books, film, and television, here in chapter 7, we are focusing on how such stories are configured at historical and heritage sites. We argue that organizing stories "on the ground," so to speak, involves issues relating to the spatial form of text that are somewhat different from those involved in telling the story on the pages of a book, e-book, or video screen.

The examples we explore are sometimes little more than brief captions on markers positioned at historical sites. Others are spread over large areas like battlefields and heritage sites and might involve elaborate collections of buildings, markers, memorials, and inscriptions positioned with care to point out key events and locations related to one or more historical events. Sites like these are a good starting point for our study because they "map" stories, at least metaphorically, onto real-life environments. The examples in figure 7.1 tell several different stories, to paraphrase the text: "Here is where a small Florida town was burned in an outbreak of racial violence 1923"; "Here is the route of many of the civil rights marches in Birmingham, Alabama, in the 1960s"; and "Here is where executed political prisoners—now martyrs—were buried secretly in Budapest, after the 1956 Hungarian uprising."

We also use historical examples because they help us make one of our principal theoretical points (mentioned briefly at the start of chapter 6)—when stories are told "on site" or "on the ground," space is often used as a surrogate for time. As stories are taken off the page and positioned as signs and inscriptions on real places, space assumes a somewhat unexpected narrative capacity. Distances between signs, the directions in which people move, and the overall spatial pattern in which signs and plaques are arranged can all serve to represent time and the temporal sequence of a narrative. Indeed, we would go further to assert that as stories are told "in place," not only must time be narrated spatially but movements that are part of the storyline must sometimes be narrated chronologically.

Configuring stories in real-life settings can pose considerable challenges in some situations. Exact temporal sequences and diachronic progressions might have to be condensed, transposed, omitted, or refigured to fit the space of particular historical sites. Two of the principal obstacles to the strict temporal sequencing of complex narratives fall at the extremes—stretching stories across large spaces and packing them into small ones. That is, it is difficult to sustain coherent landscape narratives across large areas and long distances, and equally challenging to narrate long, complex stories in confined spaces. As a result, temporal sequences are often rewritten and transformed into episodes, scenes, and vignettes, almost like developing a screenplay from a book.

Here we bump against some of the same terminological constraints we faced in chapter 6 and will see again in chapter 8. As we move away from stories on a page or screen (the focus of chapters 2 to 5) and toward stories told

FIGURE 7.1. Common strategies for using signs and inscriptions to present stories. Top: A point narrative describing the race riot and massacre of 1923 that destroyed the African American village of Rosewood, Florida. Middle: One in a sequence of markers along the Birmingham, Alabama, Civil Rights Heritage Trail indicating a site of protest against local businesses in 1963. Bottom: Some of the many markers, memorials, and signs distributed around the extensive Parcel 301 burial ground in Budapest, Hungary, honoring victims of political terror and oppression during the communist period. Photos by K. E. Foote.

through signs, inscriptions on buildings, and text on memorials (the topics of chapters 6 to 8), neither narratology nor geography offers terms ideally suited to our needs. Like Potteiger and Purinton (1998), who were among the first to address some of the topics addressed in this chapter, we use the term "landscape narrative" to refer to stories that are told by being inscribed or marked in the environment. We use "landscape" in the sense employed by geographers to refer to environments shaped and modified by human agency, a long tradition of research in the discipline but, again, not attuned to the interests of narratology. However, in using this term "landscape narrative," we need to be clear that we are *not* focusing on "stories about landscape" as, for example, John Muir's *My First Summer in the Sierra* of 1911, but rather on stories that are told by "draping" them over the places where they occurred—the markers and signs now found in Yosemite National Park (some of which refer to Muir's life in the Sierra Nevada Mountains). "Readers" (if we can use that term rather than "visitors") must walk, drive, or otherwise move about in space to enjoy the underlying stories.

Perhaps more jarringly, we are suggesting that roadside markers, memorials, tourist signage, and landscape are types of "media" for storytelling. This is a large conceptual leap to make between stories printed in books, published in magazines or newspapers, or broadcast on radio or television and those configured and inscribed in landscape. But, making this leap helps us draw parallels between traditional narrative forms and the signs and markers we consider in this chapter. We argue that these "landscape narratives" are of four broad types that revolve, in part, around the spatial and temporal scale of the events themselves. The first involves narrating an event from a single point or place with a marker and are most commonly employed for events that are constrained spatially and temporally. The second category includes linear and sequential chronologies linking time and space along routes and paths. These are frequently used for events of intermediate temporal and spatial scales. The third type is used for events involving complex spatial and temporal sequences over large areas or long periods of time that are difficult to narrate in a straightforward spatial or chronological order. The fourth category, "hybrid," simply admits that several strategies are sometimes applied together.

POINT NARRATIVES

Perhaps the most common strategy for organizing a landscape narrative is to tell a story from a single point, the roadside historical marker being the epitome of this type. The historical events being recounted are reduced to brief, usually formal or even formulaic prose. These markers are *declamations* in the second and fourth sense of the *Oxford English Dictionary*'s definition: "A public speech or address of rhetorical character . . . expressing strong feelings and addressed to the passions of the hearers" and often involving formal devices of rhetorical elocution. Such inscriptions sometimes take the style of soliloquy or of epic poetry. The Haymarket Martyr's Memorial that tells the story and honors the labor organizers executed in Chicago in the aftermath of the Haymarket Riot of 1886 includes the last words of Albert Spies, one of the men executed:

"The day will come when our silence will be more powerful than the voices you strangle today."

Historical sites of this sort are frequently framed by a fence or wall, with gates sometimes used to separate the narrative space from the surrounding area. Point narratives are common, of course, because they are relatively inexpensive, easy to create, and use such a simple means of applying text to landscape—a sign or plaque. But it is also true that point narratives are popular because many events can be localized to single, easily marked places, like this marker along the Chicago River where the excursion boat *Eastland* capsized in 1915:

THE EASTLAND DISASTER
WHILE STILL PARTIALLY TIED TO ITS
DOCK AT THE RIVER'S EDGE, THE EXCURSION
STEAMER EASTLAND ROLLED OVER ON THE
MORNING OF JULY 24, 1915. THE RESULT WAS
ONE OF THE WORST MARITIME DISASTERS IN
AMERICAN HISTORY. MORE THAN EIGHT
HUNDRED PEOPLE LOST THEIR LIVES WITHIN A
FEW FEET OF SHORE. THE EASTLAND WAS FILLED
TO OVERFLOWING WITH PICNIC BOUND WESTERN
ELECTRIC COMPANY EMPLOYEES AND THEIR
FAMILIES WHEN THE TRAGEDY OCCURRED.
INVESTIGATIONS FOLLOWING THE DISASTER
RAISED QUESTIONS ABOUT THE SHIP'S
SEAWORTHINESS AND INSPECTION OF GREAT
LAKES STEAMERS IN GENERAL.

ERECTED BY THE ILLINOIS MATHEMATICS AND
SCIENCE ACADEMY AND THE
ILLINOIS STATE HISTORICAL SOCIETY, 1988

In this case, the position of the marker is framed by the railing along the river and, indeed, the river itself. The terse, formal prose—emphasized with CAPITALIZED font—is representative of how such markers compress stories into minimalist prose. The corporate "authorship" (or sponsorship) claimed at the close is also typical of such stories. Such markers are typical of many events that can be localized in very specific places. Examples that come to mind are the death sites of leaders and famous people such as Princess Diana in Paris or Israeli Prime Minister Yitzhak Rabin in the since renamed Rabin Square in Tel Aviv.

Point narratives are also used in other situations. For example, complex events can sometimes be boiled down to key moments or decisive actions that are readily narrated at those points. And sometimes the landscape itself provides a particularly good vantage point for narrating an event. In other cases, the point of declamation holds significance in the telling of the story. The monument on the Zuran Hill in southern Moravia (Czech Republic) marks the place that served as Napoleon's command post in the early stages of the Battle of Austerlitz (Slavkoy), fought on December 2, 1805, against Austrian, Russian, and Prussian armies. The Zuran Hill offers a panoramic view of the battlefield, while the monument presents a bronze battle map. The memorial to the Scottish hero William Wallace was built on Abbey Craig, the high ground assumed to have served as his command post against the English during the Battle of Stirling Bridge in 1297 (Edensor 1997; Gold and Gold 1995). In the case of the memorial to the victims of the Ludlow massacre of strikers and their families during the in 1914 coal "war" in southern Colorado, it is the place where the worst loss of life occurred, marked as the so-called "death pit" (Saitta, Walker, and Reckner 2006). A convenient vista point for narrating the Johnstown Flood of 1889 in Pennsylvania is the abutment of the former South Fork Dam; the breach in the earthen dam that caused the flood is still visible. Narratives positioned at a single point can also be effective when the actual site of an event is inaccessible, such as the site the torpedoing of the R. M. S. *Lusitania* in 1915 off the south coast of Ireland, with the story told and victims memorialized both on the Old Head of Kinsale and in Cobh, County Cork.

SEQUENTIAL NARRATIVES

Sequential narratives are structured linearly along trails or paths, particularly when the story involves a point-to-point chronology. The starting and ending points of such narratives are frequently framed by gates or portals, and the chronological sequencing is sustained for visitors using numbered stops along paths. Fences and borders are used to suggest or enforce an appropriate sequence, although such narratives vary considerably in the options they offer. Some are highly structured while others allow great flexibility. Decisions about the relative control of sequencing can be integral to the narrative. By freeing visitors to explore a story nonsequentially or bypass some sections entirely, some amount of repetition is needed from stop to stop. In practical terms, strict control of movement is difficult over larger sites or those requiring long periods of time to visit.

Prototypes for many sequential narratives can be found in many different cultural and religious traditions. They involve travels and journeys, such as a spiritual quest, exile, banishment, or odyssey, which tests, enlightens, or illustrates lessons of social, moral, or religious significance. Pilgrimage is among the most important of these prototypes. It is a journey of moral significance in which the pilgrim visits sites or shrines to reflect on the lives of prophets, martyrs, and saints. Often the journey is meant to test the pilgrim's strength, stamina, and courage. The Stations of the Cross, or Via Dolorosa, in the old city of Jerusalem is one of the most important Christian prototypes and marks the path that is said by tradition to be the one Jesus walked from his trial to crucifixion (Halbwachs 1992). Each of the fourteen stops along the path is associated with a particular event recounted in the Gospels. The stations are duplicated symbolically inside most Roman Catholic churches, in many Lutheran and Anglican churches, as well across the landscape at sites like the Sacred Mount Calvary of Domodossola in Italy.

The Via Dolorosa as a pilgrimage serves as a prototype in two ways. First, it is a model for arranging a temporal sequence of events in space—that is, guiding visitors along a route or path followed by participants in an historical event or episode, such as Paul Revere's ride from Boston during America's Revolutionary War period. Second, the pilgrimage in its experiential or moral sense suggests paths designed to show the visitor what it might have been like to participate in an event, to experience a test of courage or sacrifice (such as stepping into a prison cell), or to gain a heightened sense of community or nation. This experiential sense of courage and sacrifice is sometimes an important part of the narrative, as, for example, in trails created in recent decades to commemorate the protests and marches of the American Civil Rights in Selma and Birmingham, Alabama, and the anti-Vietnam War movements at Kent State University, during which protestors were met with violence. In these cases, the ability of narratives to represent lived experiences, or *qualia* (i.e., what it was like) allows the visitor to identify with the participants in the events being commemorated, a point stressed by Fludernik (1996) and Herman (2009).

Time and Space Linked Sequentially Along a Path or Trail

Among the most common instances of sequential narratives are those like the Stations of the Cross, in which time and space are linked sequentially in an order specific to a particular event. Some of the best examples are the marking of paths or trails around historical sites. Typically, these narratives are intended to be experienced over a relatively brief visit lasting from an hour or two to perhaps one or two days. A case in point is the Little Bighorn Battlefield in Montana, where George A. Custer and his cavalry troops were defeated by Plains Indians on June 25, 1876. The sequence of events is portrayed along automobile and foot trails that stretch across the battlefield from the first engagement to their last stand (figure 7.2). By car, visitors can visit all the points of the narrative in about two hours. If they wish to walk or wander, they can spend a day or two studying the details of the battle.

At battlefields like Little Bighorn and other sites telling complex stories, sequential narratives have limitations. In this case, the battle involved hundreds of soldiers and warriors on two sides of the battle. A written narrative can handle this by alternating between plot lines, something more difficult to do using signs and markers. Sometimes the result is a simplification of action and movement that can be compressed into signage and inscriptions.

As we argue below in the section on narratives told over large areas and long periods of time, sequence is also used to structure stories of a slightly different sort—those that cannot be experienced in a short visit or journey. In the United States, these include narratives of the major western trails, such as the Lewis and Clark, California, Oregon, Mormon, and Santa Fe trails, all used for exploration and settlement; the Erie Canal; the Trail of Tears, tracing the expulsion of the Cherokee Nation from its homelands in the southeastern United States to Oklahoma; the routes of the major transcontinental railways; and wartime campaigns like General Sherman's March to the Sea from Atlanta to Savannah, Georgia, in the last year of the American Civil War. Enthusiasts might try to travel these routes over a week or month, but the narratives providing the common thread are different from stories experienced in an hour or a day.

Other Types of Stories Told Sequentially in Space

Sometimes landscape narratives are formed to sequentially link places without obvious chronological connections in a coherent story. Common examples

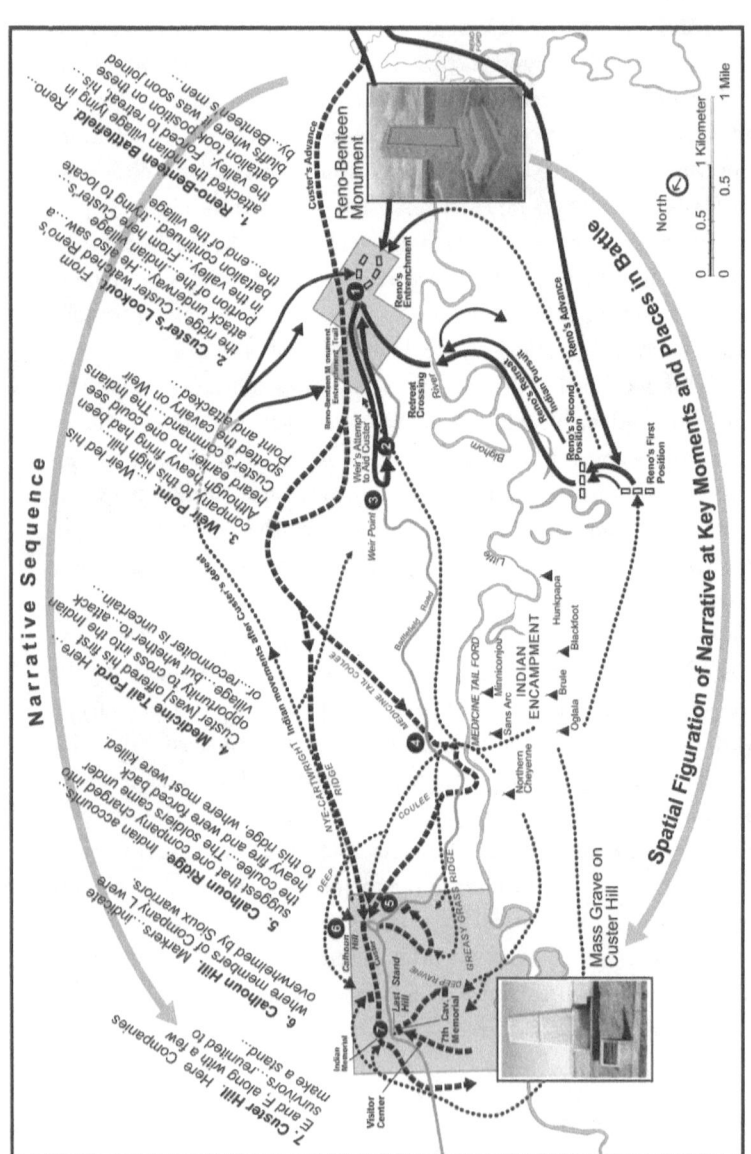

FIGURE 7.2. Little Bighorn Battlefield in Montana, an example of a sequential narrative depicting the defeat of Seventh U.S. Cavalry troops under George A. Custer during the afternoon of June 25, 1876. The spatial figuration of narrative moves from right to left across the map, highlighting key moments in the battle with signs, markers, memorials, and trails. Map by K. E. Foote using National Park Service digital base maps.

are stories that trace in space the life or achievements of famous individuals. Examples include the walking tour of Abraham Lincoln's Springfield neighborhood in Illinois, developed by the U.S. National Park Service, or "The Story of an Industrial City" in Lowell, Massachusetts, that uses Lowell to trace the history of the industrial revolution in the United States from the perspective of the New England textile industry.

The chronology of the person's life from birth to death often provides the basic framework for this type of narrative, but other types of stories can be told in this way as well. Philadelphia's "Walking in the Steps of Benjamin Franklin" was developed for the Franklin tercentenary celebration of 2006. The route developed for this anniversary tells the story of Franklin but also of early Philadelphia and the American Revolution. The key events of Franklin's life anchor the story, but his contributions to the history of Philadelphia and the United States are also highlighted with stops at the Federal Reserve Bank, the Second Bank of the United States, the Constitution Center on Independence Mall, and Elfreth's Alley, the oldest continuously inhabited street in the United States (Greater Philadelphia Tourism Marketing Corporation 2005).

Another possibility is to link existing shrines to represent a larger historical sequence. The Yad Vashem holocaust memorial in Jerusalem is situated just below Israel's national cemetery on the crest of Mount Herzl. These are two of Israel's primary national shrines, with Yad Vashem telling the story of the Holocaust and Mount Herzl representing the narrative of national independence (Yad Vashem 2007). In 2004, a trail was created to link the two shrines so that visitors can experience the narrative progression from Holocaust to independence, the same progression that is also embedded in the architectural narrative of the Yad Vashem shrine itself, as we discuss in the next chapter (Rehabilitation Department Unit for the Commemoration of Fallen Soldiers 2003, 2004). The local topography amplifies the narrative symbolism. From the entrance plaza of Yad Vashem, visitors must ascend Mount Herzl to reach the national cemetery.

NARRATIVES TOLD OVER LARGE AREAS OR INVOLVING LONG PERIODS OF TIME

Among the most difficult sites to interpret are those involving actions that stretch over large areas or long periods of time; a large number of simultaneous events over wide areas; complex spatial and temporal movement within the overall event; and layerings of events in archeological strata. These are stories that revolve around large battles and military campaigns; major social, economic, political, and cultural change; and complicated archeological and historic sites. As in one-day battle narratives, these stories contain parallel events, but rather than forming a global story arc, they encompass a large number of independent episodes, or substories. No one point or sequence provides an effective perspective for narrating the story in space. Instead, narratives are greatly simplified—temporal and spatial relationships are abridged, compressed, lengthened, embellished, straightened, or smoothed as needed to provide a sense of coherency at the historical site. Rather than presenting a sequence or chronology, strategies at these sites might involve presenting distinct "slices" of a story.

Narratives of Significant Places

We include in this category stories that are told from a series of vista or vantage points, with one element of a story told at each point, but not in strict chronological order. One vantage point might reveal a significant event from one period, another vista might expose an important episode from a wholly different period. Such a strategy offers several advantages for telling complex stories. They permit a simplification of spatial and temporal complexity—particularly the problem of narrating simultaneous events. In other media, an illusion of simultaneity can be produced using devices like visual cutaways and windows. Simultaneity can be simulated, perhaps imperfectly, at historical sites by picking particularly noteworthy places from which to tell contrasting stories about the place and its history.

Such narrative arrangements are common at multilayered archeological sites, like the Old City of Jerusalem or Roman ruins of London. The Masada National Park in Israel is a good example. The principal remains atop the plateau are those of a massive fortress built by Herod the Great in late first century BCE and the remains of the last stand of Jewish rebels who were defeated by the Roman army in 73 CE (Azaryahu and Kellerman 1999; Ben-Yehuda 1995; Zerubavel 1995). Given the geographical layering of these artifacts, a strict chronological narrative would be difficult to employ, since it would require visitors to loop several times around the site. Instead, the visitor stops are organized around a carefully framed arrangement of sights that highlight key periods and events for their individual significance and for the ways they relate to other significant elements of the local topography and history (Stiebel 2000).

Irrespective of whether they are fictional or factual stories, narratives are selective in what they represent and what they leave out. The palpability of landscape at sites like Masada highlights that the need to fit landscape narrative in physical space involves a stringent selection process: discarded options are visually evident in the form of landscape features that are not marked as sights and, accordingly, are not considered to be constituent elements of the local landscape narrative.

Narratives of Significant Moments

Just as stories told from the most important or "significant" places allow them be simplified into a series of tableaux, narratives that emphasize "significant moments" simplify temporal and spatial complexity by featuring turning points in a complex series of events that can be spread over a large area (Hawthorne 1988). Narratives of this type are related to the sequential narratives described earlier in this chapter except, perhaps, that these significant-moment narratives are more selective in highlighting only the most vital aspects in a more involved sequence.

An example is the Gettysburg National Military Park in Pennsylvania. The Battle at Gettysburg on July 1–3, 1863, during the American Civil War involved combined armies of approximately 163,000 soldiers fighting over an area of 15–20 square miles. The scope of the battle makes it difficult to narrate—in particular, simultaneous troop movements and fighting at widely removed points on the field of battle. As a solution, the self-guided tour developed by the National Park Service focuses on key moments in the battle—the points where important changes took place (National Park Service 2013b). The full eighteen-mile automobile route claims to be—and generally is—chronological; it begins at McPherson Ridge (where the troops first engaged) and ends at the High Water Mark Memorial (where the last Confederate assault was repulsed) and National Cemetery (figure 7.3). But this chronological narrative involves significant concatenations.

These sorts of significant-moment narratives can also be applied to stories spread even further apart in time and space. The Mormon Trail, mentioned earlier in this chapter under sequential narratives, is an example extending over several U.S. states from Illinois to Utah, linking many towns and cities that were of significance at different times. The trail was begun in 1846–47 under the leadership of Brigham Young after the assassination of the Mormon prophet and leader, Joseph Smith. Recognizing the need to move further west to avoid persecution, Young guided the development of the trail that, far beyond its importance in providing a path to freedom, proved to be

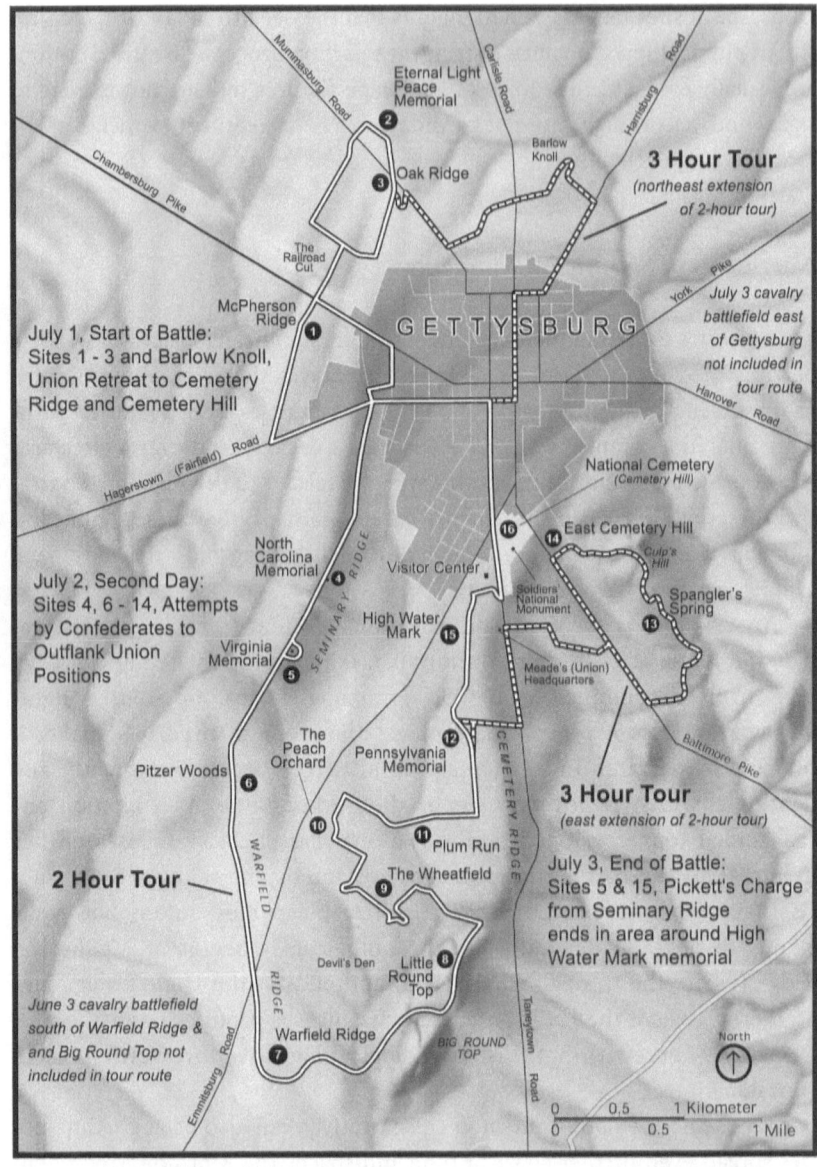

FIGURE 7.3. The two- and three-hour automobile tour routes of the Gettysburg, Pennsylvania, battlefield. Gettysburg can be seen as an example of a chronological narrative of significant moments that has been developed to tell the story of a very complex battle. In this case, events that occurred simultaneously are narrated sequentially, particularly the events of the second day, July 2, 1863 (sites 4, 6–14). Some events and engagements are left out, such as the cavalry battles to the east and south on July 3, or are included only in the three-hour tour. Map by K. E. Foote using National Park Service digital base maps.

of tremendous importance to the settlement of the western United States. It became the key corridor across the central Great Plains and into the Rocky Mountains for settlers emigrating to Utah, California, and Oregon until the rise of transcontinental railroad connections after 1869. The trail's history has been extensively marked by a wide range of local, state, and national government agencies, private organizations such as the Oregon-California Trails Association, as well as individuals and families (Berrett 2001, 2005; Brown 2004). At the federal level, a narrative was developed when the Mormon Trail became the first U.S. historical trail to be marked in 1978. The legislation that recognized the trail specified that the first year's struggle of 1845–46 should be the focus of the narrative, rather than the stories of subsequent groups in later years. The decision to focus on the first year simplified what would otherwise be a complex narrative. The segment of the trail running across Iowa and connecting Nauvoo, Illinois, to Winter Quarters, Nebraska, highlights twenty-eight sites as key moments in the first wave of emigration (figure 7.4).

Themed Visits

What we term here as "themed visits" allow perhaps the greatest freedom in structuring landscape storytelling. They involve weaving a sometimes disparate set of events, issues, periods, perspectives, and places into a unifying story, for example, the "rise of New York" or the "maritime history of New England." In the absence of some sort of overarching story, the elements of the narrative would simply be a miscellany of superficially unrelated sites. As we will note again in the next chapter, with respect to museums, temporal ordering is present to some degree in these themed visits. Sometimes this ordering is only implied or very loosely built into the story—a sense of "before" and "after," perhaps dates inscribed on labels, or references to time periods and the like. A themed visit does not have to follow an explicit chronological storyline, but the existence of such a storyline is brought to mind by other means.

Some good examples are the various themed tours that have developed through time in Boston, Massachusetts, particularly around Beacon Hill, one of the city's oldest neighborhoods. The Freedom Trail is one of the most famous and links places tied to the American Revolutionary War (Bahne 2005; Dunwell and Linden 2005; National Park Service 2013a). The paths of at least three other themed heritage walks intersect the Freedom Trail at Beacon Hill:

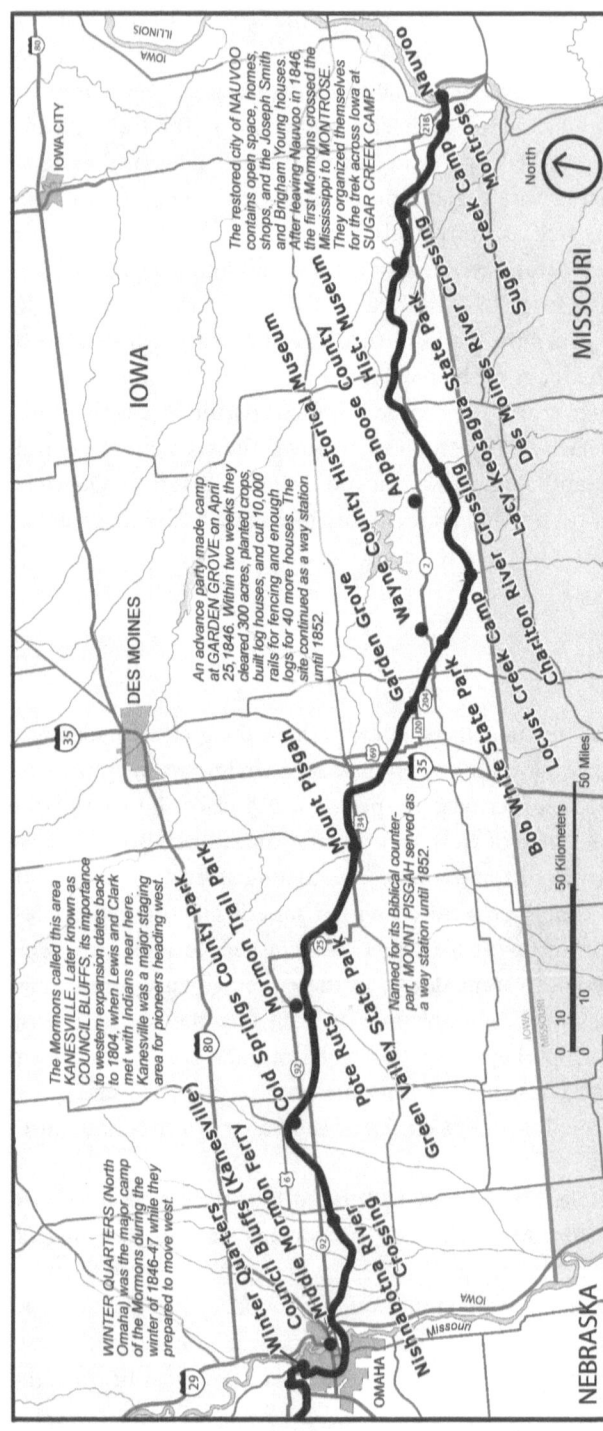

FIGURE 7.4. The Mormon Trail across Iowa, an example of a sequential narrative arranged spatially over a large area. The narrative highlights the sites of camps, farms, settlements, and river crossings important in 1846, as the first Mormon pioneers left Nauvoo, Illinois (right), for Winter Quarters, Nebraska (left), not arriving in Utah until 1847. This narrative comes from the National Park Service. On the ground, the sites are marked and maintained by many different groups, including the Latter-Day Saint Church; state and local government; and private associations. Map by K. E. Foote using National Park Service digital base maps and National Park Service (2005).

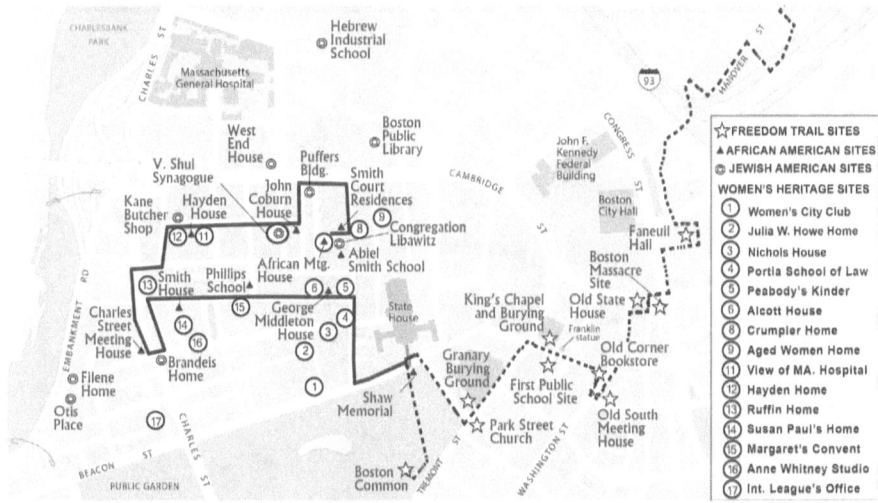

FIGURE 7.5. The intersection of several thematic narratives on Beacon Hill, Boston, Massachusetts. One of the oldest neighborhoods in Boston, Beacon Hill is a place where many stories intersect. Although some places are included in more than one narrative, visitors could follow a single narrative unaware that the others exist. Map by Martha Lorena Davis.

the Boston Black Heritage Trail (National Park Service 2013a), one segment of the Boston Women's Heritage Trail (Kaufman et al. 2006), and a Jewish-American heritage trail (Ross 2003) (figure 7.5). All three of these weave together a miscellany of sites into stories that highlight the contributions of these groups to the city, state, and nation.

Themed visits can be used in other situations as well, as they are at the Buchenwald concentration camp memorial in Germany (figure 7.6). As decided in the early 1990s, the official tour of Buchenwald distinguishes among three successive periods: the National-Socialist concentration camp (1937–45); the Soviet detention camp (1945–50); and the memorial created by the East German government during the period of communist regime (1950–89). Rather than a single trail or one for each period, visitors are offered four trails and one monument to visit (Stein and Stein 1993). The titles of the trails signify their particular focus and, by implication, their chronology. The National-Socialist camp is presented through three trails: "The Way to the Prisoners' Camp," "Remains of the Camp Barracks," and "In the Footsteps of the Perpetrators." "Graveyard of Special Camp No. 2" presents the Soviet detention camp, and "The Monument" presents Buchenwald when it served as an East German memorial site.

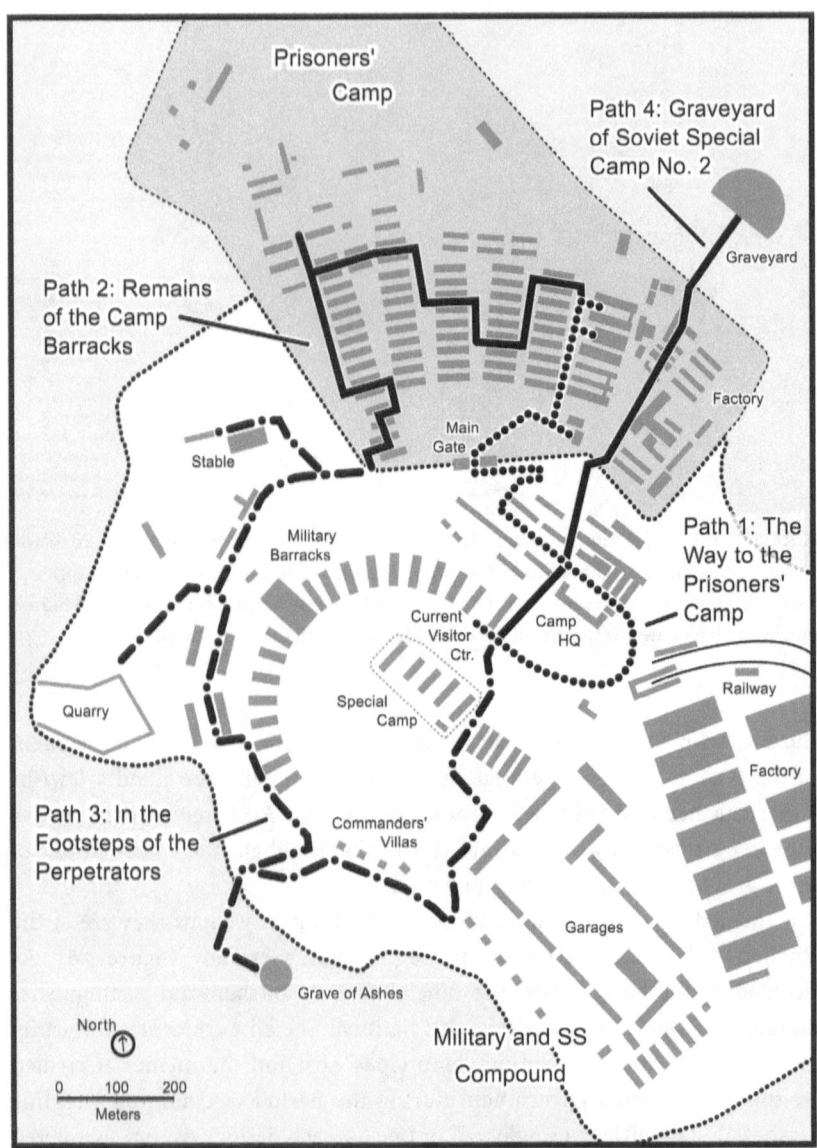

FIGURE 7.6. Tours of the Buchenwald concentration camp near Weimar, Germany. Visitors can choose between four routes, each developed around a thematic narrative. When these routes were developed during the redesign of the site in the mid-1990s, they distinguished between the two successive periods in the site's history: the Nazi concentration camp (1937–45) and the Soviet detention camp, also known as Special Camp 2 (1945–50). The key distinction was between the victims and the perpetrators but emphasizing the perspective of the prisoners. Map by K. E. Foote.

HYBRID NARRATIVES

Some narratives fall between those described above, and hybrids can emerge where categories blur together. A case in point is Arlington National Cemetery in Arlington, Virginia, just across the Potomac River from Washington, DC, and adjacent to the Pentagon. The property, an estate confiscated at the start of the U.S. Civil War from confederate general Robert E. Lee and used as a cemetery during the war, has gradually emerged as a shrine to America's military and political heroes. Point, sequential, and themed tours are all used to tell stories about different aspects of the cemetery and those buried there. At the microscale, the case could be made that each of the gravestones alludes to a personal story. But some markers and memorials are more explicit in their storytelling, like the monument honoring the sailors who died in the sinking of the U.S.S. Maine in Havana harbor in 1898 at the start of the Spanish-American War or the victims of the terrorist bombing of Pan Am flight 103 over Lockerbie, Scotland, in 1988. Trails connect many of the cemetery's important graves, and visitors are offered many different options for touring the grounds (Arlington National Cemetery 2007; Bigler 2005).

In some respects hybrid narratives are more in keeping with a postmodern design ethos, which questions attempts to impose a single story on historical sites. Instead, they can be used to present visitors with a range of evidence, ideas, and perspectives that invite them to confront an event or site on their own. The Sixth Floor Museum in the Texas School Book Depository in Dallas tells the story of President John F. Kennedy's assassination. Overlooking Dealey Plaza, the museum is situated on the floor that Lee Harvey Oswald used as his sniper's nest. The assassination remains contested even today, and visitors hold many different, often strong, views about what happened in November 1963. As a result, the curators took care to present a range of evidence and interpretations in the displays so that visitors can consider the controversies from a variety of points of view. So here in the sniper's aerie, visitors are offered a bird's-eye view of the assassination site and an overview of the contested interpretations of the shooting.

Similarly, the abstract memorial commissioned for Parcel 301 in Budapest, Hungary, is positioned adjacent to the once anonymous graves of the political prisoners executed in the two years after the 1956 Hungarian uprising. The design includes an abstract representation of the scaffolding on which the martyrs were hanged, a black obelisk recessed underground, and the graves of the martyrs themselves, together playing off the stark contrast between national memory and the executions but not attempting to narrate the events of the uprising.

In some cases, these hybrid narratives involve creating metaphoric or symbolic relationships among inscriptions, monuments, buildings, landscape elements, and design, as well as letting visitors make the connections as they wish. For example, at the Little Bighorn battlefield, the recent monument to the Cheyenne, Lakota, and Arapahoe warriors was placed about one hundred yards from the obelisk positioned over the mass grave of U.S. cavalry. The two are of equal visual prominence and connected axially to form a spirit gate for the cavalry dead as well as for the Crow Indian scouts who died with the soldiers. Additionally, memorials at the death sites of Native American warriors began to be marked in 1999. The red granite tablets contrast symbolically with the white marble used to mark where the cavalrymen fell.

DISCUSSION AND CONCLUSION

These categories and classifications are only a first step in landscape narratives. Certainly one reason we have examined them in this book is because their spatial configurations differ so greatly from stories narrated in more conventional media. Like other types of stories, landscape narratives help to share the experiences of characters in the story; explain the causes and consequences of historical events; transport visitors to past times to make history more seem more personal; honor and remember members of a community; enlighten; amuse; and serve many other purposes. Stories told as landscape narratives vary from the ways they are told in literature, film, television, drama, and other media.

Even the examples that might seem closest to landscape narrative, such as the visual arts and museum design, differ in important ways. Telling a story spatially in landscape involves critical choices about position, distance, direction, perspective, and movement on the ground. The geography of the site is a constraint: stories have to be woven around well-defined historical locations. Of course, the need to divide, segment, and pace are constraints faced by other forms of storytelling. But arranging stories around the "facts on the ground" at historical sites presents considerably different challenges.

As we alluded to earlier, one of the key constraints is sustaining a temporal sequence in space. In so many other media, the storyteller can assume that the viewer, listener, or reader will pursue the narrative from start to finish, even if not in one sitting. Landscape narratives are not so readily structured. Apart from point narratives, it would be difficult to assume that visitors will start at a given place and follow the narrative from beginning to end. This means that landscape narratives frequently use spatial, visual, and geographical cues to direct visitors along particular trails around historical sites. Gates, rails, walkways, borders, and curbs are all used to varying degrees to guide visitors from place to place.

Designers and writers of the narrative seem very conscious of the difficulties of serializing stories into many episodes that will be read in part or whole, in sequence and out of sequence, by visitors who might differ considerably in background, with respect to a particular narrative. This means that creating a landscape narrative is not, of course, simply the writing of a story on place, but rather the rewriting of this story to make connections among significant moments and places that would otherwise remain unconnected spatially and temporally.

Authorship is another difference between landscape narratives and storytelling in conventional media. Landscape narratives are more frequently coauthored than other types of narrative. Though of course other types of narrative, like films and computer games, are also coauthored, landscape narratives are often created by committees that include writers, artists, architects, historians, politicians, and members of the general public. There are advantages to committee authorship of landscape narratives in that knowledge and experience can be pooled, but the ensuing written-by-committee signage might involve compromises of content and form.

Landscape narratives also differ from many other story forms in that they are often composed, edited, and reshaped over long time periods, perhaps a bit like epic poems and stories that were (and sometimes still are) embellished in their telling by skilled readers and raconteurs. For landscapes, this means that authorship can extend over years, but more typically, decades, generations, and centuries as stories change. This is a different process than the translation or editing of stories from one language into another, but it means that the configuration of landscape narratives, more than others, can readily be changed as a result of social or political pressures, an issue we have written about in other contexts (Azaryahu 1996b; Bodnar 1992; Foote 2003; Foote and Azaryahu 2007; Foote, Tóth, and Árvay 2000; Linenthal 1991).

At the same time, we recognize that there are several issues about landscape narratives that suggest further study. Narrative theory points to the important role played by the reader, viewer, or listener in constructing meaning from narrative forms. Interestingly, relatively little research has been undertaken on the experience of visitors and tourists at historical sites (Hanna and Del Casino 2003; Lamme 1989; Till 1999). Urry's (2002) notion of the "tourist gaze" and Dicks's (2004) idea of tourism as a form of cultural display focus on issues other than narrative and tourist experiences. Our contention is that future studies should also take into account how landscape narratives partake in shaping the experience of historical sites. For example, in chapter 4, we suggested that readers often develop cognitive maps of the narratives they read and, indeed, that these spatial conceptions of plot and action are essential to apprehending many nuances of the narrative itself. Is it the case then that visitors develop the same sorts of cognitive map as they visit historical sites? What schema do they form about the causes and consequences of the events being narrated?

Attention might also focus on how landscape narratives change and hybridize through time, as is true of many of the examples discussed in this chapter—the Little Bighorn battlefield, Buchenwald, the Kent State University shootings of May 4, 1970. These social and political motives are important in shaping narrative, but stories also change for other reasons. These days, some reshaping is occurring because of technological advances, specifically, the adoption of digital media is having an impact on how narratives are told (as discussed in chapter 5).

This chapter has focused on historical sites, but landscape narratives are also used in nature and ecotours, architectural tours, and other types of excursion organized around narrative. Noteworthy in this regard are so-called "discovery tours," types of adventure tourism that employ movement to lend a sense of progression and plot development. This sort of narrative can be organized to provide a sense of spatial order, direction, linearity, and temporal progression, but may also allow for more serendipitous exploration than some of the historical cases examined in this chapter.

Finally, there is a connection between the landscape narratives discussed in this chapter and the so-called "museum narratives" discussed in the next. Stories told in museums rely on many of the same strategies used in landscape to organize their narratives—spatial order, direction, linearity, and progression. At the same time, museums can use text, audio-visual aids, and artifacts that offer additional storytelling potential (Crane 2000; Kirschenblatt-Gimblett 1998; Samuel 1994; Sherman 1995). Increasingly, the architectural plans of new museums are even incorporated into the storytelling. And sometimes, there is only a fine line between landscape and museum narratives, as, for instance, when an historical site is itself a building or building compound that is configured as a museum.

CHAPTER 8

Museum Narratives

WHEREAS CHAPTERS 6 AND 7 explored the arrangement of narratives across cityscapes and landscapes, this chapter explores storytelling in history museums with an emphasis on built-in museum features: the permanent exhibition and the building's architecture. Not all museums are organized around narratives, but history museums often are. In recent years, storytelling has become increasingly important in the design of these museums, and some are quite explicit about using stories as a means of encouraging visitors to explore historical events. Our reason for focusing on narratives found in museums (what we will call "museum narratives" in this chapter), relates to the theoretical concerns outlined in chapter 1. Of the four ways we described space, text, and narrative intersecting, two are of particular interest in this chapter: the space taken by the text itself; and, especially, by the spatial form of the text. This means that we are interested in how museums planners and designers arrange text and stories along circulation paths that direct the movement of visitors and invest museum space with a sense of sequential, narrative order. Indeed, some contemporary museum buildings have been designed around the stories they are designed to tell. This means that a museum's interior (and sometimes exterior) form provides an environment in which text "comes off the page" to be arranged in novel spatial configurations, a conception quite different than Joseph Frank's (1991 [1945]) original notion of the spatial form of text.

Whereas the spatial configuration of narratives at historical sites (discussed in chapter 7) and in history museums have similarities, museums allow complex narratives to be told with the assistance of artifacts, text (on inscriptions, labels, and signs), reconstructions, audiovisual aids, and human guides in a carefully controlled setting designed specifically for this purpose. Notably, storytelling in narrative history museums is not usually constrained by the same spatial or temporal realities underlying the spatial configuration of narratives at the sites themselves, where "facts on the ground" and landscape features pertaining to the history of the site have to be taken into account. In contradistinction to historical sites, history museums can tell history through the arrangement of exhibits in museum space and in the idiom of architectural design.

At the same time, we are not suggesting that there is necessarily a sharp divide between the landscape narratives presented at historical sites and those found in the interior spaces of museums. As was mentioned in the previous chapter, museums are often found at historical sites, and these interior spaces are often designed to complement the narratives found outside. Also, there are examples that fall between landscapes and museums, for example, rural folklife museums and open-air museums like Colonial Williamsburg in Virginia. Similarly, some types of historical storytelling fall squarely between museum and landscape. The President Franklin Roosevelt Memorial dedicated in 1997 in Washington, DC, frames twelve years in U.S. history, using a sequence of four outdoor rooms, one for each of Roosevelt's terms of office, yet the site of the memorial along the Potomac is not itself directly connected to the events depicted. Not far away, on Pennsylvania Avenue between the U.S. Capitol Building and the White House, the U.S. Navy Memorial uses a set of bas-relief sculptures to depict key moments and events in its history.

Another possibility is a historical site that is converted into and performs as a historical museum. To this category belong buildings dedicated to the commemoration of an important event that took place there. A prominent example is the Hall of Independence in Philadelphia. This is also the case when the residence of a famous individual is converted into a museum. Such sites freeze historical time in a historical place, where mundane artifacts ostensibly left in their original location offer access to the life-story of the famous resident. The rhetoric of authenticity reigns supreme. Such sites overlay the domestic with greatness and veneration: artifacts are relics suffused with their association with their famous owner. The spatial arrangement of artifacts does not correspond to a storyline, and no chronology is implied.

Clearly, not all museums are organized around principles of storytelling and narrative. Our analysis does not then entail a survey of all museums.

We focus here largely on history museums and on contemporary museums with strong storylines—for reasons similar to those that led us to consider historical sites in the previous chapter on landscape narratives. First, history museums tend to stress storytelling more than some other types of museum, although there is certainly a contemporary trend to use storytelling as a means of organizing museums of other kinds. And here, we are not just discussing museums labeled "historical" like the German Historical Museum or the National Museum of American History. Instead, we are casting our net widely to encompass a broad range of institutions that focus on telling stories about time and history. This means that we also touch in passing on some natural history and anthropological museums; science, industrial, and technology museums; art museums; and a few types involving temporal themes such as the lives and works of writers, artists, and political leaders. Second, history museums provide examples of the contemporary trend of designing museum buildings around the stories they tell. From the perspective of the spatial form of the text, these cases allow us to examine how architecture, exhibits, and text are interwoven spatially to redefine the relationship between narrative sequence and circulation, as we discuss below.

Originating in royal collections of extraordinary objects, museums emerged as institutions dedicated to the preservation and public display of authentic objects in their particular fields of interest. But, as we mentioned above, new approaches to museum making have emerged more recently that offer intriguing alternatives to the traditional commitment of museums to the preservation and display of their collection, especially the growing popularity of the conception and design of the museum as a means for the purpose of storytelling (Bedford 2001; Karp 1991; Kelly 2010; Rounds 2002; Weinberg and Elieli 1995). Carter (2011) provides a fascinating discussion of the modern origins of the narrative history museum in the late eighteenth century. In contrast to conventional collection-based museums, where the public display of the collection reigns supreme, in a contemporary narrative-based museum the display of artifacts is secondary to the poetics of storytelling, while issues of exhibition sequence and museum architecture underlie the spatial configuration of narratives. Another significant shift in museum making has been the use of multimedia and interactive devices to enrich and update the experience offered to visitors. In some quarters, these changes are lamented as the "Disneyfication" of the museum (Galant 2004), but we see this in a different way. Many of the changes underway in museums involve using a broader range of media to offer a technologically up-to-date and versatile narrative experience. These might have been pioneered in commercial tourist attractions, but that makes them no less valuable to storytelling strategies.

Despite recent trends, permanent exhibitions at contemporary history museums vary across a wide spectrum in how they employ narrative as an organizing principle. At one end of the spectrum are those museums where the display of artifacts reigns supreme. Exhibits in halls and galleries are organized by type, artist, place, or period, but the contents of the exhibits do not follow a strict temporal sequence. For example, in an art museum where different periods and artists are displayed in different galleries, these galleries might be scattered about the building to fit the room plan and the size of the collection rather than according to a clear principle of succession. At the other end of the spectrum are history museums designed from the outset to lead visitors through a narrative based on a coherent storyline, while the storytelling is related to but somewhat independent of the display of artifacts. In such a case, the exhibition is built upon a preconceived narrative framework and movement in space that corresponds to progression in time. Along the spectrum are hybrid forms of history museums that combine displays of artifacts belonging to the museum's collection, some employing a strict chronological progression and others more a themed approach, which, though still organized—even if loosely—in some sort of temporal sequence, focuses on perhaps several stories within the museum space.

Our work is related to, but also expands upon recent work in museum theory (Black 2005; Buschmann 2010; Geoghegan 2010; Hooper-Greenhill 1995; Maclead 2005; Macleod, Hanks, and Hale 2012; Marstine 2006; Witcomb 2003). These works address the challenges of developing compelling museum exhibits and the ways in which text (as inscriptions, labels, and signs), space, and objects interact in museum space. Others have drawn attention to the challenges of writing text for different audiences (Marcus, Stoddard and Woodward 2012; Ravelli 2006; Serrell 1996). Although all of these writers are, in a sense, dealing with the issue of storytelling and narrative, they tend to link their work to theories of communication and education. Here we focus more explicitly on linking spatial arrangement and architectural design of exhibitions and museums to narrative and storytelling. At the same time, we recognize that spatial arrangement of displays and storytelling are only one aspect of the museum experience. As Falk and Dierking (1992) pointed out long ago, there is not a clear connection between designer intent and visitor experience. Many visitors read little of the text provided in museums and, when they do, it is not always in the order intended. As a consequence, our focus here is on the designers' intents and how these are spatialized in the museum.

THEMATIC ARRANGEMENT AND PARATACTIC STRUCTURE IN COLLECTION-BASED HISTORY MUSEUMS

A basic question with regard to storytelling in history museums is whether the organization of a display corresponds to a coherent or explicit storyline. Some exhibits are more loosely narrated; the temporal chronology is more implied than stated. Whether the arrangement of thematic displays illustrates the history of expressionist painting or explores the end of the age of dinosaurs, the exhibit might choose not to use an explicit storyline linking one element of an exhibit to the next. The themes do not "follow" one another in strict serial order. Although the arrangement of such exhibits might seem devoid of explicit narrative structure, an ordering can be implied by their arrangement within the spatial frame of the museum.

In this chapter, we term this sort of loosely structured narrative "thematic." Temporal ordering is present, to some degree, and chronological sequencing, the sense of "before" and "after," is implicit—its existence is signified in the dates inscribed on labels, in references to time periods, in historical accounts provided in guidebooks, or in the texts inscribed on plaques. The thematic arrangement of exhibits and objects does not follow an explicit chronological storyline, but the existence of such a storyline is repeatedly brought to mind. We can use the term "thematic" to describe the arrangement of a permanent exhibition often found in art, ethnographic, and archaeological museums. One example is Berlin's Neues Museum. Built in the mid-nineteenth century and severely damaged in World War II, the museum was reopened in 2009 after a thorough renovation. In its new version, the Neues Museum features a cluster of archeology collections that belonged to the Egyptian Museum, the Prehistory and Early History Museum, as well as artifacts from a collection of classical antiquities. The official Web site describes the arrangement as follows:

> The various collections are no longer kept strictly apart, but are instead merged together in a novel display which affords visitors a fascinating insight into the origins of humankind.
> The geographical breadth, historical richness and exceptional quality of the archaeological collections bring to life the history of the Old World, stretching from the Near East to the Atlantic, from North Africa to Scandinavia, across several millennia at once, in the form of both the remains of material culture and written sources. (Neues Museum 2013)

Obviously the fact that the museum accommodates different archaeological collections in its premises contributes to the "geographical breadth and historical richness" advertised in the Web site. However, it also undermines the possibility of configuring the museum's entire collection and exhibition space according to a strict chronological progression.

Another example is the Pitt Rivers Museum in Oxford, England. As is pointed out in its Web site, "In most ethnographic and archaeological museums the displays are arranged according to geographical or cultural areas. Here they are arranged according to type: musical instruments, weapons, masks, textiles, jewelry, and tools are all displayed in groups to show how the same problems have been solved at different times by different peoples" (Pitt Rivers Museum 2013). Though grouped by object type rather than chronology, each exhibit supports the museum's broader story about how through human history "the same problems have been solved at different times by different peoples."

The Science Museum in London or the adjacent Natural History Museum also use this sort of themed approach to the arrangement of a permanent exhibition. The Science Museum organizes its exhibits around different realms of science and technology, such as agriculture, flight, medicine, energy, electronics and computing, materials, and telecommunications. Some, but not all, of these exhibition areas include an implied chronological sequence. This is because chronology is not by itself always a useful means of explaining, say, principles of flight. An exhibit on the history of flight can be organized in a generally chronological sequence, but viewers also have to understand some of the physical principles of flight, propulsion, airfoil design, and other physical properties and mechanical systems that do not necessarily fit into a strict chronological sequencing.

Although a thematic approach offers considerable latitude for structuring a narrative, considerable variation exists in how closely or loosely designers try to guide visitors through exhibit spaces in sequential order. This is clearly evident when a fixed circulation path is offered in signs and orientation maps to direct the movement of visitors. The obvious advantage of a recommended circulation path is that it imposes spatial orientation and sequential order onto exhibition space, but more loosely organized exhibits can still have an implied narrative structure.

A champion of the narrative-based history museum, Jeshajahu Weinberg, suggested that a fundamental characteristic of such a museum "is the imposition of a certain necessary sequence on the arrangement of the exhibits" (Weinberg and Elieli 1995, 51). However, the existence of sequence does not necessarily entail a coherent storyline. When the spatial arrangement of an exhibition along a circulation path is not predicated on a chronological sequential order, the arrangement of consecutive thematic displays along the path corresponds to a paratactic aggregate. According to Paul Feyerabend (1993, 173), "The elements of such an aggregate are all given equal importance, the only relation between them is sequential, there is no hierarchy, no part is presented as being subordinate to and determined by others" (although we might argue that the total amount of space devoted to particular exhibits, their placement in relationship to one another within the museum space, the design elements such as lighting, color, font, and font size can establish hierarchy).

The term "parataxis" (in Greek: "an arranging side by side") is commonly applied to the arranging of rhetorical and literary elements one after the other but independently of each other. In a paratactic structure of a literary text, the arrangement of consecutive thematic units lacks a temporal form of sequential order and the causal connections it entails (on poems, see Herrnstein Smith 1968). Paratactic structure of an exhibition means that since spatially consecutive displays do not "follow" from one another chronologically, movement along a recommended circulation path may express spatial expediency rather than provide for a continuous storyline.

A case in point is the Israel Defense Forces (IDF) History Museum (figure 8.1). Situated in Tel Aviv, Israel, the museum showcases Israel's military history. Its exhibition presents the museum's vast collection of artifacts, most prominently weapons used by the infantry, artillery, and armored corps (aircraft and navy vessels are not included). Opened to the public in 1991, the museum consists of outdoor displays of heavy weapons and pavilions for particular categories of exhibits such as machine guns, uniforms, and communication equipment. Originally created as a storehouse for the collection of a future IDF history museum, the spatial arrangement of exhibits and pavilions was not built on a narrative framework. The circulation path offered to visitors invests the display with a notion of spatial sequence, but it does not conform to chronology or an explicit logic of thematic development, and hence it is not aligned with any discernible storyline.

Regardless of the narrative capacity of the spatial arrangement of displays along a circulation path, storytelling at museums can also be performed by tour guides. In her study of Israeli pioneering museums, Tamar Katriel observes that artifacts often inspire tour guides to tell about them: "Museum guides then operate within the parameters set by the display, injecting narrative segments into their interpretative accounts along the tour route" (1997, 144). This is of special significance in museums where the paratactic structure of the spatial arrangement of exhibits does not allow a circulation path that follows a storyline. The stories woven around artifacts activate the narrative

188 • CHAPTER 8

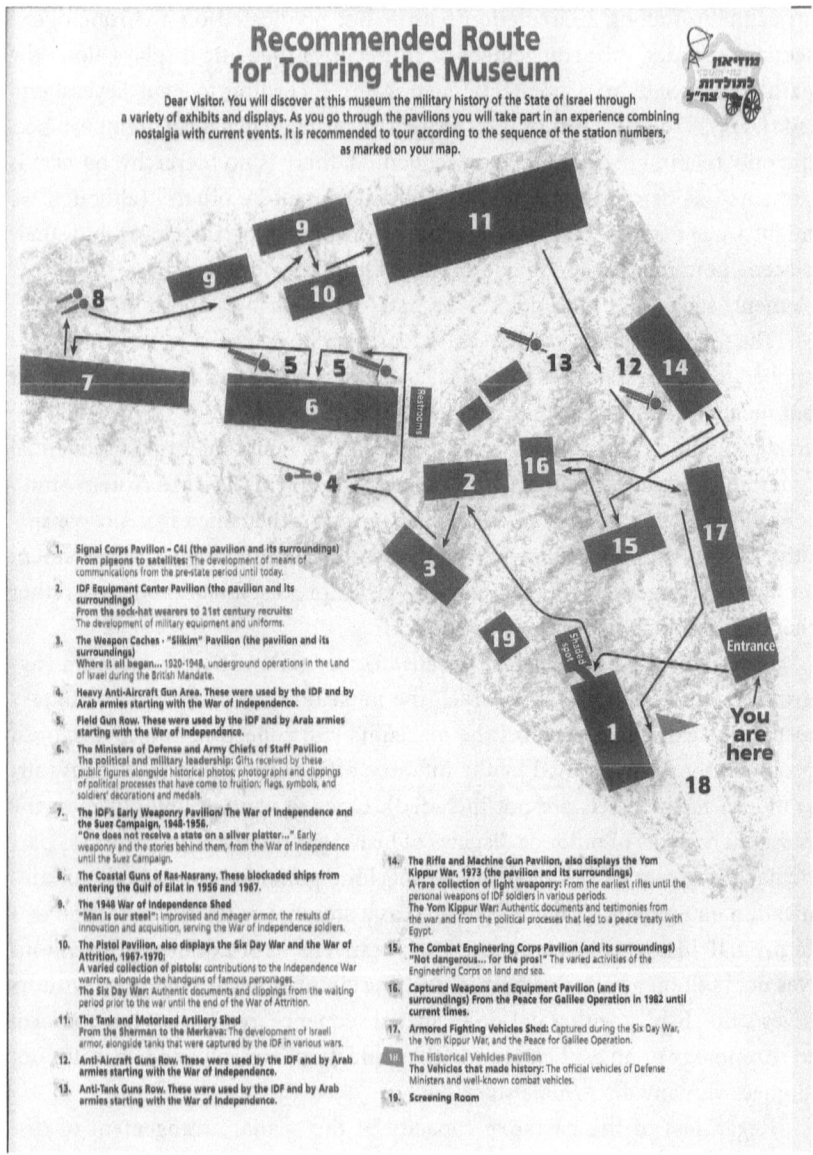

FIGURE 8.1. Tourist guide to the Israel Defense Forces History Museum, Tel Aviv. Used with the permission of the Museums Unit of the Israeli Defense Ministry.

potential of the display and occasion of storytelling in the form of "narrative insertions" that belong to the repertoire of each guide. Notably, beyond their association with the overarching theme of the museum, these stories are not joined together in a unified narrative framework. Yet, at the same time, this sort of open format allows visitors and particularly guides more flexibility in matching visitor interests to exhibits. The role of guides goes beyond the current discussion but is receiving increasing attention (National Association for Interpretation 2012).

SPATIAL STORYLINES IN NARRATIVE-BASED HISTORY MUSEUMS

Circulation paths in narrative-based museums serve the presentation of a story to the effect that "essentially the circulation path is an alter ego of the storyline" (Weinberg and Elieli 1995, 56). Whereas paratactic arrangements of displays do not follow storylines, narrative-based history museums are built on them. The intention is to lead visitors through a narrative mapped onto the sequential configuration of displays in successive exhibit areas. The premise is that the storyline flows along the circulation path, which, in Jennifer Carter's succinct formulation, thus figures as a "narrative itinerary" (2011, 93).

The chronological approach to spatial storyline is based on the continuous passage of time as a structural principle; consequently, the storyline is arranged along the historical time axis. The chronological arrangement of the storyline provides an ostensibly simple and accessible principle of succession that readily acquiesces with modern notions of history as progression along the time axis, since, as Hannah Arendt notes, "The thread of historical continuity" is a conventional means for recording "the unilinear, dialectically consistent development" (qtd. in Kermode 1967, 56). The chronological approach to spatial storyline in permanent exhibitions at history museums means that planners are engaged in creating an exhibition space in which time moves forward while allowing for the possibility that this movement is potentially punctuated by discontinuities. Chronological storytelling does not necessarily imply a strict linear circulation path or a coercive arrangement of displays, since there are many ways the narratives can be arranged spatially.

Examples of the use of a chronological approach to spatial storylines in history museums abound. Affiliated with the Imperial War Museum, the Churchill Museum (since 2010, called the Churchill War Rooms) in London features the life-story of the British statesman. At the center of the hall is the 15-meter chronological "Lifeline," which offers an interactive exploration of each year of Churchill's life. Around the "Lifeline," the biography of Churchill is displayed. The chronologically arranged storyline consists of five chapters: "Young Churchill" (1874–1900), "Maverick Politician" (1900–1929), "Wilderness Years" (1929–39), "War Leader" (1940–45), and "Cold War Statesman" (1945–65). Another example is the permanent exhibition at the National Museum of American Jewish History in Philadelphia, where the chronological

190 • CHAPTER 8

sequence of the storyline consists of three chapters: "Foundations of Freedom: 1654–1880"; "Dreams of Freedom: 1880–1945"; and "Choices and Challenges of Freedom: 1945–Today."

The storyline of Abraham Lincoln's biography on display at the Abraham Lincoln Museum in Springfield, Illinois, is chronologically progressive, yet it is divided into two "journeys," each in a different gallery. One tells Lincoln's life from his childhood to his election as president of the United States in 1860. The other presents his presidency and the Civil War. The two "journeys" are chronologically continuous but are not spatially arranged along a continuous path. This spatial arrangement of the storyline is about choice, since it allows visitors to skip Lincoln's career before 1860, should they wish to do so, and focus on his presidency and leadership during the Civil War (Decker 2005).

The Palmach Museum in Tel Aviv tells the story of an elite paramilitary organization formed within the Jewish community of British Mandate Palestine (figure 8.2). Founded in 1941, the Palmach operated until the establishment of the State of Israel in 1948. A distinction of this narrative-based museum is the choice of a specially arranged film as the primary storytelling vehicle. Cinematic storytelling is at center stage, while no artifacts belonging to the museum's collection are on display along the circulation path. In this

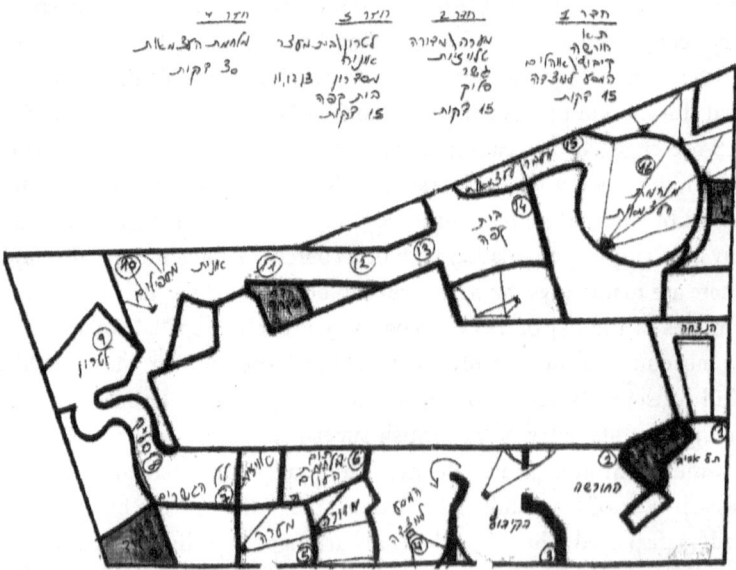

FIGURE 8.2. Design sketch of the Palmach Museum, Tel Aviv. Used with permission of the Palmach Museum, Tel Aviv.

sense, the experience offered to visitors defies the expectations of those familiar with conventional history museums. The "Palmach story" on view features segments of a film screened in consecutive locations along the circulation path. The locations along the path where segments of the film are screened are designed to serve as backdrop for particular scenes of the film featured there. Visitors are moved from tableaux to tableaux by a guide and are not allowed to move forward or backward on their own. The circulation path itself has a symbolic role to play in the story. At the start of the tour, visitors are led to an underground passage emphasizing the Palmach's origins in clandestine, underground efforts by Jewish settlers to protect their settlements. The path then zigs and zags through the museum space, reflecting the Palmach's successes and setbacks and with the various exhibition rooms themselves shaped and sized to fit the attending narrative.

The film's story is a period drama about a fictional yet representative group of young people who joined the Palmach and took part in its work. The historical drama on view is embedded in the larger picture of the unfolding dramatic history. The storyline is strictly chronological, and movement along the circulation path is therefore movement along the historical timeline. As mentioned above, movement is closely regulated both in space and time: the sole task of museum guides is to see to it that each group moves forward from one screening area to the next at the right moment, making sure that no one gets ahead or is left behind. Accordingly, walking along the storyline is performed in a rigid space/time matrix: it takes approximately seventy minutes to "transport" a group through the display.

According to the planners of the permanent exhibition of Berlin's German Historical Museum, "The decision in favor of chronological display of exhibits is based on experience and is the result of visitor surveys in other exhibition projects of the German Historical Museum that showed that chronologically organized paths meet the reception possibilities and wishes of the visitor" (Czech 2009, 12). A chronological approach to storytelling in space is a default option for planners of permanent exhibitions in narrative-based history museums. However, planners can also opt to include a linear sequence of major themes inherent in the story. Notably, without a clear sense of explicit logic of thematic development, such a sequence is susceptible to parataxis. However, a purely chronological approach to storytelling is potentially reductive, since it limits the possibility to present thematic continuities that transcend the periodization imposed by the chronological structure of the storyline.

The combination of the two approaches is evident in hybrid forms. The interplay between a thematic display and chronological storytelling assumes different forms according to what story these museums intend to tell, and no

192 • CHAPTER 8

less importantly, according to the creative capacities of the designers of the exhibition. Most common is the insertion of the thematic sections in a predominantly chronological organization. In the words of Ralph Applebaum, the head of the design team of the permanent exhibition at the U.S. Holocaust Memorial Museum in Washington, DC, the aim was to present the Holocaust as "a play in three acts": "Nazi Assault, 1933–1939," "Final Solution, 1940–1945," and "Last Chapter" (qtd. in Linenthal 1995, 168). Underlying the narrative structure is a chronologically arranged storyline. However, the final part of the exhibition also includes three thematic sections that are outside the historical sequence: the rescue of Jews by non-Jews, Jewish resistance, and the fate of children (Weinberg and Elieli 1995, 54). Berlin's Jewish Museum offers another variation (figure 8.3). The museum's permanent exhibition tells the story of German Jews within a chronological framework, beginning in medieval times and ending in the "present," which is post-1945 Germany. The storyline is divided into three parts. The first and the last comprise chronologically

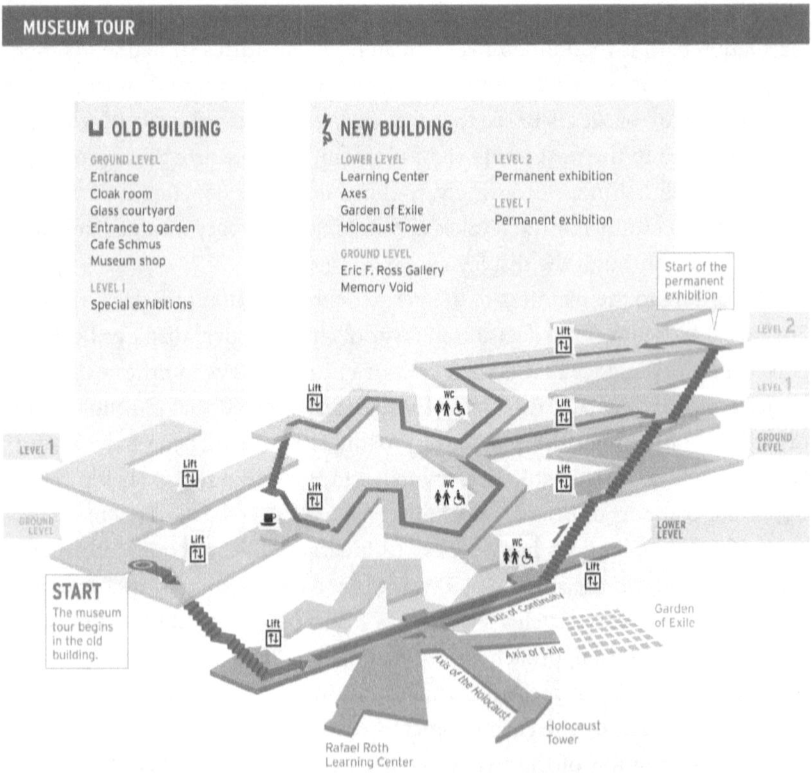

FIGURE 8.3. Plan of the Jewish Museum, Berlin. Used with the permission of the Jewish Museum Berlin.

consecutive sections. The middle part of the exhibition's sequence is a paratactic aggregate of themes inherent to the story of German Jews in the period 1800–1933 as the story of integration, assimilation, and segregation. Notably, consecutive sections of this part of the exhibition sequence are partially synchronous.

In principle, there is always the option to spatially separate chronologically arranged and thematically organized displays in exhibition space. The story told at the Imperial War Museum North in Manchester, England, is how war influenced the life of citizens in Great Britain and the Commonwealth since the outbreak of World War I in 1914. The museum's permanent exhibition on the first floor combines a chronological display configured around the perimeter of the main gallery and six thematic displays in the inner space of the gallery. A similar approach is taken at the In Flanders Field Museum in Ieper (Ypres), Belgium, which was first opened in 1998 and substantially redesigned in 2012 for the centenary of the Great War of 1914–18. Because Ieper was one of the towns devastated by the war, the museum is a natural point from which to narrate its history. But the museum has always done more than narrate the war from a chronological perspective. It has sought to personalize the war in ways that help visitors appreciate the wartime experience of people on many sides of the conflict. Personal impressions of soldiers, artists, and ordinary people are included, and the impact of the war on the local environment is also considered. The works of poets, authors, painters, photographers, and sculptors are also included, both from the World War I period and later. The problem of combining the chronological and the thematic is not unique to museum displays: in text-based biographies and biographical novels, the author must often interrupt the sequential presentation of the events in the life of the biographical subject to develop themes such as the subject's personality, opinions, attitude toward certain kinds of people, and other people's opinion of him or her.

With some 8,000 artifacts out of the 80,000 stored at the museum's collection on display (Ottomeyer 2009, 5), the permanent exhibition at Berlin's German Historical Museum combines both a chronological storyline and thematic displays, yet the primacy of the chronologically arranged storyline is evinced in its alignment with the main path leading visitors through successive periods showcased in consecutive areas. According to the official Web site, "The real core of these display spaces are the *period rooms*, in which visitors are walking through the epochs from the beginnings of German history up to the present" (Deutsches Historisches Museum 2013). In accordance with the primacy of a chronological storyline, the most important exhibits from each era are displayed along the main path and showcase significant events, rulers, and processes. Thematic displays are also included, but these are subordinate to the chronological arrangement of the main storyline: The diachronic configuration of time periods along the main path is complemented by thematic showrooms, which, arranged parallel to the main path, showcase political, social, and cultural processes and phenomena of each time period. Some examples: "Art and Science in the Renaissance" in the 1500–1650 time period ("Reformation and the Thirty Years' War"); "Biedermeier and Middle Ages Romanticism" in the 1789–1871 time period ("From the French Revolution to the Second German Empire"); "Society in the Empire" in the 1871–1918 time period ("The German Empire and World War I"); "Modern Life" in the 1918–33 time period ("Weimar Republic").

The idea that a chronologically arranged spatial sequence should correspond to successive time periods is based on a clear concept of historical periodization. The two millennia of German history featured are divided into nine successive time periods. These are housed in consecutive areas of the exhibition and are each distinguished by a different color. In historical exhibitions, periodization is not only about the sequential structure of the timeline but also about the space allocated to each time period. The correlation is straightforward: the weight given to a certain historical period in exhibition space accords with the space allocated to displaying this period. The planners of the permanent exhibition at the German Historical Museum allocated a tenth of exhibition space that showcases two millennia of German history to the twelve years of the Third Reich (1933–45) (Czech 2009, 15–16). The emphasis on the display of the Third Reich in exhibition space belongs to the politics of representation: the allocation of space for the Third Reich is an unequivocal statement about the significance assigned to this particular chapter of German history.

When history is conceived of as a chronological succession of disparate, discrete time periods, periodization means that the beginning and end of each time period represent discontinuities in the flow of time. In a chronologically arranged historical exhibition periodization also takes shape in how discontinuities in the storyline are demarcated in exhibition space. The planners of the permanent exhibition at the German Historical Museum use the square-shaped floors of the building as a narrative device. The exhibition is spatially configured in such a way that turning points and decisive political disruptions in German history, such as the founding of the German Reich in 1871, are positioned at corner zones, which is also where the exhibition's main path is making a change of direction (Czech 2009, 13). This kind of arrangement is designed to make turning points in political history discernible in space.

FIGURE 8.4. Exhibition entitled "Crossroads of Czech and Czechoslovak Statehood" at the National Memorial on Vítkov Hill, Prague. Used with permission of the National Museum and National Memorial at Vítkov Hill, Prague, Czech Republic.

In contrast to the conventional emphasis on successive time periods punctuated by discontinuities, a distinction of the permanent exhibit at the National Memorial on Vítkov Hill in Prague is its focus on discontinuities as an organizing principle of the storyline (figure 8.4). The exhibit presents the history of the Czechoslovak state between the creation of the first republic in 1918 and the dissolution of the Czechoslovak Federation in 1992. The storyline is constituted as a chronological sequence of "crossroads" in the history of Czech and Czechoslovak statehood that represent discontinuities in the linear flow of historical time. As featured at the exhibition, the course of Czechoslovak political history is a succession of turning points: the birth of Czechoslovak statehood in 1918; the Munich agreement and the end of the first republic in 1938–39; the reconstitution of an independent state in 1945; the communist takeover of 1948; the creation of the Czechoslovak Federation in 1968; the end of the communist regime in 1989; and the dissolution of the Czechoslovak federation in 1993.

Despite the original concept, the permanent exhibition at the German Historical Museum does not present thematic displays that extend across consecutive time periods, the official reason for this being lack of available exhibition space (Czech 2009, 12). An original and innovative answer to the question of whether it is possible to set chronological and thematic approaches to the spatial arrangement of the display as both separate but equal options is presented at the Mercedes-Benz Museum in Stuttgart, Germany. Underlying this museum, a presentation of a collection of 160 cars, is a novel concept: two separate circulation paths that run through the museum. One path takes visitors through "Legend Rooms" that present the brand's highlights in chronological sequence. The timeline is divided into five successive chapters. The other path leads visitors through a series of "Collection Rooms" that "thematically document the breadth and diversity of the brand portfolio and collection" (Mercedes-Benz Museum, 2014) under titles like "Voyagers," "Carriers," "Helpers," "Celebrities," and "Heroes." The two paths are arranged in a double-helix form and meet at every level so that visitors can decide if they want to continue or switch to another path. This unique spatial arrangement allows the museum to offer visitors two modes of organization: one largely chronological, the other thematic, focusing on stories within particular categories.

NARRATIVE ARCHITECTURE IN HISTORY MUSEUMS

Narratives of history in museums are also constituted through architecture, as we remarked at the start of this chapter. Regardless of architectonic style in fashion in particular periods, the main contribution of architecture to the configuration of spatial narratives in museums seems to have traditionally been in the spatial organization of the interior spaces, such as halls, galleries, and passageways and the décor of showrooms and staircases. Of much importance in this regard is also the arrangement of movement between spaces and different levels of the building. Yet how should we describe the narrative function of these spaces? Both narratology and architecture use distinct disciplinary terms that are not necessarily well suited to describing the overlaps between the two fields. Writings on the rhetoric and semiotics of architecture (Hattenhauer 1984; Preziosi 1979) and on architecture as a language or "pattern language" (Alexander et al. 1977) are useful to a point, but are not focused on precisely the same issues of narrative, space, and storytelling that are the focus of this chapter. Here we suggest, at least tentatively, some possible points of overlap between narrative, text, museums, and space.

Transforming existing buildings into museums often amounts to the creation of new space within the "outer shell" of the building: a prominent example is the creation of the Musée d'Orsay in the 1980s in a building that had been built to serve as a railway station (Schneider 1998) or the Tate Modern Gallery developed from London's iconic Bankside Power Station on the

Thames. The transformation of old buildings into museums sometimes places constraints on the narrative structure of the exhibits but, at times, provides opportunities to integrate the building's history into the museum's story. This is of special significance when the history of the building is thematically related to the history told by the museum it currently inhabits. The exhibition "Crossroads of Czech and Czechoslovak Statehood" is housed in the historical premises of the National Memorial on Vítkov Hill in Prague, a building that is an important icon of Czechoslovak statehood. The above-mentioned In Flanders Fields Museum in Ieper, Belgium, presents the story of World War I in west Flanders. The museum is housed in the Cloth Hall, one of the largest medieval guildhalls in Europe, which was destroyed in the war and was later restored to its former glory to become "an important symbol of wartime hardship and later recovery" (In Flanders Fields Museum 2013).

A different issue is when new buildings are constructed to serve as museums. As Volker Welter notes, "At the turn to the current century eclectic and unique architectural designs, so-called signature buildings, became synonymous with museum architecture" (Welter 2010, 3689). A recent trend is toward innovative designs that invest the building's architecture with narrativity, namely evoke and associate the story told there. The Web site of the National Museum of the American Indian in Washington, DC, states that the museum building is filled "with details, colors, and textures that reflect the Native universe" (2013). The growing popular view of the museum as a storytelling institution accords with architectural designs that shape newly commissioned history museums as narrative environments: the building does not serve merely to accommodate the permanent exhibition but is explicitly designed to concur with the story told by and at the museum. An outstanding example is the building of the Imperial War Museum North in Manchester, England:

> The design concept is that of a globe which has been shattered into fragments and then reassembled. The building's form is the interlocking of three of these fragments which represent earth, air, and water. These three shards together concretize the twentieth-century conflicts which have never taken place on an abstract piece of paper, but rather have been fought by men and women by land, sky and sea. (Studio Daniel Libeskind 2013)

In his commentary on the Holocaust Memorial Center in Budapest, Hungary, architect István Mányi shares his view on the relationship between the permanent exhibition and the architectural features of the building: "The design of the permanent exhibition was not our task, but we have created its mental and physical frame, because without it, the whole building can't be interpreted" (Holocaust Memorial Center 2013). Shaping the interior of a museum building as a narrative environment entails the sequencing of spaces within the building and the use of architecture to shape a particular atmosphere and to manipulate the experience of visitors. Importantly, it also includes the explicit integration of architectural elements into the museum sequence and hence to its narrative structure. Employing architecture in the service of narrative comes to the fore in three landmark historical museums that feature or revolve around the Holocaust: the U.S. Holocaust Memorial Museum in Washington, DC; Berlin's Jewish Museum, and the Holocaust History Museum at Yad Vashem in Jerusalem. Offering different solutions to the challenge of finding a contemporary architectural language to express the Holocaust, the architects of these museums came up with designs for signature buildings that showcase original and novel approaches as to how to involve architecture in recounting the Holocaust as a historical process and as a calamitous event.

The U.S. Holocaust Memorial Museum in Washington, DC, is an example of how architecture is employed to serve storytelling by the use of materials and design that resonate with the museum's story. For James Ingo Freed, the architect, his design expresses his conviction that the building should be "more than just a box of artifacts" that has nothing to tell in its own terms about the Holocaust (Linenthal 1995, 86). According to Freed, the building is not meant to provide literal references to the geography and history of the Holocaust. The official Web site of the museum explains that "Freed wanted the visitor to experience the Museum building 'viscerally'" and further that the Museum's "architecture of sensibility" is "intended to engage the visitor and stir the emotions" (U.S. Holocaust Memorial Museum 2013).

In his appraisal of the building, the architectural critic Herbert Muschamp (1993, H1) wrote that "it provides far more than a neutral background for the tale that must be told." The impact of architecture on storytelling was in "the feel and rhythm of space and the setting of mood" (Linenthal 1995, 169) but also in architectural allusions to the Holocaust. The building's "raw materials" are brick, steel, and glass. Structural features such as brick walls and steel trusses paraphrase what Herbert Muschamp called the "hard industrial forms" (1993, H1) of the Final Solution. For instance, the architectural space of the permanent exhibition in the upper floors of the building consist of bridges, towers, and corridors that allude to key architectural features of the Warsaw ghetto and of concentration camps (Weissberg 2001, 19). The floating glass bridges evoke a sense of insecurity and danger. As observed by James E. Young, the architectural space of the museum's interior features discontinuity and fragmentation (1993, 342). According to Linenthal, "Freed's building, from its outward appearance and its interior mood and insistence on certain ways visitors inhabit and move through space is designed as a space of disorientation" (1995, 89).

The use of narrative architecture is a hallmark of Daniel Libeskind's design for the extension building of Berlin's Museum of Jewish History (figure 8.3). Underlying Libeskind's design of the zigzag-shaped building are two lines: one winding, similar to a lightning bolt, the other straight and crisscrossing the meandering building. According to Libeskind, that straight line serves as "one element of continuity throughout the complex form of the building" (qtd. in Young 2000, 175). The straight line suggests the uninterrupted continuity of time; the jagged, open-ended line suggests the ruptured history of German Jews.

These two lines intersect in the form of six empty spaces—designated "voids" by the architect—that run vertically through the building and traverse different levels. As empty structural features of the building that only occasionally can be looked into, the voids signify the absence of Berlin's Jews. Proper treatment of the voids in the spatial arrangement of the historical exhibition in the museum building was considered crucial by the museum's custodians. In an essay on the building's design, Rolf Bothe, the director of the Berlin Museum, wrote:

> Therefore the main exhibition rooms can't be granted spatial sequence in a conventional fashion, as otherwise the "voids" would lose their significance to the visitor and would be reduced to the status of dividing walls. . . . The presentation in the exhibition halls must develop independently of the "voids" to a large extent. The "voids" do not mark boundaries which occur naturally in the course of history, but cut into the exhibition sequence independently of these. (1992, 52)

In this conception, whenever voids intersect the exhibition space, they are meant to serve as "gaps" that punctuate the linear progression of history on display in the exhibition rooms. The concept was that the voids should be visually recognizable throughout the building and their different character be made explicit in areas of the future permanent exhibition. Notably, the idea was that walls of the voids in areas of the exhibition should be left empty and not used for the purpose of display, thereby rendering visual the gaps in the linear progression of storytelling.

The design of the permanent exhibition required the addition of walls, display cabinets, panels, and columns through space and hence necessitated changes in the interior architecture. As a result, some of the singular architectural features of the interior are concealed: angular elements are rounded and the unique curvature of the zigzag-formed building is largely obscured. These changes notwithstanding (which were envisioned by the architect and stipulated by the director of the Berlin Museum at a stage where the building was yet to be built), the spatial continuity of the exhibition round is interrupted by the black and empty walls of the "voids" that traverse the building. In this manner, the flow of storytelling is interrupted by "silences" that suspend the spatial sequence with no apparent relationship to chronological or thematic sequences.

A prominent narrative feature of Libeskind's design consists of what the architect labeled "axes," which are placed at the beginning of the circulation path, before the stairs leading to the permanent exhibition. Entering through the adjacent baroque building, visitors are led through a staircase to the underground level of the new building. The story of Jewish history in Germany begins at the bottom of the staircase, where visitors are faced with three axes—paths in the form of three corridors—arranged in such a geometric form that only two can be seen at a time. The architect conceived of the three axes as the spatial embodiment of the three major experiences in the history of German Jews: exile, death, and continuity. Walking in the labyrinth of corridors tests the visitor's sense of orientation, since the configuration of corridors offers patterns of circulation that are not in a sequence and therefore defies the expectations of visitors. Of the three paths, only the "axis of continuity" leads through a long staircase to the museum galleries in the upper floors of the building where the permanent exhibition is housed.

Opened in 2005, the new Holocaust History Museum at Yad Vashem, Jerusalem is another example of narrative architecture where lines and "voids" figure prominently (figure 8.5). The triangular, prism-like structure designed by Moshe Safdie cuts through Har HaZikaron [Mount Remembrance] from south to north. Both ends of the 175-meter structure protrude from the hillside, seemingly floating over the slope. The southern end of the "tube" is closed, while the northern end, where the hitherto compact structure seemingly unravels to form two spatially divergent "wings," is open. The exterior, interior walls, and floor of the elongated, triangular edifice are made of reinforced concrete. A glass skylight at the top of the structure allows light to enter the structure. The underground structure contains ten successive chambers that serve as exhibition spaces and are situated on both sides of the axis created by the prism-shaped "tube" running through the entire museum complex. A tunnel-like empty space running through the museum becomes narrower as the story of the Final Solution unravels to create the impression of mounting pressure. The exhibition chambers are not identical in size, and their positioning in relation to the spatial axis is not symmetrical.

MUSEUM NARRATIVES • 201

FIGURE 8.5. Holocaust History Museum at Yad Vashem. Photo by Maoz Azaryahu.

Whereas the tube that cuts through the structure represents the linear continuity of the timeline, the storyline is aligned with a zigzag-shaped circulation path leading through consecutive exhibition spaces on opposite sides of the tube. Notably, the tube forms a void that is inaccessible to visitors but clearly seen when visitors enter the museum and again when they cross it while moving along the circulation path. Unlike the voids embedded in the building of Berlin's Museum of Jewish History, the void at the Holocaust History Museum at Yad Vashem is constitutive of the exhibition's sequence, since it marks and facilitates transition between successive chapters of the history of the Holocaust on display. A backbone of the structure, the void is a physical obstacle that forces a zigzag movement along the path. However, since the tube opens to the landscape and the sky at its end, the void mitigates the horrific story on display by making the proverbial "light at the end of the tunnel" an omnipresent visual aspect of the storyline.

BEGINNINGS AND ENDINGS: FRAMING THE BOUNDARIES OF MUSEUM NARRATIVES

A circulation path leading visitors through a historical exhibition entails clear spatial boundaries—a beginning and an ending. The issue of beginning and ending is of little relevance when a historical exhibition is arranged as a paratactic aggregate, since the sequential order of exhibits positioned along the circulation path does not follow a coherent storyline. Things are different in museums organized around a single storyline largely based on a temporal sequence.

Edward Said (1975, 2) noted that beginnings involve "reversal, change of direction, the institution of a durable movement that increasingly engages our interest: such a beginning *authorizes*; it constitutes an authorization for what follows from it." The story of Czechoslovak statehood on display at the National Memorial at Vítkov Hill in Prague begins in 1918, with the birth of independent Czechoslovakia. The story of Abraham Lincoln in the museum bearing his name in Springfield, Illinois, begins with the birth of the future president. The cinematic story of the Palmach presented to visitors at the Palmach Museum in Tel Aviv begins with the founding of the force in 1941. Importantly, the beginning of visual storytelling in exhibition space does not have to coincide with the beginning of the story in historical time. As in drama and fiction, a conventional poetic device is to begin visual storytelling not at the beginning of the historical narrative but at a later point in time. A case in point is the U.S. Holocaust Memorial Museum in Washington, DC, where monitors installed in the elevators transporting visitors to the permanent exhibition in the upper floors of the building tell the story of the American soldiers' encounter with the horrors of Nazi concentration camps in the last weeks of World War II, an encounter that occurred some twelve years after the first concentration camp had been built in Germany (Linenthal 1995, 193).

Obviously, every circulation path leading visitors through a historical exhibition has a point of termination, yet convention requires a closure: that the ending of the story told along the path should not be arbitrary. Frank Kermode observes that closure "makes concord with what had preceded it" (Kermode 1967, 178). Barbara Herrnstein Smith suggests that closure "announces and justifies the absence of further development; it reinforces the feeling of finality, completion, and composure" (1968, 36). German history on display at the German Historical Museum in Berlin ends in 1990, with the reunification of Germany (Czech 2009, 16). Since German history is open ended, the current ending of the permanent exhibition is actually a turning point only, albeit important in German history, which suggests a possible extension of the storyline in the future to include post-1990 developments.

Hayden White (1981, 20) offers an important insight: "The demand for a closure in the historical story is a demand that sequences of real events be assessed as to their significance as elements of a moral drama." This entails the possibility of an emotional relief or a sense of vindication. This aspect is hugely relevant to the design of permanent exhibitions in Holocaust museums. The issue of ending figured during the design stage of the permanent exhibition at the Holocaust museum in Washington, DC. In contrast to the demand of many members of the board who wanted a hopeful ending with an emphasis on resistance and rescue, Martin Smith, the director of the exhibition department, favored an "ending that would intentionally not bring closure to the narrative" (Linenthal 1995, 252). The compromise solution was a film that features interviews with survivors. Additionally, the Hall of Remembrance provides visitors with a quiet setting for reflection, even prayer, at the end of the tour.

The permanent exhibition at the museum at Yad Vashem concludes with an "Epilogue." Entitled "Facing the Loss," it is a video art display of excerpts from letters, poems, and diaries written during the Holocaust. Notably, a sense of closure is also embedded into the architecture of the building. The tour of the museum does not end with the epilogue. After crossing a glass door separating the exhibition space from the outer world, visitors arrive at a large balcony that offers a place of quiet contemplation and a panoramic view of the Jerusalem hills and the implied promise of new Jewish life in the ancestral homeland.

SPECIAL QUALITIES OF MUSEUM NARRATIVE

Compared to the landscape narratives discussed in the previous chapter, museum narratives are not tied to place in the same ways. Not constrained by the geography of local history, as is the case in historical sites, the designers of permanent exhibitions in history museums have the option to invest exhibition space with a built-in narrative structure. Of much significance is the possibility to design the exhibit along a circulation path that accords with a storyline and narrative progression.

Museum narratives offer opportunities that are not possible with landscape narratives. Perhaps foremost among these is the range of storytelling media that can be drawn together in museums, particularly in complex assemblages of text, graphics, artifacts, and audiovisual and electronic media. The idea of using all the senses to tell stories is far more alive in contemporary museums than in landscape narratives at historic sites, where the story is largely anchored in and constrained by local geography. And it is true that some overlap is apparent between storytelling in digital media as discussed in chapter 5 and some of the efforts among curators and designers to use multimedia assemblages to create a rich and encompassing experience for visitors. The virtue of museums then is that they offer a sort of three-dimensional canvas or stage from which stories can be told from many different spatial angles and perspectives, and at a temporal/spatial pacing suited to a particular storyline. The ideal might be something like the CAVE (cave automatic virtual environment) environments developed to simulate immersive virtual reality environments within which a story could be told, watched, or experienced. CAVEs use three to six video projects (controlled by computers) to project perfectly scaled images onto the walls of a room-sized cube, with each image in true perspective to the viewer's line of sight. Of course the idea of a totally immersive museum experience is not entirely new. The Jorvik Viking Center in York, England, was one of the first to experiment successfully with a visitor ride that sought to simulate the sights, sounds, and even smells of Viking York.

Already in 1991, Ivan Karp noted that museum makers think of museums "as conforming to one of two models: either a vehicle for the display of objects or a space for telling a story" (1991, 12). The rise of narrative architecture in museum design increases considerably the ability of museums to serve as multidimensional and multimedia stage sets. Of all the examples explored in this chapter, the Palmach Museum in Tel Aviv is probably the best illustration of this trend. Even the exterior architecture of the museum is designed to look like a rough-hewn bunker or defensive redoubt. Notwithstanding their appeal to museum makers and audiences, immersive narrative environments using state-of-the-art multimedia do not necessarily herald the end of more traditional history museums where storytelling involves objects and texts arranged along a circulation path. The unique power of artifacts in a history museum is that they are both involved in storytelling and serve as material fragments of the story itself. At times, the collection is still at center stage. In the Mercedes-Benz Museum near Stuttgart, the chronological and thematic storylines along the circulation paths offered to visitors invest the display with narrative coherence, yet in this case, it seems that the main attraction is not the carefully arranged storyline or architecture but the vehicles on display.

THE INTERPLAY OF TOPONYMS, LANDSCAPE, AND MUSEUM NARRATIVES

We have addressed toponyms, landscape narratives, and museum narratives in separate chapters, but here at the close of these three chapters, it is useful to consider how they are sometimes used in combination to structure narratives. For instance, at the Gettysburg National Battlefield in Pennsylvania, discussed in the previous chapter, significant moments in the battle have been inscribed on the landscape as place names—places such as the Devil's Den, Peach Orchard, and Wheatfield. These place names signify locations but also figure as "titles" of the stories of the events that took place there. The story of Masada is told in the local landscape of the historical site as well as in guide books and even in an American miniseries screened for the first time in 1981. The place and its (hi)story are evoked not only in street signs in numerous Israeli cities but also in American towns, such as Franklin township (NJ), Anniston (AL), Grass Valley (CA), Virginia Beach (VA), and Chesterfield (VA).

The memorial site of Lidice, in the Czech Republic, demonstrates how the story of a site and the atrocity that took place there is told in the local landscape, in a local museum, and through local street names. The Czech village was razed by the Nazis on June 10, 1942 and its inhabitants massacred in retaliation for the assassination of Schutzstaffel (SS) General Heydrich, the Deputy Reich protector of Bohemia and Moravia, by members of the Czech resistance. After the war, the site where the village had stood was transformed into a memorial site dedicated to the commemoration of the tragedy. The story of Lidice is told in the local landscape, where some archeological remains testify to the former village. The local museum acquaints visitors with historical details and the fate of the village's residents. It is a narrative-based museum, where the story unfolds chronologically. Meant as commemorations, local street names also belong to the story. Avenue Barnett Stross, within the perimeter of the memorial site, honors the British MP who was at the head of the humanitarian campaign "Lidice shall live." The street leading away from the parking lot of the memorial site to the new Lidice built after the war bears the date of the massacre (figure 8.6).

A different blending of landscape and museum narratives can be found in the example of the "Topographie des Terrors" compound and museum in central Berlin on the former site of the Reich Main Security Office—home of the Secret State Police, more commonly known as the Gestapo, between 1939 and 1945. The ruins of the buildings were demolished at the end of the war, and the site remained in limbo for many years. Beginning in 1987, the site was opened to the public. Preliminary excavations had revealed building remains, including prisoner cells, and these relics were made accessible under the name "Topographie des Terrors." The permanent exhibition, housed in a new documentation center, focuses on the institutions of the SS and Gestapo during the Nazi period and the crimes committed by these organizations throughout Europe. The exhibition combines a chronological narrative and thematic displays. Text and photographic materials dominate, but a few audio and film recordings and maps are also used.

FIGURE 8.6. Street name in Lidice bearing the date of the massacre: June 10, 1942. Photo by Maoz Azaryahu.

We end with these examples because, perhaps in the long run, these mixed and blended narrative strategies are particularly interesting from the standpoint of narrative theory. They help to show the fluidity of available forms and how often they can be used in combination with new types of narrative form. We address some of these challenges and opportunities in our next, concluding chapter.

CHAPTER 9

Into the Future

IN LOOKING AHEAD, it is worth revisiting the relations between narratology and geography in terms of future research opportunities. These extend in two directions, one leading from geography to narratology and representing what Fredric Jameson (1991) has called the spatial turn of late twentieth-century culture, and the other leading from narrative to geography and representing the narrative turn that took place in the humanities around the 1980s. In this chapter, we look ahead in both directions to consider possibilities for future research. The first section focuses on issues deriving from chapters 2 to 5, which we see as some of the most promising opportunities for moving forward toward a more encompassing geographical narratology. The second section extends some of the themes of chapters 6, 7, and 8 to sketch out some promising paths for advancing narrative geography. In the third and final section, we explore possible collaborations between geography and narratology that might lead into territories that have not yet been claimed by either discipline. Here we consider topics that crosscut both narrative geography and geographical narrative.

As we noted in the first chapter, not all work that deals with aspects of space in a narrative text can be considered narratological. As a theoretical and descriptive project, narratology is not the interpretation of individual works but the exploration of regularities found in multiple narrative texts. Furthermore, not all discourse about the role or the theme of space in narrative represents a convergence of geography and narratology. Geographers are not alone in their focus on spatial patterns and processes. Disciplines across the humanities and social and natural sciences also deal with space in a variety of ways. Therefore, attempts to address the manifestations of space in narrative can be inspired by several disciplines other than geography. So although we focus here on issues that bridge narratology and geography, our discussion extends to other fields as well.

TOWARD A GEOGRAPHICAL NARRATOLOGY

Based on the strength of their connection to geography, we can distinguish three groups of approaches to space, place, and narrative that deserve further attention: (1) independent from geography, (2) geocritical, and (3) cartographic. These categories correspond roughly to those identified by Michel Collot, who, in his 2014 book *Pour une géographie littéraire,* proposes the following types of approaches: geopoetical, geocritical, and properly geographic (or cartographic).

Whereas Collot conceives geopoetics as the study of how literary texts, especially poetry, embody a particular way of inhabiting the world, our category of "geography-independent" approaches is a much more prosaic grab bag of topics that might concern any one of the four issues identified in the first chapter: (1) space of the storyworld, or narrative space; (2) contextual and referential space; (3) space taken by the text; and (4) spatial form. Furthest removed from the concerns of geography is a research area that is now beginning to attract interest among narratologists: the investigation of the narrative affordances of various types of physical supports, such as lines, pages, screens, books, the stage, or the human body. The physical support of narrative corresponds to the fourth of our types of space: the space taken by the text itself. Inquiries devoted to this kind of space may ask not only what kind of stories are best fitted to specific types of material support (book, screen, stage, audio stream) but also questions like: How do the arrangement of the frames of comics on a page or the design of an illustrated children's book guide the eye and the mind? How do the gestures of oral narrators or the choreography of actors on a stage use space? How do gestures complement the information conveyed by language?

The space of the storyworld has inspired the most extensive narratological activity, yet many of its domains remain unexplored or underexplored. An area that has been relatively neglected so far is the plot-functional, strategic design of space in narrative. A plot-functional approach to narrative space will ask questions such as: Why is there a balcony off the victim's room? Why does the house of Santiago Nasar have a front door facing the square and a back door near the river? Where is Gregor Samsa's bed located with respect to the door of his room, which way does the door open, and why do these details matter? Sometimes spatial features are motivated by the plot, while other times their purpose is mainly to suggest a particular type of storyworld. Contrary to the principle of Chekhov's gun, in certain genres the gun mentioned early in the text will not fire later; in a detective novel, it might be mentioned in order to attract suspicion toward the wrong character, and in a realistic novel, it might serve what Roland Barthes called a "reality effect."

The investigation of the cognitive mapping is still in its early stages, but experimental methods for this type of study are rapidly improving. In chapter 4, we contrasted the methods of psychological science, which are only feasible with artificially simplified texts, with our own informal approach to the construction of space in a complex literary text. Now a new player has entered the field: fMRI studies of the reading mind (Goldman 2012; Speer et al. 2009). Can this type of research, which shows that the same regions of the brain are activated when reading about, watching, or performing actions involving movement, throw light on the processes of storyworld construction and mental simulation of narrative information? Is there a way to pass from the level of neurons shown by brain imaging to the level of symbols that forms the concern of narratology and psychology, or are the two approaches incommensurable (Richardson 2010; Vermeule 2011; Zunshine 2010)?

Our second category, geocriticism, is conceived as the investigation how fictional worlds intersect with the world of human geography in its concern for how the earth supports human cultures, how behavior is affected by the physical properties of the environment, how human activity impacts the environment, and how people experience and organize space and place. Also falling within the domain of geocriticism are the narrative manifestations of phenomena that span wide areas of the earth, such as globalism, colonialism, migration, and diaspora, as well as the kind of studies known as ecocriticism (Heise 2005).

Bertrand Westphal (2011), who coined the term, has a narrower conception of geocriticism. Whereas what Collot calls geopoetics is mainly concerned with the subjectivity of the authors who describe space and place, geocriticism is the study of the impact of real-world geography on the collective imagination. "For example," writes Robert T. Tally, "instead of looking at the ways in which Dickens represents London in his novels, Westphal's geocritic starts with London . . . and then proceeds to look at various texts which attempt to represent it" (2013, 141). But geocriticism does not have to limit itself to the traces of real places on the literary and narrative imagination; it could just as well focus on generic places or landscape types, such as deserts, mountains, seashores, steppes, the Great Plains of North America, or the contrast between the city and the country. An example of this landscape orientation is the recent interest in oceanic studies, as evidenced by a special set of nine papers published in *PMLA* with an introductory essay by Margaret Cohen (2010).

A concrete example of what geocriticism could be is the study of how stories, or corpora of stories, infuse physical space with symbolic meaning. As an example of this type of investigation, consider the folklore that relates to the Rhine River, more precisely to the stretch that flows through middle Germany (roughly, from Mainz to Cologne). This corpus includes some of the most celebrated tales of German culture, such as the story of Siegfried and Kriemhild (itself an important part of the *Nibelungenlied*), the legend of the Lorelei, or the tale of Lohengrin. Several of these stories inspired Wagner's operas and became cultural icons. They all relate to specific places, mainly to the numerous castles that dot the Rhine in the spectacular narrow gorge between Bingen and Coblence: "The Mouse Tower in Bingen," "The Master Trick at Castle Sooneck," "Where Does the Name Marksburg [a castle] come from," and so on (Hollerbach 2004). The symbolic landscape that emerges from these tales pits the left bank of the Rhine, as the site of order, civilization, and Christianity, against the forested right bank, a pagan realm of dark forces populated with supernatural creatures. On the left bank rise industrious cities, from the right bank come robbers who raid the cities at night. On the left bank live priests, kings, and knights, on the right bank prowl dragons and evil dwarves (there are also good dwarves, but they work on the left bank). Siegfried, a hero from the left bank, must cross the Rhine in order to kill a dragon, while the Lorelei, who sits on a rock on the right bank, lures boaters to their death by distracting them from treacherous currents. On the left bank, wealth is created through hard work and craftsmanship; on the right bank, gold is mined from the depth of the earth and brings only war and corruption to mankind. This division of the global storyworld into good and bad, light and darkness, Christianity and Paganism not only reflects the geographic configuration of the territory—nowadays opposing the industrial left bank to the forested, relatively wild right bank—it also sends roots deep into history; for the Rhine marked the limit of the Roman conquest of Germany and consequently of "civilization." When the Roman general Varus crossed the Rhine in the year 9 CE to suppress a reported rebellion of local tribes, his legions were annihilated by the Germanic chieftain Arminius (also known as Hermann) at the appropriately named Battle of the Teutoburger Forest. Far from being unique to the

Rhine region, this intertwining of landscape, narrative, and history should be found in many other areas around the world, and it provides geographic narratology with an exciting field of investigation.

The domain that might benefit the most from a collaboration between geography and narratology is literary (or narrative) cartography. Geography has not only inspired literary theory with its critical discourse on maps (Mitchell 2008), it provides concrete tools for the mapping of storyworlds. The Literary Atlas of Europe, a research project conducted at the Institute of Cartography and Geoinformation, ETH Zurich, in collaboration with the Georg August University in Göttingen and the Charles University in Prague, gives a preview of some of the possibilities of collaboration between narratology and geography (Literary Atlas of Europe 2013; Piatti et al. 2008). Using advanced cartographic techniques, this project maps hundreds of literary texts onto real-world geography on the basis of the actual place names found in the narratives. When a text combines actual places with invented ones that cannot be precisely located on maps, the project uses special visualizations such as fuzzy shapes or animations that propose several possible locations for purely fictional places. Through a variety of interactive tools, users can scrutinize the database in multiple ways, such as comparing the maps of different texts, displaying the passages in the text that refer to a certain location, or scaling the maps, so that the world-spanning travels or thoughts of characters can be as efficiently studied as their wanderings in a small neighborhood. As Barbara Piatti and her colleagues (2009) argue, the mapping is not an end in itself but a research tool that should allow the investigation of many new questions: for instance, which areas are heavily populated with literary texts and which ones are relatively empty, which areas inspire foreign authors and which one are mainly selected by local authors (the St. Gotthard region of Switzerland is an example of the former, North Friesland of the latter), and how far-ranging is the network of place names mentioned in the stories inspired by a certain area (it was found [Piatti 2012] that stories whose main action is located in Prague cast a much wider network than stories whose setting is North Friesland). In addition to mapping purely literary texts, a geography of narrative could locate myths and legends on the maps of the real world, or include texts of other media such as films, graphic novels, and computer games.

More problematic than the mapping of realistic texts is the geographic treatment of fantastic texts, since these texts create their own world from scratch and do not share it with other texts, except in the case of prequels, sequels, and transmedial storytelling (i.e., the spreading of stories across different media; see Jenkins 2006). It would be necessary to create a separate map or set of maps for every fantastic text, and these maps would contain large blank areas, since they cannot be filled in on the basis of the principle of minimal departure. The principle tells us that real-world geography is only included in storyworlds when the text mentions at least one real-world location, so that Paris and New York exist, at least in the background, in the world of James Joyce's "Eveline," but they do not in J. R. R. Tolkien's Middle Earth. Still, certain fantastic texts, such as *The Lord of the Rings,* are so detailed in their spatial information that they have inspired an extensive mapping activity, both from the author and from readers (Fonstad 1991). It would therefore be useful to create digital databases that collect maps of fully imaginary storyworlds, whether these maps are intra- or extradiegetic, and author-, editor-, or reader-created. Named locations could be connected to textual segments, so as to facilitate the analysis of their description, or to allow the visualization of the movements of characters.

But why stop narrative mapping at the visual representation of spatial information? As Piatti (2009, 25) and her coauthors argue, "Maps have always asked the question 'where,' in the information era they must also answer new questions such as 'why,' 'when,' 'by whom' and 'for what purpose'—and they must convey to the user an understanding of a much wider variety of topics than was previously the case." The ultimate goal of narrative cartography should be the design of dynamic models of plot that answer the types of questions formulated by Piatti. This project would require an interactive database comprising multiple interconnected diagrams, such as a geographic map of the storyworld, a time line showing the succession of events and diagrams representing the private worlds of characters, which includes their thoughts, emotions, feelings toward each other, goals, and plans after every major event. (Such diagrams are proposed in Ryan 2007). Clicking on various buttons would locate the events on the map, reveal the itineraries of characters, overwrite the map with lines and shapes that show the symbolic structure of space, or display the private worlds of characters for each significant state of the storyworld. The ultimate diagram that shows everything we know about narrative is a chimera, because it would be so cluttered with information that it would become unreadable; but we can split the representation of stories into many diagrams, and by interlinking them, we can let the user produce a dynamic simulation of plot.

TOWARD A NARRATIVE GEOGRAPHY

As we push the narratological turn of geography forward in chapters 6 to 8, we discuss a number of topics that suggest further research. For example, in the chapters focusing on toponymic, landscape, and museum narratives, we focused mainly on historical sites with strong temporal storylines. The next step in this kind of analysis would consist of examining a larger range of cases, such as nature walks in parks or architectural tours of cities. Such stories—whether of ecological relationships or building types—have to develop sequential narratives around the somewhat arbitrary locations of the phenomena they are narrating. This makes the creation of a coherent storyline somewhat challenging, since most such tours are relatively short (one or two hours) and are constrained by how far people can walk, bike, or drive in a limited amount of time. In the case of nature walks, plants and animals live in particular ecological settings that cannot simply be moved to different locations to build a stronger story. For example, telling the story of the declining habitat of the giant sequoia tree at Yosemite National Park in California involves visiting particular redwood habitats in the park that are distributed according to ecological conditions rather than narrative convenience. In the case of architectural tours in Tel Aviv, excellent examples of Bauhaus style can be found throughout the city, but they aren't arranged spatially by date, architect, or building type. It is therefore necessary to create a storyline about Tel Aviv's architectural heritage that carefully selects which buildings to visit in the span of a single walking tour. As discussed in chapter 7, such issues can also arise at large, complex historical sites like Gettysburg or Buchenwald, where tours and guides must edit their scripts to fit the spatial realities of the locations.

Once these stories are moved off the trail and into museums, this distinction between historical and other thematic narratives becomes less important. The exhibits at zoos, aquariums, and botanical gardens can be designed and arranged so that stories are easier to narrate about the species under display, their ecological relationships, and broader themes relating to the natural world. The same can be done for architecture, for example, in open-air museums such as Old Sturbridge Village in Massachusetts, Colonial Williamsburg in Virginia, or Skansen near Stockholm, the prototype for these sorts of folk architecture and heritage parks. But nature walks and architectural tours are but two examples of the many types of stories told in space. Technological museums use text and objects to explain how, for instance, a steam engine works or how steel is made. Such examples are important to consider because they might employ interesting narrative strategies different from many of the historical examples used in this book.

We have prioritized the written word in much of our discussion. Expanding the analysis to consider the spoken word would be an important next step, particularly in respect to the topics of chapters 7 and 8. Such analysis would consider how tour guides, museum docents, and the reenactors at living history museums and other such attractions present their stories in space. In some cases, there is relatively little difference between spoken and written scripts. Guides are asked to memorize or read scripts that could be presented as written text. The difference between the written text and the live performance lies in the contributions of the inflections, tone, nonverbal cues, and gestures of the guides to the interpretive experience. In other cases, guides have almost complete freedom to change, invent, and embellish stories, depending on visitor interest. This is closer to some of the "ghost tours" that are popular in cities like New Orleans, Louisiana; Charleston, South Carolina; Savannah, Georgia; and Gettysburg, Pennsylvania. Such tours can be easily customized to fit visitor interest. Between scripted and unscripted tours are those in which guides have some flexibility—a knowledge of an attraction deep enough to answer spontaneous questions—but still follow the same general text and path during each tour. Examining such tours is important not only for identifying how guides use their acting and speaking skills to draw visitors into their stories but also to find out where the guides stop and why; which places the guides highlight and why; and how they organize their tours or walks to tell a coherent, interesting story. In this regard, it might be interesting to try to map out guided tours on the model of the maps presented in chapter 7. Rather than present only the routes and text as we have done in chapter 7, multimedia maps could be created that would show videos of the gestures and dramatic elements used by guides to tell their stories about place.

The issue of guides and spoken narrative also raises issues about the performative elements of space and narrative. On many occasions, the location of a speech, public address, or story is just as important as the text itself. Martin Luther is said to have posted his ninety-five theses on the door of the All Saints' (or Castle) Church of Wittenberg, Germany, in 1517 as a protest against church authorities but also because the church itself held a major collection of religious relics. These relics had become a major source of income for the church, as had the sale of indulgences. In terms of its spatial symbolism, Luther's mythologized "hammering" of his theses onto the door of All Saints' is triply significant. It was directed at the major emblem of local ecclesiastical authority; at Frederick III of Saxony's vast collection of religious relics; and, most symbolically, at the church's doorways as symbols of the gateway to redemption, salvation, and heaven.

Many opposition movements—historic and contemporary—choose similarly symbolic locations for their protests, marches, and announcements (Stangl 2010). The Occupy Wall Street movement of 2011 focused its protest against the powerful collection of financial institutions headquartered in New York City. Taking a stand against social and economic inequality as well as the greed, corruption, and influence of corporations on government, the movement was based in Zuccotti Park, adjacent to Wall Street. Similarly, the U.S. Civil Rights Movement of the 1950s and 1960s consistently followed the Quaker adage of "speaking truth to power" in selecting the targets for their protests. Many of the most famous protest marches were aimed at the seats of local, state, and national power. In Birmingham, Alabama, this meant marching toward the city hall and county courthouse, buildings that faced each other across Linn Park in the center of town. Martin Luther King Jr.'s famous "Letter from Birmingham City Jail" of 1963 gains much of its impact from where it was written. The Selma, Alabama, marches of 1965 were aimed at the state capital of Montgomery, and the March on Washington of 1963, where Martin Luther King Jr. delivered his "I Have a Dream" speech, was in the heart of the nation's capital on the National Mall. Each of these sites had its own symbolic meaning, which reinforced the underlying messages. For example, King spoke on the steps of the Lincoln Memorial, symbolizing the legacy of the American Civil War and Lincoln's emancipation of slaves, but also, within eyesight to the east of the U.S. Capitol Building where Lincoln delivered both his first and second inaugural addresses.

The symbolic meaning of a site is a function of its narrative potential, namely, it is a measure of how the site resonates with stories about events that took place there, stories that are potentially inscribed on the local landscape. The place where Martin Luther King Jr. stood in 1963 to deliver his "I Have a Dream" speech is now inscribed in the stone steps of the Lincoln Memorial. President Barack Obama stood on the same spot when he spoke on the fiftieth anniversary of the March on Washington, not to reenact King's speech but to speak out again on civil rights. But other similarly symbolic locations have been used on many other occasions—for example, President Abraham Lincoln's Gettysburg Address, which more clearly than any of his previous orations defined the rationale for the American Civil War; President John Kennedy's "Ich bin ein Berliner" speech in Berlin in 1963 at the height of the Cold War; or the speech by then-student (but now prime minister) Viktor Orbán in Heroes Square in Budapest, Hungary, in 1989 at the reburial ceremony for political prisoners killed after the 1956 uprising. The reburial ceremony was one of the key protests that helped spur the fall of the communist government. These symbolically significant locations often serve as a means of amplifying the narrative power of the text.

It is interesting to note in this context that many key declarations and documents, whether of protest or assent, are known by where they were written or signed, with the locations taking on symbolic significance through time.

A few of these are Runnymede and the signing of the Magna Carta in 1215; Philadelphia and the signing of the American Declaration of Independence in 1776; or Abraham Lincoln's Gettysburg address of 1863. Sometimes there are spatio-rhetorical aspects to struggles for power as words and places collide. On November 9, 1919, Karl Liebknecht declared the creation of a Free Socialist Republic of Germany from a balcony (still preserved) of Berlin's royal palace only hours after Philipp Scheidemann declared the creation of a German Republic from a balcony of the Reichstag only a short distance away.

As these examples suggest, ignoring the political overtones of these stories is nearly impossible. Much recent research in geography and critical studies has indeed focused on the political dimensions of narrative—that is, on how the narration of historical events expresses hegemonic relations of power and authority and their contestation. A major emphasis of these investigations has been the critical examination of how relationships of political, economic, and social power are expressed in both performative and representational forms (Azaryahu 2011a; Azaryahu and Foote 2008; Foote and Azaryahu 2007). Although we alluded to the political dimensions of some of the cases used in previous chapters, we have hardly scratched the surface of how such narratives are created, debated, and changed. This is not just a question of comparing official and unofficial stories or contrasting hegemonic with subaltern narratives, since power relationships are usually more than simple top-down hierarchies. Influence, control, and authority can be woven into narrative in complex and subtle ways. By drawing attention to rhetorical devices and strategies, narrative theory offers a more nuanced perspective on power relationships as they develop, are contested, and change through time and across space. One example might be the rhetoric used in the abolitionist movement in Europe and the Americas beginning in the eighteenth century. In part, this was a war of words and stories that eventually undermined one of the most powerful economic institutions of its time. Slave narratives presented harrowing accounts of brutality and dehumanization, as did the fiction of writers like Harriet Beecher Stowe and the lectures of ex-slaves like Frederick Douglass and Sojourner Truth. Supporters of slavery countered with their own stories and narratives, whether drawn from biblical texts or the scientific theories of the time but in the end, the abolitionists prevailed.

A different issue that arises in chapter 6, 7, and 8 is that the notion of "authorship" is complicated when considering street names, landscape narratives, and museum narratives. In contrast to many of the works of literature considered in the first chapters of this book, landscape and museum narratives often have multiple (uncredited) authors or are written by committee. The stories are compromises and, in the case of many historical markers, the resulting captions are often short, even brusque texts that attempt to pack as much information as possible in the smallest amount of space typically using formal, almost formulaic prose: "On this site in . . ." Typically the authoring of landscape and museum narratives also extends (and changes) over long periods of time as stories grow and change or are removed and replaced with new text (though such changes are never noted onsite in the way books are identified by edition).

Research on these processes has appeared in a variety of fields, but more is needed. Aden's (2010) analysis of the President's House Controversy on Independence Mall in Philadelphia provides one model for examining the interplay of rhetoric, politics, and place. The controversy involves the discovery that President George Washington not only kept slaves in Philadelphia (the U.S. capital before being moved to the District of Columbia), but that he worked assiduously during his tenure in Philadelphia to circumvent Pennsylvania's laws of manumission so as to keep his servants enslaved. Parallel research has been published by Marcuse (2001) on the changing meaning of the Dachau concentration camp near Munich; Azaryahu (2003) on the ideological reorientation of the Buchenwald concentration camp following German reunification; Spielvogel (2013) on the rhetoric of U.S. national Civil War parks and battlefields; Linenthal and Engelhardt (1996) on the controversy surrounding the display of the B-29 bomber Enola Gay on the fiftieth anniversary of the bombing of Hiroshima; Leib (2006) on the controversy of placing a statue of Arthur Ashe along Monument Avenue in Richmond, Virginia; and Hoskins (2007) about the museum on Angel Island in San Francisco Bay telling the story of Chinese migration to the United States in the context of the exclusion laws of the nineteenth and twentieth centuries. The rhetoric of museums and memorials has been taken up by a broader range of scholars in communication and media studies (Dickinson, Blair, and Ott 2010).

These examples suggest looking more closely at how other narrative media are used to augment toponyms, landscape and museum narratives. For example, as urban commemorations, street names evoke biographies and past events, yet their narrative dimension can also be augmented by other commemorative media, such as memorial plaques, monuments, maps, and guidebooks. The spatial convergence and possible concurrence of toponymic and monumental commemoration offers new insights into how history is told in urban space. As the case of Trafalgar Square in London shows, toponymic and monumental commemorations that are associated with the same location might refer to different aspects of the same story. Built in the early 1840s, the name of the new square built at the center of London commemorated the victory of the British Fleet over the French Fleet in the Battle of Trafalgar in 1805.

The Nelson Column at the center of the square was built in 1842 to commemorate Vice Admiral Horatio Nelson, who lost his life in the battle. The name and the monument told a story of imperial glory: the geographic designation was a namesake of the historical event and celebrated the victory, while the 6-meter-high statue of Nelson, positioned on a 52-meter-high column, honored the venerated hero.

Monumental commemoration on such sites enhances the storytelling capacity of a street name itself. The case of Leninplatz in East Berlin offers insights into the strategic use of name, monument, and urban design to create a themed environment which, in effect, tells the story of the effects of regime change in Germany. On April 22, 1950, on the occasion of Lenin's seventieth birthday, a main thoroughfare and a square in Prenzlauer Berg and Friedrichshain in East Berlin, the capital city of communist East Germany, were renamed Leninallee and Leninplatz, respectively. The communist regime transformed Leninplatz into a communist showcase. The toponymic commemoration was augmented by an ambitious housing project and a Lenin monument built at the center of the square. Standing in front of the 75-meter-high housing project, the 19-meter-high figure of Lenin made of Ukrainian red granite was unveiled in a mass event on April 19, 1970, a few days before Lenin's one hundredth birthday (Horandt and Horn 1970). With the unveiling of the Lenin monument, the organ of the ruling communist party explained that "the square that bore [Lenin's] name received the architectural design decided upon by the Party and the Government" (*Neues Deutschland* 1970). The commemorative composite of place name and monument did not survive the demise of the communist East Germany in 1990. Following German reunification, the square in the former East Berlin was renamed Platz der Vereinten Nationen [Square of the United Nations]. In November 1991, the Lenin monument, a symbol of the communist past, was dismantled, and Lenin's story as well the story of its commemoration by the Communist state were erased from the local landscape.

The *stolpersteine* [stumbling blocks] memorials created by artist Gunter Demnig are another example of how text, space, and place intersect in complex ways. Begun in Cologne in 1992 on the fiftieth anniversary of the deportation of Germany's Sinti and Roma population to extermination camps, Demnig's project has spread across Europe as a way of recognizing the victims of the Holocaust. Each *stolperstein* is the size of a paving stone but faced with a brass plaque noting the name and birthdate of a Holocaust victim, including a brief caption about the person's fate: date of deportation, incarceration, and death. The blocks are set flush with the pavement where the victims last lived or worked. First used as memorials in Germany, *stolpersteine* have now been placed in many cities in Europe. These memorials resonate with many of the themes we have raised about place and narrative. They are somewhat like street names, somewhat like historical plaques, but also serve as tropes of loss that allude to a huge story extending far beyond the individual blocks. Their evocative power arises not only from their placement but also from the subtle balance they sustain between what is stated and is left unsaid, between the narrated, which is minimal, and the pregnant silence of what Gerald Prince (1988) calls the disnarrated. As Joseph Pearson (2010) has written, "It is not what is written which intrigues, because the inscription is insufficient to conjure a person. It is the emptiness, void, lack of information, the maw of the forgotten, which gives the monuments their power and lifts them from the banality of a statistic."

Underlying all these suggestions for future research is the goal of encouraging geographers to engage more thoroughly with narrative theory. The term "narrative" is now frequently used in geographic theory, but its meaning varies considerably (Price 2004). In some contexts, narrative is used as a synonym for "explanation" or "theory," in others narrative refers to the stories and information elicited from respondents in ethnographic research. Perhaps more generally, it is sometimes used as a synonym for "discourse" and the sorts of discourse analysis now popular in some areas of geography when, in fact, narrative is only one type discourse (albeit, a very well-studied type). Such definitional confusions are not uncommon in cross-disciplinary research, and such borrowings of terms and concepts often lead to deeper engagement across theoretical divides. We see our work as a step in this direction.

CROSSCUTTING ISSUES

Many of the lines of research that are sketched in this book should extend far into the future. Perhaps the most important of them is the need to relate our work to many different types of media. Narrative theory was originally elaborated for language, the medium (or type of signs) in which storytelling originated and that presents the richest narrative resources, but it has recently been extended to film, television, comics, painting, the theater, computer games, and even music, with particular emphasis on those media that allow a combination of signs (commonly referred to as "multimodality"). "Transmedial narratology" (i.e., the study of the realization of narrative in different media), whether these media are semiotically, culturally, or technologically conceived, is currently one of the most active areas of narrative theory (Ryan 2004b; Ryan and Thon 2014). Here we focused not only on fiction, the traditional domain of narratology, but also on maps, digital media, landscape stories, toponyms, and museums. This choice of topics was not merely a matter of intellectual convenience (given our previous research and writings) but also an opportunity to address issues that haven't been thoroughly covered in either narratology or geography, as well as a chance to bridge the divide between these two disciplines.

The most obvious area for future development is the study of how different media, especially film and television, affect our conceptions of space and place. As many scholars have argued, the social construction of knowledge, consciousness, and awareness of the world is shaped and reshaped by experience and perception, but especially by media and narrative forms of many types (Anderson 1991; Lowe 1982). The work of scholars such as Cosgrove (2001, 2008), Schulten (2001), Stafford (1984), and Lutz and Collins (1993) suggests indeed that literature, newspapers, visual art, travelogues, magazines, television, and film all have powerful effects on the way people frame and interpret the world. Much can be gained by focusing on how landscape narratives interact with other media to shape modern and postmodern conceptions of space, place, and history to create a broadened notion of visual rhetoric (Olson, Finnegan, and Hope 2008).

Among the most promising avenues of media-conscious research relate to the work by geographers on movies and television (Adams 1992, 2009; Aitken and Zonn 1994; Lukinbeal and Zimmermann 2008; Zonn 1990) as well as on the visual arts, such as painting (Daniels 1993; Norwood and Monk 1987; Sandweiss 1987). This research in geography and neighboring fields has focused especially on issues of regional identity, place making, sense of place, place images, and the role of film and television in mediating the experiences of space and place. At the same time, many of these same writers draw attention to the key role space plays in film and television narratives. We noted in chapter 2 that space plays not one but many roles in narrative fiction. This is no less true of visual media like film and television. Classic films as varied as John Ford's *The Searchers* (1956), Werner Herzog's *Aguirre, the Wrath of God* (1972), Francis Ford Coppola's *Apocalypse Now* (1979), and Ridley Scott's *Bladerunner* (1982) use space as an essential element of their screenplays.

To understand these many roles, it is necessary to unpack these different layers of use and meaning. In chapter 2, we proposed five basic levels of narrative space: (1) spatial frames, (2) setting, (3) story space, (4) storyworld, and (5) narrative universe. Considerable research attention has been devoted to both the setting and story space of visual narrative media, for example Stuart Aitken's (2002) examination of cities in science fiction horror films or Larry Ford's (1994) close reading of the use of light and shadow in the depiction of cities in film. By focusing on particular aspects of film narrative, such studies support the broadened definition of narrative for which we argue in this book.

Beyond television and film, it is equally important to devote more attention to connections between narratives and innovations in digital media. In the discussion of locative narrative in chapter 5, the example of the [murmur] project was used to consider how digital media are being used to change the way people explore and experience place. As one of the [murmur] (2013) Web sites explains:

> [murmur] is a documentary oral history project that records stories and memories told about specific geographic locations. We collect and make accessible people's personal histories and anecdotes about the places in their neighborhoods that are important to them. In each of these locations we install a [murmur] sign with a telephone number on it that anyone can call with a mobile phone to listen to that story while standing in that exact spot, and engaging in the physical experience of being right where the story takes place. Some stories suggest that the listener walk around, following a certain path through a place, while others allow a person to wander with both their feet and their gaze.

Although [murmur] is the work of volunteers, many commercial firms and travel writers are developing comparable mobile guides. Companies like Walking Papers Media (2013), Geogad (2013), Audio Travel (2013), and Visual Travel Tours (2013) create mobile sites for a wide range of customers including city governments and chambers of commerce, shopping malls, museums, hotels, restaurants, and special audiences.

Looking ahead, some of the most important changes for narrative might arise in the domain of what is coming to be termed "locative media," the consequence of the widespread use of digital networks and archives with ever more powerful mobile devices (Alexander 2011; Farman 2014; Wilken and Goggin 2014). Commercial and crowd-sourced projects like [murmur] set precedents for intentional efforts to tell stories in space, but the gradual emergence of the Web as a massive, searchable archive of stories and information about events and places also changes the experience of landscape narratives. Visitors standing at historical sites can use their phones and other mobile devices to access all sorts of primary and secondary material, including narratives, counternarratives, comments, and criticism. For example, visitors to Emily Dickinson's house in Amherst, Massachusetts, or Samuel Clemens's (Mark Twain) in Hartford, Connecticut, can access the entire corpus of their writings as well as the works of all their contemporaries and commentators from their cell phones as they walk through the buildings.

These networks of information free the visitor from the landscape narrative arranged on the ground. Thanks in part to the rise of geo-tagging, location-based information is becoming much easier for people to find. Geo-tagging involves assigning geographical coordinates to information stored on the Web and is now a popular way of sharing photographs and information in Google Maps and Google Earth. These systems allow users to overlay geo-tagged information on top of base maps and satellite images in what are called "mash-ups." At the time of this writing, geo-tagging is used mostly for sharing photographs and, in the commercial world, as the basis for advertising location-based services. But the expansion of geo-tagging into the tagging of textual and other types of graphic materials has the potential to change the way narratives are created and presented.

Virtual reality is another digital technology that might substantially change the nature of landscape narratives. Although the dream of a complete, immersive virtual reality system that provides users with a sense of the presence of an environment has not materialized, despite the hype of the 1990s, many lesser degrees of simulation can lead to compelling and realistic engagement with virtual worlds. One of these, as Adams (2004) points out, is when a player "gets immersed in a narrative [to the point where] he or she starts to care about the characters and wants to know how the story is going to end."

Other writers like Björk and Holopainen (2004) use the term "spatial immersion" to describe experiences in which users feel that the simulated world looks and feels "real." Both of these types of immersion might gradually impact landscape narratives. This is not to say that narratives based on virtual displays will supplant landscape narratives but rather that virtual reality does offer possibilities that are difficult to achieve in other media, particularly for historical and archaeological sites. One example is the Theban Mapping Project (2013), which allows visitors to move through detailed reconstructions of ancient tombs in the Theban necropolis in Egypt. Here visitors can see the archaeological sites in ways that are otherwise difficult to achieve.

Similarly, the Robie House Interior Restoration Project (2013) allows visitors to see how Frank Lloyd Wright used space, furnishings, fixtures, fabrics, and lighting to create a masterpiece of domestic design. And many virtual battlefield tours are beginning to appear, like Virtual Gettysburg (2013), which allows visitors to see the places and events from perspectives difficult to achieve on the ground. Although some of these digital technologies are still in their infancy, they suggest how landscape narratives might develop and change in the future. The still rudimentary and not particularly immersive experiments of today might lead to cybernetic or bionic forms of narrative that will link place, space, and story in new and interesting ways.

These suggestions point to ways our work might support emerging themes in the digital and spatial humanities. Our first and foremost goal for this book is to strengthen the link between narrative theory and geography, but our broader purpose is to promote similar cross-disciplinary collaborations that will help to advance narrative theory. Given the insistence of both this chapter and chapter 5 on the increasing role of digital media in people's lives, one of the many possible extensions of our work is in the area of the digital humanities. Currently the notion of digital humanities is somewhat of a catchall category for a wide range of experimental approaches to an equally broad range of theoretical topics, but even at this early stage in its development, there are some points of overlap with the issues we have raised in this book.

At the most general level, the digital humanities focus on theoretical and methodological issues lying at the intersection of computing and the humanities, including the disciplines of history, the ancient and modern languages, philosophy, linguistics, literature, art, archaeology, music, and cultural studies. The point is to address research questions arising from traditional humanities disciplines by using computational tools such as those developed for data visualization, data mining, statistical analysis, content analysis, and other techniques. The ability of researchers to work with massive textual databases—for example, the body of materials digitized by Google or the literary texts made electronically available by Project Gutenberg—help support the work of researchers such as Franco Moretti (1998), who pose hypotheses that can only be addressed using large textual databases. Some of the ideas we have advanced in this book might profit from careful scrutiny of large textual databases.

Sources like Google Maps, Google Earth, and Bing Maps allow access to a body of toponyms and geo-coded addresses, names, and places never before assembled. This database can be easily improved and expanded every day. It is now possible to search worldwide for occurrences of particular names as well as detailed local historical and archival information that was formerly hard to find or costly to access. And while the ability to visit the sites of landscape narratives through Google's Street View does not replace firsthand experience, it does allow detailed comparisons of sites that would be time-consuming or very difficult to visit in person.

Similar textual developments allow researchers to "harvest" information from online discussions, tweets, and Facebook posts, making it possible to track how narratives and stories develop and evolve in real time. Much of what we write and theorize nowadays is based on a relatively limited range of materials, such as manuscripts, personal papers, and autobiographical writings that vary considerably in coverage and completeness. Digital media are changing this world by providing scholars with far more dynamic entrée into the creative process, with blog posts, tweets, RSS feeds, and Facebook pages serving as a sort of stream of consciousness for studying the narrative and storytelling.

While some of our ideas relate to the digital humanities, at the broadest level our work belongs to an emerging field known as the "spatial humanities" or "geohumanities" (Daniels et al. 2011; Dear et al. 2011). Like "digital humanities," the label "spatial humanities" is a bit of an omnibus term and, to some extent, the two areas overlap. Grouped together under the spatial humanities banner is research on geographic information science (GIScience), geographic information systems (GIS), and spatial analysis in the humanities; time-space geography; historical GIS; qualitative GIS and emerging semantic web; representations of space and place in the humanities; mapping text; e-science; and grid computing (Bodenhamer 2010; Bodenhamer, Corrigan, and Harris 2010; Offen 2013). As one of the leaders in the field makes clear, the spatial humanities and digital humanities are interlinked conceptually:

> New technologies such as Geographic Information Systems (GIS) have facilitated the (re)discovery of space for humanists [through] . . . advances in spatial multi-media, in GIS-enabled web services, geo-visualization, cyber geography, and virtual reality that provide capabilities far exceeding the abilities of GIS on its own. . . . This convergence of technologies promises to revolutionize the role of place in the digital humanities by allowing us to move far beyond the static map. . . . The result may be termed "deep mapping," a process and platform that enables an exploration of multiple perspectives and deep contingencies over various spatial and temporal scales. (Bodenhamer 2013)

However, GIS technologies are not always well suited to the questions and materials with which humanists work (Griffiths 2013). In summarizing one recent conference, the organizers sought to bridge this divide by focusing on "two innovative forms—spatial narratives and deep maps—that bend spatial and other digital technologies to the intellectual traditions of humanists, thereby constituting a bridge between diverse avenues of investigation" (Bodenhamer, Harris and Corrigan 2013, 170). The focus on spatial narratives and deep maps is a clear connection between the spatial humanities and the themes we have explored in this book. Our contribution is to sharpen the analytical tools that might play a role in advancing these intellectual frontiers.

In the end, our goal is not to propose a grand theory to subsume all perspectives on the importance of space and place for narrative, but rather to initiate a dialogue between geographers and narratologists that will encourage the exploration of common interests. By emphasizing the complementarity of their concerns, we hope to encourage geographers to learn from narratology and narratologists to learn from geography. We see this book as promoting space as a key concept for narrative theory, and narrative as a key concept for geography. This task is fulfilled in two different ways. First, rather than arguing for a single point of intersection between space and narrative, we have proposed multiple perspectives on the relations between these two fields of study. Second, we have demonstrated that narrative is a type of meaning that transcends disciplines and media by bringing together examples from fiction, cartography, games, toponymy, historical sites, and museums. In each instance, we have sought to demonstrate how general concepts from narrative theory help frame and explain the phenomena under study. But as we have noted in this final section, many topics remain to be explored. More than a conclusion, this chapter is really an introduction to future research.

Above all, we hope to have demonstrated that narratology and geography have much to gain from each other at a more fundamental level. Narratology gains from geography because the essence of narrativity can be described as bringing a concrete world to the imagination, an evolving world inhabited by active characters who relate emotionally to it and to each other. Geography provides narratology not only with the concepts of space and place but also with tools to describe storyworlds (maps and other visual representations of data), with a critical examination of these tools (critical cartography), with systems to anchor stories in the real world (GPS), and with a rich corpus of work on how people experience space and place (Hubbard and Kitchin 2011). This work can teach narratology new ways to approach texts (Prieto 2013; Mehigan and Corkhill 2013). As for geography, it needs narratives and narratology because, if it wants to capture the experience of space and place in its emotional, existential, and phenomenological dimensions, its richest source of data are the stories people create involving space and place.

REFERENCES

Aarseth, Espen. 2001. "Allegorien des Raumes: Räumlichkeit in Computerspielen [Allegories of space: The question of spatiality in computer games]." *Zeitschrift für Semiotik* 23 (3–4): 301–18. English version available online at http://cybertext.hum.jyu.fi/articles/129.pdf (accessed March 9, 2015). Page numbers refer to the English version.

Abbott, Edwin. 2006 [1884]. *Flatland: a romance of many dimensions*. Oxford: Oxford University Press.

Adams, Ernest. 2004. "Postmodernism and the three types of immersion." http://designersnotebook.com/Columns/063_Postmodernism/063_postmodernism.htm (accessed January 1, 2013).

Adams, Paul. 1992. "Television as a gathering place." *Annals of the Association of American Geographers* 82 (1): 117–35.

———. 2009. *Geographies of media and communication: A critical introduction*. Malden, MA: Wiley-Blackwell.

Aden, Roger. 2010. "Redefining the 'Cradle of Liberty': The president's house controversy in Independence National Historical Park." *Rhetoric & Public Affairs* 13 (2): 251–80.

Aiken, Charles S. 2009. *William Faulkner and the southern landscape*. Athens: University of Georgia Press.

Aitken, Stuart. 2002. "Tuning the self: City space and science fiction horror movies." In *Lost in space: Geographies of science fiction*, edited by Rob Kitchin and James Kneale, 104–22. London: Continuum.

Aitken, Stuart C., and Leo E. Zonn, eds. 1994. *Place, power, situation, and spectacle: A geography of film*. Lanham, MD: Rowman & Littlefield.

Alber, Jan. 2013. "Unnatural spaces and narrative worlds." In *A Poetics of Unnatural Narrative*, edited by Jan Alber, Henrik Skov Nielsen, and Brian Richardson, 45–66. Columbus: The Ohio State University Press.

Alderman, Derek H. 2000. "A street fit for a king: Naming places and commemoration in the American South." *Professional Geographer* 52: 672–84.

———. 2002a. "School names as cultural arenas: The naming of U.S. public schools after Martin Luther King Jr." *Urban Geography* 23: 601–26.

———. 2002b. "Street names as memorial arenas: The reputational politics of commemorating Martin Luther King Jr. in a Georgia county." *Historical Geography* 30: 99–120.

———. 2003. "Street names and the scaling of memory: The politics of commemorating Martin Luther King Jr. within the African American community." *Area* 35: 163–73.

Alexander, Bryan. 2011. *The new digital storytelling: Creating narratives with new media*. New York: Praeger.

Alexander, Christopher, Sara Ishikawa, Murray Silverstein, Max Jacobson, Ingrid Fiksdahl-King, and Shlomo Angel. 1977. *A pattern language: Towns, buildings, construction*. New York: Oxford University Press.

Anderson, Benedict. 1991. *Imagined communities: Reflections on the origin and spread of nationalism*. London: Verso.

Applebome, Peter. 2010. "A local street and a lesson in history. *New York Times*. March 8: A16.

Aristotle. 1996. *Poetics*. Translated by Malcolm Heath. London: Penguin.

Arlington National Cemetery. 2007. "Arlington National Cemetery." http://www.arlingtoncemetery.mil/ (accessed July 4, 2014).

Audio Travel. 2013. http://www.audiotravel.com/mobile-travel-guide (accessed January 1, 2013).

Augé, Marc. 1995. *Non-places: Introduction to an anthropology of supermodernity*. New York: Verso.

Azaryahu, Maoz. 1986. "Street names and political identity: The case of East Berlin." *Journal of Contemporary History* 21: 581–604.

———. 1992. "The purge of Bismarck and Saladin: The renaming of streets in East Berlin and Haifa, a comparative study in culture-planning." *Poetics Today* 13: 352–67.

———. 1996a. "The power of commemorative street names." *Environment and Planning D: Society and Space* 14: 311–30.

———. 1996b. "The spontaneous formation of memorial space: The case of *Kikar Rabin*, Tel Aviv." *Area* 28 (4): 501–13.

———. 1997. German reunification and the politics of street names: The case of East Berlin. *Political Geography* 16: 479–93.

———. 2003. Replacing memory: The reorientation of Buchenwald. *Cultural Geographies* 10 (1): 1–20.

———. 2011a. "The critical turn and beyond: The case of commemorative street naming." *ACME: An International E-Journal for Critical Geographies* 10 (1): 28–33.

———. 2011b. "The politics of commemorative street renaming: Berlin 1945–1948." *Journal of Historical Geography* 37 (4): 483–92.

———. 2012a. "Renaming the past in post-Nazi Germany: Insights into the politics of street naming in Mannheim and Potsdam." *Cultural Geographies* 19 (3): 383–98.

———. 2012b. "Rabin's road: The politics of toponymic commemoration of Yitzhak Rabin in Israel." *Political Geography* 31: 73–82.

Azaryahu, Maoz, and Kenneth E. Foote. 2008. "Historical space as narrative medium: On the configuration of spatial narratives of time at historical sites." *GeoJournal* 73 (3): 179–94.

Azaryahu, Maoz, and Aharon Kellerman. 1999. "Symbolic places of national history and revival: A study of Zionist mythical geography." *Transactions of the Institute of British Geographers* 24 (1): 109–23.

Bachelard, Gaston. 1969 [1957]. *The poetics of space: The classic look at how we experience intimate places.* Translated by Maria Jolas. Boston: Beacon Press, 1994.

Bahne, Charles. 2005. *The complete guide to Boston's Freedom Trail.* 3rd ed. Cambridge, MA; Newtowne Publishing.

Bakhtin, Mikhail. 1973 [1938]. "Forms of Time and of the Chronotope in the Novel." In *The dialogic imagination: Four essays,* edited by Michael Holquist. Translated by Michael Holquist and Cary Emerson. 84–258. Austin: University of Texas Press, 1981.

Bal, Mieke. 1985. *Narratology.* Translated by Christine van Boheemen. Toronto: University of Toronto Press.

Balzac, Honoré de. 1955. *Eugénie Grandet.* Translated by Marion Ayton Crawford. London: Penguin.

Barnes, Trevor, and James Duncan, eds. 1992. *Writing worlds: Discourse, text, and metaphor in the representation of landscape.* New York: Routledge.

Barrett, Andrea. 2002. *Servants of the map.* New York: W. W. Norton.

Barthes, Roland. 1972 [1957]. "Introduction to the structural analysis of narrative." In *Image, music, text,* translated by S. Heath, 79–124. New York: Hill and Wang.

Baudelaire, Charles. 1995. *The painter of modern life.* Translated and edited by J. Mayne. London: Ohaidon Press.

Bedford, Leslie. 2001. "Storytelling: 'The real work of museums.'" *Curator* 44 (1): 27–34.

Belknap's waterproof Grand Canyon river guide. N.d. Evergreen, CO: Westwater Books.

Bellamy, Liz. 2005. "Novel of circulation (it-narrative, circulation narrative)." *The Literary Encyclopedia.* http://www.litencyc.com/php/stopics.php?rec=true&UID=1535 (accessed March 19, 2015).

Ben-Yehuda, Nachman. 1995. *The Masada myth: Collective memory and myth making in Israel.* Madison: University of Wisconsin Press.

Ben-Yishai, Aharon Zeev. 1952. "Tel Aviv and its streets: A monograph." *Yediot Iryat Tel Aviv* 22 (1–2): 37–39 (Hebrew).

Berg, Lawrence, and Jani Vuolteenaho, eds. 2009. *Critical toponymies. The contested politics of place naming.* Farnham, UK: Ashgate.

Bergonia.org. 2015. http://www.bergonia.org/why.htm (accessed April 2, 2015).

Bernaerts, Lars. 2012. "Narrative disorientation: Representations of space in experimental fiction." Paper presented at the conference of the Society for the Study of Narrative, March 15–17, in Las Vegas.

Berrett, LaMar C., ed. 2001. *Ohio and Illinois.* Vol. 3 of *Sacred place: A comprehensive guide to early Latter Day Saint historical sites.* Salt Lake City: Deseret Book Co.

———, ed. 2005. *Iowa and Nebraska.* Vol. 5 of *Sacred place: A comprehensive guide to early Latter Day Saint historical sites.* Salt Lake City: Deseret Book Co.

Bertin, Jacques. 1998. *Sémiologies graphique. Les diagrammes—les réseaux—les cartes,* 3rd ed. Paris: Éditions de l'École des Hautes Études en Sciences Sociales.

Bigler, Philip. 2005. *In honored glory: Arlington National Cemetery, the final post.* 4th ed. St. Petersburg, FL: Vandamere Press.

Björk, Staffan, and Jussi Holopainen. 2004. *Patterns in game design.* Newton Center, MA: Charles River Media.

Bjornson, Richard. 1981. "Cognitive mapping and the understanding of literature." *Sub-Stance* 30: 51–62.

Black, Graham. 2005. *The engaging museum: Developing museums for visitor involvement.* New York: Routledge.

Bodenhamer, David J. 2010. "The potential of spatial humanities." In *The spatial humanities: GIS and the future of humanities scholarship,* edited by David J. Bodenhamer, John Corrigan, and Trevor M. Harris, 14–30. Bloomington: Indiana University Press.

———. 2013. "Deep maps, emergent realities: The promise of spatial humanities." http://ias.umn.edu/2013/04/22/david-bodenhamer/ (accessed December 1, 2013).

Bodenhamer, David J., John Corrigan, and Trevor M. Harris, eds. 2010. *The spatial humanities: GIS and the future of humanities scholarship.* Bloomington: Indiana University Press.

Bodenhamer, David J., Trevor M. Harris, and John Corrigan. 2013. "Deep mapping and the spatial humanities." *International Journal of Humanities and Arts Computing* 7 (1–2): 170–75.

Bodnar, John. 1992. *Remaking America: Public memory, commemoration, and patriotism in the twentieth century.* Princeton, NJ: Princeton University Press.

Bolter, Jay David. 1991. *Writing space: The computer, hypertext, and the history of writing.* Hillsdale, NJ: Lawrence Erlbaum.

Borges, Jorge Luis. 1983 [1944]. "Partial magic in the Quixote." In *Labyrinths: Selected stories and other writings,* translated by James E. Irby, 193–96. New York: Modern Library.

———. 1998. "On exactitude in science." *Collected fictions,* translated by Andrew Hurley, 325. New York: Viking,

Bothe, Rolf. 1992. The Berlin Museum and its extension. In *Daniel Libeskind: Extension to the Berlin Museum with Jewish Museum Department,* edited by Kristin Feireiss, 32–52. Berlin: Ernst & Sohn.

Bower, Gordon, and Daniel Morrow. 1990. "Mental models in narrative comprehension." *Science* 247: 44–48.

Bracher, Frederick. 1944. "The maps in *Gulliver's travels.*" *Huntington Library Quarterly* 8 (1): 59–74.

Bradbury, Malcolm. 1998. *The atlas of literature.* New York: Stewart, Tabori, and Chang.

Brown, Randy. 2004. *Historic inscriptions on western emigrant trails.* Independence, MO: Oregon-California Trails Association.

Buchan, John. 2013 [1915]. *The 39 steps.* Las Vegas, NV: CreateSpace (independent publishing platform).

Buchholz, Sabine, and Manfred Jahn. 2005. "Space in narrative." In *The Routledge Encyclopedia of Narrative Theory,* edited by David Herman, Manfred Jahn, and Marie-Laure Ryan, 551–54. London: Routledge.

Bulson, Eric. 2006. *Novels, maps, modernity: The spatial imagination.* London: Routledge.

Burgess, Jacquelin, and John Gold, eds. 1985. *Geography, the media and popular culture.* London: Croom Helm.

Buschmann, Heike. 2010. "Geschichten im Raum: Erzähltheorie als Museumsanalyse." In *Museumsanalyse: Methoden und Konturen eines neuen Forschungsfeldes*, edited by Joachim Baur, 149–69. Bielefeld: Transcript Publishers.

Caïra, Olivier. 2007. *Jeux de rôles: les forges de la fiction*. Paris: CNRS Editions.

Cameron, Emilie. 2012. "New geographies of story and storytelling." *Progress in Human Geography* 36 (5) 573–92.

Campbell, Joseph. 1973 [1949]. *The hero with a thousand faces*. 2nd ed. Princeton, NJ: Princeton University Press.

Carroll, Lewis. 1982. *Sylvie and Bruno: The complete illustrated works of Lewis Carroll*. Edited by Edward Guiliano. New York: Avenel Books.

Carter, Jennifer. 2011. "Narrative and imagination: Remaking national history at the Musée des monuments français, Paris." In *National museums: New studies from around the world*, edited by Simon Knell, Peter Aronsson, Arne Bugge Amundsen, Amy Jane Barnes, Stuart Burch, Jennifer Carter, Viviane Gosselin, Sally Hughes, and Alan Kirwan, 89–104. London: Routledge.

Castronova, Edward. 2005. *Synthetic worlds: The business and culture of online games*. Chicago: University of Chicago Press.

Caviedes, César. 1996. Guest editorial. *GeoJournal* 38 (1): 1–2.

Chatman, Seymour. 1978. *Story and discourse: Narrative structure in fiction and film*. Ithaca, NY: Cornell University Press.

Child, Lee. 2010. *Worth dying for*. London: Bantam Books.

City of Memory. 2013. http://www.cityofmemory.org/map/index.php (accessed March 9, 2013).

City of Toronto. 2013. "City of Toronto honourific and street naming policy." http://www.toronto.ca/mapping/street_naming/ (accessed June 14, 2013).

Cohen, Margaret. 2010. "Literary studies on the terraqueous globe." *PMLA* 125 (3): 657–62.

Collectif Microtruc. 2013. "Les Trucs." http://www.jeudepaume.org/index.php?page=article&idArt=1404&lieu=3 (accessed March 9, 2015).

Collot, Michel. 2014. *Pour une géographie littéraire*. Paris: Editions Corti.

Conan Doyle, Sir Arthur. 1994 [1892]. "The speckled band." In *The adventures of Sherlock Holmes*, 171–97. New York: Oxford University Press.

Cortázar, Julio. 1967. "Continuity of parks." In *Blow-up and other stories*, translated by Paul Blackburn, 63–65. New York: Pantheon.

Cosgrove, Denis E. 2001. *Apollo's eye: A cartographic genealogy of the Earth in the Western imagination*. Baltimore: Johns Hopkins University Press.

———. 2008. *Geography and vision: Seeing, imagining and representing the world*. London: I. B. Tauris.

Cosgrove, Denis E., and Veronica della Dora. 2005. "Mapping global war: Los Angeles, the Pacific, and Charles Owens's pictorial cartography." *Annals of the Association of American Geographers* 95 (2): 373–90.

Cowan, James. 1996. *A Mapmaker's dream: The meditations of Fra Mauro, cartographer to the court of Venice*. New York: Warner Books.

Crane, Susan A., ed. 2000. *Museums and memory*. Stanford, CA: Stanford University Press.

Cumming, Charles. 2008. *The 21 steps*. http://wetellstories.co.uk/stories/week1/ (accessed March 9, 2015).

Czech, Hans-Jörg. 2009. "Deutsche Geschichte in Bildern und Zeugnissen: Ziele und Struktur der ständigen Ausstellung." In *Deutsche Geschichte in Bildern und Zeugnissen*, edited by Hans Ottomeyer and Hans-Jörg Czech, 8–17. Munich: Minerva.

Danielewski, Mark Z. 2000. *House of leaves*. New York: Pantheon.

Daniels, Stephen. 1993. *Fields of vision: Landscape imagery and national identity in England and the United States*. Princeton, NJ: Princeton University Press.

Daniels, Stephen, Dydia DeLyser, J. Nicholas Entrikin, and Douglas Richardson, eds. 2011. *Envisioning landscapes, making worlds: Geography and the humanities*. New York: Routledge.

Dannenberg, Hilary. 2008. *Convergent and divergent lives: Plotting coincidence and counterfactuality in narrative fiction*. Lincoln: University of Nebraska Press.

Dante Alighieri. 1960. *The divine comedy. I: Hell*. Translated by Dorothy Sayers. London: Penguin Books.

Darby, H. Clifford. 1948. "The regional geography of Thomas Hardy's Wessex." *Geographical Review* 38: 426–43.

Dear, Michael, Jim Ketchum, Sara Luria, and Douglas Richardson, eds. 2011. *GeoHumanities: Art, history, text at the edge of place*. New York: Routledge.

Debord, Guy. 1981. "Theory of the dérive." In *Situationist international anthology*, edited by Ken Knabb, 62–65. Berkeley, CA: Bureau of Public Secrets.

De Certeau, Michel. 1984. *The practice of everyday life*. Translated by Steven Randall. Berkeley: University of California Press.

Decker, John R. 2005. "Abraham Lincoln Presidential Library and Museum." *The Journal of American History* 92 (3): 934–38.

Deleuze, Gilles, and Félix Guattari. 1987. *A thousand plateaus: Capitalism and schizophrenia*. Translated by Brian Massumi. Minneapolis: University of Minnesota Press.

DeLyser, Dydia. 2005. *Ramona memories: Tourism and the shaping of southern California*. Minneapolis: University of Minnesota Press.

Dennerlein, Katrin. 2009. *Narratologie desRaumes*. Berlin: Walter De Gruyter.

Deutsches Historisches Museum. 2013. "Concepts governing the museum and its exhibitions." http://www.dhm.de/ENGLISH/dhm_konzeption.html (accessed February 4, 2013).

Díaz-Migoyo, Gonzalo. 1988. "Truth disguised: Chronicle of a death (ambiguously) foretold." In *Gabriel García Márquez and the powers of fiction*, edited by J. Ortega and C. Eliot. 74–85. Austin: University of Texas Press.

Dickinson, Greg, Carole Blair, and Brian L. Ott, eds. 2010. *Places of public memory: The rhetoric of museums and memorials*. Tuscaloosa: University of Alabama Press.

Dicks, Bella. 2004. *Culture on display: The production of contemporary visitability*. Maidenhead, UK: Open University Press.

Döblin, Alfred. 2003 [1929]. *Berlin Alexanderplatz: The story of Franz Biberkopf*. Translated by Eugene Jolas. New York: Continuum International.

Dodge, Martin, and Rob Kitchin. 2001a. *Atlas of cyberspace*. London: Addison-Wesley.

———. 2001b. *Mapping cyberspace*. London: Routledge.

Doležel, Lubomír. 1998. *Heterocosmica: Fiction and possible worlds*. Baltimore: Johns Hopkins University Press.

Dong, Aixia. 2013. "212576: NW area of Grange Park." http://murmurtoronto.ca/place.php?212576 (accessed March 11, 2013).

Dublin City of Literature. 2013. "Honouring Dublin's writers." http://www.dublincityofliterature.ie/dublin-writers/honouring-dublins-writers.html?d6f9900c6abf5559408ec51f5523a7ea=df20cce5a0a3f18ca85d58a32aef9b75 (accessed June 14, 2012).

Duncan, James, and David Ley, eds. 1993. *Place/culture/representation*. New York: Routledge.

Dunwell, Steve, and Blanche M. G. Linden. 2005. *Boston Freedom Trail*. Boston: Back Bay Press.

Duvert, Elizabeth. 1986. "Faulkner's map of time." *Faulkner Journal* 2 (Fall) 14–28.

Edensor, Tim. 1997. "National identity and the politics of memory: Remembering Bruce and Wallace in symbolic space." *Environment and Planning D: Society and Space* 15 (2): 175–94.

Eliade, Mircea. 1998. "Myth and reality." In *The myth and ritual theory*, edited by Robert Segal, 180–89. Oxford: Blackwell.

Epstein, Andrew. 2012. "Found poetry, 'uncreative writing,' and the art of appropriation." In *The Routledge companion to experimental literature*, edited by Joe Bray, Alison Gibbons, and Brian McHale, 310–22. London: Routledge.

Esri. 2012. "Storytelling with maps." http://storymaps.esri.com/wordpress/ (accessed June 30, 2012).

Esrock, Ellen. 1994. *The reader's eye: Visual imaging as reader response*. Baltimore: Johns Hopkins University Press.

Falk, John H., and Lynn D. Dierking. 1992. *The museum experience*. Washington, DC: Whalesback Books.

Faraco, J. Carlos Gonzalez, and Michael Dean Murphy. 1997. "Street names and political regimes in an Andalusian town." *Ethnology* 36: 123–48.

Farman, Jason, ed. 2014. *The mobile story: Narrative practices with locative technologies*. New York: Routledge.

Fauconnier, Gilles. 1985. *Mental spaces: Aspects of meaning construction in natural language*. Cambridge, MA: MIT Press.

———. 1997. *Mapping in thought and language*. Cambridge: Cambridge University Press.

Faulkner, William. 1948. *Intruder in the dust*. New York: Random House.

Ferguson, Erika, and Mary Hegarty. 1994. "Properties of cognitive maps constructed from texts." *Memory and Cognition* 22 (4): 455–73.

Ferguson, Priscilla Parkhurst. 1988. "Reading city streets." *French Review* 51: 391.

Feyerabend, Paul. 1993. *Against method*. 3rd ed. London: Verso.

Fludernik, Monika. 1996. *Towards a "natural" narratology*. London: Routledge.

Fonstad, Karen. W. 1991. *The atlas of Middle Earth*. Rev. ed. New York: Houghton Mifflin.

Foote, Kenneth E. 2003. *Shadowed ground: America's landscapes of violence and tragedy*. Rev. ed. Austin: University of Texas Press.

Foote, Kenneth E., and Maoz Azaryahu. 2007. "Toward a geography of memory: Geographical dimensions of public memory and commemoration." *Journal of Political and Military Sociology* 35 (1): 125–44.

Foote, Kenneth E., Attila Tóth, and Anett Árvay. 2000. "Hungary after 1989: Inscribing a new past on place." *Geographical Review* 90 (3): 301–34.

Ford, Larry. 1994. "Sunshine and shadow: Lighting and color in the depiction of cities on film." In *Place, power, situation and spectacle: A geography of film*, edited by Stuart Aitken and Leo Zonn, 119–36. Lanham, MD: Rowman & Littlefield.

Forster, E. M. 1990 [1927]. *Aspects of the novel*. Harmondsworth, UK: Penguin.

Foucault, Michel. 1995. *Discipline and punishment*. New York: Vintage Books.

Frank, Joseph. 1945. "Spatial form in modern literature: An essay in two parts." *Sewanee Review* 53 (2): 221–40.

———. 1991 [1945]. *The idea of spatial form*. New Brunswick, NJ: Rutgers University Press.

Friedman, Susan Stanford. 1993. "Spatialization: A strategy for reading narrative. *Narrative* 1 (1): 12–23.

Friel, Brian. 1981. *Translations*. London: Faber and Faber.

Frishbach, Bob. 2011. "Ayn Rand column really gets a reaction from readers." *Omaha World-Herald*. May 12. http://www.randex.org/index.php/weblog/auth/Qm9iIEZpc2NoYmFjaA== (accessed July 2, 2014).

Furst, Lilian R. 1995. *All is true: The claims and strategies of realist fiction*. Durham, NC: Duke University Press.

Galant, Debra. 2004. "Young look. Child-friendly or child-frenzied? Turn Down the Interactivity, Please!" *New York Times*. March 31.

Galbraith, Keith Chesterton. 1907. "Drift of London literary gossip." *New York Times*. October 19.

García Márquez, Gabriel. 1982. *Chronicle of a death foretold*. New York: Ballantine Books.

Genette, Gérard. 1972. *Narrative discourse: An essay in method*. Translated by Jane Lewin. Ithaca, NY: Cornell University Press.

Geogad. 2013. http://www.geogad.com/ (accessed January 1, 2013).

Geoghegan, Hilary. 2010. "Museum geography: Exploring museums, collections and museum practice in the UK." *Geography Compass* 4 (10): 1462–76.

Gerrig, Richard. 1993. *Experiencing storyworlds: On the psychological activities of reading*. New Haven, CT: Yale University Press.

Gibson, William. 1984. *Neuromancer*. New York: Ace.

Giese, August. 1934. "Unsere Helden und ihre Taten in den Straßennamen von Gross-Berlin." *Berlinische Blätter für Geschichte und Heimatkunde* 1 (10–11): 122–23 and 1 (12): 134–40.

Gill, Graeme. 2005. "Changing symbols: The renovation of Moscow place names." *Russian Review* 64 (3): 480–503.

Gold, John R., and Margaret M. Gold. 1995. *Imagining Scotland: Tradition, representation and promotion in Scottish tourism since 1750*. Aldershot, UK: Scolar Press.

Goldman, Corrie. 2012. "This is your brain on Jane Austen, and Stanford researchers are taking notes." Stanford/News http://news.stanford.edu/news/2012/september/austen-reading-fmri-090712.html (accessed December 3, 2013).

Goralick, Shlomo. 1934. "A street named after Halpern." *Ha'Aretz*. September 26 (Hebrew).

Gould, Peter, and Rodney White. 1974. *Mental maps*. London: Penguin.

Greater Philadelphia Tourism Marketing Corporation, Official Visitor Site for Greater Philadelphia. 2005. "Walking in Benjamin Franklin's footsteps." http://www.gophila.com/C/Things_to_Do/211/Itineraries_and_Tours/428/Itineraries/429/I/Walking_in_Benjamin_Franklins_Footsteps/8.html (accessed November 7, 2007).

Greimas, Algirdas Julien. 1966. *Sémantique structurale*. Paris: Larousse.

Griffiths, Sam. 2013. "GIS and research into historical 'spaces of practice': Overcoming the epistemological barriers." In *History and GIS: Epistemologies, considerations and reflections,* edited by Alexander von Lunen and Charles Travis, 153–71. London: Springer.

Grynbaum, Michael M. 2011. "After 3 decades, a Bronx historian loses his road." *New York Times.* April 11.

Halbwachs, Maurice. 1992. *On collective memory.* Translated by L. A. Coser. Chicago: University of Chicago Press.

Hanna, Stephen P. and Vincent J. Del Casino, eds. 2003. *Mapping tourism.* Minneapolis: University of Minnesota Press.

Harley, John Brian. 1989. "Deconstructing the map." *Cartographica* 26 (2): 1–20.

Harmon, Katharine. 2004. *You are here: Personal geographies and other maps of the imagination.* New York: Princeton Architectural Press.

———. 2009. *The map as art: Contemporary artists explore geography.* New York: Princeton Architectural Press.

Harrison, Todd. 2013. "212573: NE area of Grange Park." http://murmurtoronto.ca/place.php?212573 (accessed March 11, 2013).

———. 2006. "Space as a keyword." In *David Harvey: A critical reader,* edited by Noel Castree and Derek Gregory, 270–93. London: Blackwell.

Hattenhauer, Darryl. 1984. "The rhetoric of architecture: A semiotic approach." *Communication Quarterly* 32 (1): 71–77.

Hawthorne, Frederick W. 1988. *Gettysburg: Stories of men and monuments as told by battlefield guides.* Gettysburg, PA: Association of Licensed Battlefield Guides.

Heat-Moon, William Least. 1991. *PrairyErth (a deep map).* Boston: Houghton-Mifflin.

Heftman, Yosef. 1940. "Weekly conversation." *HaBoker.* November 27 (Hebrew).

Heise, Ursula K. 2005. "Eco-narratives." 2005. In *Routledge encyclopedia of narrative theory,* edited by David Hermann, Manfred Jahn, and Marie-Laure Ryan, 129–30. London: Routledge.

Hendrix, Harald. 2008. *Writers' houses and the making of memory.* New York: Routledge.

Herbet, Aurélie, and Edith Magnan. 2011. "Dispositifs et fictions géographiques: Une experience immersive?" Paper presented at the conference Fictions, immersions et univers virtuels, Paris. April 27.

Herman, David. 2002. *Story logic: Problems and possibilities of narrative.* Lincoln: University of Nebraska Press.

———, ed. 2003. *Narrative theory and the cognitive sciences.* Stanford, CA: Center for the Study of Language and Information.

———. 2009. *Basic elements of narrative.* Malden, MA: Wiley-Blackwell.

———. 2012. "Formal models in narrative analysis." In *Circles disturbed: The interplay of narrative and mathematics,* edited by Apostolos Doxiadis and Barry Mazur, 447–80. Princeton, NJ: Princeton University Press.

———. 2013. *Storytelling and the sciences of mind.* Cambridge, MA: MIT Press.

Herrnstein Smith, Barbara. 1968. *Poetic closure: A study in how poems end.* Chicago: University of Chicago Press.

Holden, Gregg. 2011. *Literary Chicago: A book lover's tour of the Windy City.* Chicago: Lake Claremont Press.

Hollerbach, Eugen. 2004. "Legendes rhenanes: Le Rhin raconte ses légendes." [Rhine legends: Father Rhine tells his sagas.] Pulheim, Germany: Rahmel-Verlag.

Holocaust Memorial Center. 2013. http://www.hdke.hu/en/building/exhibition-hall (accessed February 4, 2013).

Homer. *The Odyssey.* Translated by Robert Fagles. New York: Penguin Books, 1997.

Hones, Sheila. 2008. "Text as it happens: Literary geography." *Geography Compass* 2 (5): 1301–17.

Hooper-Greenhill, Eilean, ed. 1995. *Museum, media, message.* New York: Routledge.

Horandt, A., and G. Horn. 1970. *Sie ehrten Lenin, indem sie Häuser bauten: Vom Werden und Wachsen des Leninplatzes.* [They honored Lenin by building houses: On the development and growth of Lenin Square.] Berlin: Bezirksvorstand der Gesellschaft für Deutsch-Sowjetische Freundschaft in der Hauptstadt der DDR.

Hoskins, Gareth. 2007. "Materialising memory at Angel Island Immigration Station, San Francisco." *Environment and Planning A* 39: 437–55.

Houellebecq, Michel. 2010. *La carte et le territoire.* Paris: Flammarion.

Hubbard, Phil, and Rob Kitchin. 2011. *Key thinkers of space and place.* 2nd ed. Los Angeles: Sage.

Huizinga, Johan. 1950. *Homo ludens: A study of the play-element in culture.* Boston: Beacon Press.

In Flanders Fields Museum. 2013. http://www.inflandersfields.be/en/discover (accessed February 4, 2013).

Iser, Wolfgang. 1980. "The reading process." In *Reader-response criticism: From formalism to post-structuralism,* edited by Jane P. Tompkins, 50–69. Baltimore: Johns Hopkins University Press.

Jacob, Christian. 2006 [1992]. *The sovereign map: Theoretical approaches in cartography through history.* Edited by Edward H. Dahl. Translated by Tom Conley. Chicago: University of Chicago Press.

James, Henry. 1880. *Washington Square.* New York: Harper and Brothers.

Jameson, Fredric. 1988. "Cognitive mapping." In *Marxism and the interpretation of culture,* edited by N. Cory and L. Grossberg, 347–60. Urbana: University of Illinois Press.

———. 1991. *Postmodernism; or, the cultural logic of late capitalism.* Durham, NC: Duke University Press.

Jenkins, Henry. 2004. "Game design as narrative architecture." In *First person: New media as story, performance, and game,* edited by Noah Wardrip-Fruin and Pat Harrigan, 118–30. Cambridge, MA: MIT Press.

———. 2006. *Convergence culture: Where old and new media collide.* New York: New York University Press.

Joyce, James. 1914. "Eveline." http://www.online-literature.com/james_joyce/959/ (accessed April 3, 2015).

———. 1993 [1916]. *A portrait of the artist as a young man.* New York: Garland.

Juul, Jesper. 2005. *Half-real: Video games between real rules and fictional worlds.* Cambridge, MA: MIT Press.

———. 2014. "On absent carrot sticks: The level of abstraction in video games." In *Storyworlds across media: Toward a media-conscious narratology,* edited by Marie-Laure Ryan and Jan-Noël Thon, 173–92. Lincoln: University of Nebraska Press.

Kafka, Franz. 1978. *The trial.* Translated by Willa and Edwin Muir. New York: Knopf.

Kaplan, Frédéric. 2009. *La métamorphose des objets.* Limoges, France: FYP éditions.

Karp, Ivan. 1991. "Culture and representation." In *Exhibition cultures: The poetics and politics of museum display*, edited by Ivan Karp and Steven D. Lavine, 11–24. Washington, DC: Smithsonian Institution Press.

Katriel, Tamar. 1997. *Performing the past: A study of Israeli settlement museums*. Mahwah, NJ: Lawrence Erlbaum.

Kaufman, Polly W., Jean Gibran, Sylvia McDowell, and Mary H. Smoyer. 2006. *Boston women's heritage trail: Seven self-guided walks through four centuries of Boston women's history*. 3rd ed., revised. Jamaica Plain, MA: Boston Women's Heritage Trail.

Kelly, Lynda. 2010. "The role of narrative in museum exhibitions." *Australian Museum*. http://australianmuseum.net.au/BlogPost/Audience-Research-Blog/The-role-of-narrative-in-museum-exhibitions (accessed February 5, 2013).

Kermode, Frank. 1967. "The sense of ending: Studies in the theory of fiction." New York: Oxford University Press.

Kerouac, Jack. 1997 [1957]. *On the road*. New York: Viking.

Kirschenblatt-Gimblett, B. 1998. *Destination culture: Tourism, museums, heritage*, Berkeley: University of California Press.

Kitchin, Rob, and James Kneale, eds. 2002. *Lost in space: Geographies of science fiction*. New York: Continuum.

Klanten, Robert, Nicholas Bourquin, Sven Ehmann, F. van Heerden, and Thibaud Tissot, eds. 2008. *Data flow: Visualising information in graphic design*. Berlin: Gestalten.

Klanten, Robert, Sven Ehmann, and Floyd Schulze, eds. 2011. *Visual storytelling: Inspiring a new visual language*. Berlin: Gestalten.

Klevjer, Rune. 2002. "In defence of cut scenes." Proceedings of Computer Games and Digital Cultures Conference, edited by Frans Mäyrä, 191–202. Tampere, Finland: Tampere University Press.

Krzywinska, Tanya. 2008. "World creation and lore: World of Warcraft as rich text." *Digital culture, play and identity*, edited by Hilde G. Corneliussen and Jill Walker Rettberg, 123–41. Cambridge, MA: MIT Press.

Kwan, Mei-Po, and Guoxiang Ding. 2008. "Geo-Narrative: Extending geographic information systems for narrative analysis in qualitative and mixed-method research. *Professional Geographer* 60 (4): 443–65.

Labitzke, Nicole. 2013. "Das Alternate Reality Game." In *Medien, Erzählen, Gesellschaft. Transmediales Erzählen im Zeitalter des Medienkonvergenz*, edited by Karl N. Renner, Dagmar von Hoff, and Matthias Klings, 191–214. Berlin: De Gruyter.

Labov, William, and Joshua Waletsky. 1973. *Language in the inner city: Studies in the Black English vernacular*. Philadelphia: University of Pennsylvania Press.

Lakoff, George, and Mark Johnson. 1980. *Metaphors we live by*. Chicago: University of Chicago Press.

Lamme, Ary J., III. 1989. *America's historic landscapes: Community power and the preservation of four national historic sites*. Knoxville: University of Tennessee Press.

Lando, Fabio. 1996. "Fact and fiction: Geography and literature." *GeoJournal* 38 (1): 3–18.

Larsen, Reif. 2009. *The Selected works of T. J. Spivet*. London: Penguin Books.

Lefebvre, Henri. 1991 [1974]. *The production of space*. Translated by Donald Nicholson-Smith. London: Blackwell.

Leib, Jonathan. 2006. "The witting autobiography of Richmond, Virginia: Arthur Ashe, the Civil War, and Monument Avenue's racialized landscape." In *Landscape and race in the United States,* edited by Richard H. Schein, 187–211. New York: Routledge.

Lessing, Gotthold Ephraim. 1984 [1766]. *Laocoön: An essay on the limits of painting and poetry.* Translated with introduction by Edward A. McCormick. Baltimore: Johns Hopkins University Press.

Light, Duncan. 2004. "Street names in Bucharest, 1990–1997: Exploring the modern historical geographies of post-socialist change." *Journal of Historical Geography* 30: 154–72.

Light, Duncan, and Craig Young. 2014. "Habit, memory, and the persistence of socialist-era street names in postsocialist Bucharest, Romania." *Annals of the Association of American geographers* 104 (3): 668–85.

Linde, Charlotte, and William Labov. 1975. "Spatial networks as a site for the study of language and thought." *Language* 51 (4): 924–39.

Linenthal, Edward T. 1991. *Sacred ground: Americans and their battlefields.* Urbana: University of Illinois Press.

———. 1995. *Preserving memory: The struggle to create America's Holocaust Museum.* Harmondsworth, UK: Penguin.

Linenthal, Edward T., and Tom Engelhardt, eds. 1996. *History wars: The Enola Gay and other battles for the American past.* New York: Metropolitan Books.

Literary Atlas of Europe. 2013. http://www.literaturatlas.eu/en/2012/01/02/the-geographie-of-fiction-the-project-a-literary-atlas-of-europe/ (accessed December 5, 2013).

Loewy,—. 1927. Protocol, meeting of Berlin's municipal assembly, session on April 7.

Lotman, Jurij M. 1970. *The structure of the artistic text.* Translated by G. Lenhoff and R. Vroon. Ann Arbor: University of Michigan Press, 1977.

Lowe, Donald M. 1982. *History of bourgeois perception.* Chicago: University of Chicago Press.

Lukinbeal, Chris, and Stefan Zimmermann, eds. 2008. *The geography of cinema: A cinematic world.* Stuttgart: Franz Steiner Verlag.

Lutwack, Leonard. 1984. *The role of place in literature.* Syracuse, NY: Syracuse University Press.

Lutz, Catherine A., and Jane L. Collins. 1993. *Reading National Geographic.* Chicago: University of Chicago Press.

Lynch, Kevin. 1960. *The image of the city.* Cambridge, MA: MIT Press.

Macleod, Suzanne, ed. 2005. *Reshaping museum space: Architecture, design, exhibitions.* New York: Routledge.

Malraux, André. 1970. *Antimemoirs.* Translated by Terence Kilmartin. Harmondsworth: Penguin.

Macleod, Suzanne, Laura Hanks, and Jonathan Hale, eds. 2012. *Museum making: Narratives, architectures, exhibitions.* New York: Routledge.

Mallory, William E., and Paul Simpson-Housley, eds. 1987. *Geography and literature: A meetings of the disciplines.* Syracuse, NY: Syracuse University Press.

Mann, Thomas. 1961 [1901]. *Buddenbrooks.* Translated by H. T. Love-Porter. New York: Vintage Books.

Marcus, Alan S., Jeremy D. Stoddard, and Walter Woodward. 2012. *Teaching history with museums: Strategies for K-12 social studies.* New York: Routledge.

Marcuse, Harold. 2001. *Legacies of Dachau: The uses and abuses of a concentration camp, 1933–2001.* New York: Cambridge University Press.

Marschark, Mark, and Cesare Cornoldi. 1991. "Imagery and verbal memory." In *Imagery and cognition*, edited by C. Cornoldi and M. A. McDaniel, 133–82. New York: Springer.

Marstine, Janet, ed. 2006. *New museum theory and practice: An introduction*. Malden, MA: Blackwell.

McAuley, Gay. 1999. *Space in performance: Making meaning in the theatre*. Ann Arbor: University of Michigan Press.

McCloud, Scott. 2000. *Reinventing comics: How imagination and technology are revolutionizing an art form*. New York: Perennial.

McDiarmid, Angus. 2013. "Carnock." http://www.flickr.com/photos/angusmcdiarmid/4557625632/ (accessed March 9, 2013; on March 10, 2015, the map was still available, but the annotations had disappeared).

McGonigal, Jane. 2011. *Reality is broken*. London: Penguin.

Mehigan, Tim, and Alan Corkhill, eds. 2013. *Raumlektüren: Der Spatial Turn und die Literatur der Moderne*. Bielefeld, Germany: Transcript.

Memory Maps. 2013. http://www.vam.ac.uk/page/m/memory-maps/ (accessed March 9, 2013; in 2015 the site had vastly changed).

Mercedes-Benz Museum. 2014. http://barrierefrei.mercedes-benz-classic.com/en/museum/museum.php (accessed June 14, 2014).

Mikkonen, Kai. 2007. "The 'narrative is travel' metaphor: Between spatial sequence and open consequence." *Narrative* 15 (3): 286–305.

Mitchell, David. 2012 [2004]. *Cloud atlas*. New York: Random House.

Mitchell, Peta. 2008. *Cartographic strategies of postmodernity: The figure of the map in contemporary theory and fiction*. London: Routledge.

Moore, John Robert. 1941. "The geography of *Gulliver's travels*." *The Journal of English and Germanic Philology* 40 (2): 214–28.

Moretti, Franco. 1998. *Atlas of the European novel, 1800–1900*. London: Verso.

———. 2005. *Graphs, maps, trees: Abstract models for literary theory*. London: Verso.

Morgan, Bill. 2003. *Literary landmarks of New York: The book lover's guide to the homes and haunts of world famous writers*. New York: Universe.

Morrow, Daniel, Gordon Bower, and Steven Greenspan. 1989. "Updating situation models during narrative comprehension." *Journal of Memory and Language* 28: 292–312.

Mosher, Harold F. 1991. "Towards a poetics of descriptized narration." *Poetics Today* 12 (3): 425–45.

Mounin, George. 1980. "The semiology of orientation in urban space." *Current Anthropology* 21 (4): 491–501.

Mssv. 2008. "Stories, games and the 21 steps." http://mssv.net/2008/03/18/stories-games-and-the-21-steps/ (accessed March 9, 2015).

Muehrcke, Phillip C., and Juliana O. Muehrcke. 1974. "Maps in literature." *Geographical Review* 64 (3): 317–37.

[murmur] 2013. http://murmurtoronto.ca/about.php (accessed January 1, 2013).

Murray, Janet. 1997. *Hamlet on the holodeck: The future of narrative in cyberspace*. New York: Free Press.

———. 2011. *Inventing the medium: Principles of interaction design as cultural practice*. Cambridge, MA: MIT Press.

Muschamp, Herbert. 1993. "Architecture view: Shaping a monument to memory." *New York Times*. April 11.

Museum of Communism. 2013. http://www.muzeumkomunismu.cz/ (accessed July 2, 2014).

Nabokov, Valdimir. 1980. *Lectures on literature*. Edited by Fredson Bowers, introduction by John Updike. New York: Harcourt Brace Jovanovich.

Nagel, Thomas. 1989. *The view from nowhere*. Oxford: Oxford University Press.

National Association for Interpretation. 2012. http://www.interpnet.com/ (accessed December 31, 2012).

National Library Board Singapore. 2012. "Inspiring stories promote discovery of Singapore's history and heritage at the National Library's stories behind Singapore streets exhibition." http://en.eistudy.com/news/20120811/110479.html (accessed July 2, 2014).

National Museum of American Jewish History. 2013. http://www.nmajh.org/ (accessed February 4, 2013).

National Museum of the American Indian. 2013. http://nmai.si.edu/visit/washington/architecture-landscape/ (accessed February 4, 2013).

National Park Service, U.S. Department of the Interior. 2005. *The Mormon pioneer trail across Iowa in 1846: Auto tour route interpretive guide*. Salt Lake City: National Park Service, National Trails System Office.

———. 2013a. *Bunker Hill*. Harpers Ferry, WV: National Park Service.

———. 2013b. *Gettysburg National Military Park Pennsylvania*. Harpers Ferry, WV: National Park Service.

Nell, Victor. 1988. *Lost in a book: The psychology of reading for pleasure*. New Haven, CT: Yale University Press.

Neues Deutschland. 1970. "Symbol der kraft und des sieges der ideen Lenins" [Symbol of power and victory of Lenin's ideas] https://www.nd-archiv.de/artikel/768605.symbol-der-kraft-und-des-sieges-der-ideen-lenins.html (accessed December 5, 2013).

Neues Museum. 2013. http://www.neues-museum.de/ausstellung.php (accessed February 4).

Nitsche, Michael. 2008. *Video game spaces: Image, play and structure in 3D worlds*. Cambridge, MA: MIT Press.

Norwood, Vera, and Janice Monk, eds. 1987. *The desert is no lady: Southwestern landscapes in women's writing and art*. New Haven, CT: Yale University Press.

Offen, Karl. 2013. "Historical geography II: Digital imaginations." *Progress in Human Geography* 37 (4): 564–77.

Olson, Lester C., Cara A. Finnegan, and Diane S. Hope, eds. 2008. *Visual rhetoric: A reader in communication and American culture*. Los Angeles: Sage.

Ottomeyer, Hans. 2009. "Vorwort." In *Deutsche Geschichte in Bildern und Zeugnissen*, edited by Hans Ottomeyer and Hans-Jörg Czech, 5–7. Munich: Minerva.

Padrón, Richard. 2007. "Mapping imaginary worlds." In *Maps: Finding our place in the world*, edited by James R. Akerman and Rovert W. Karrow Jr., 255–87. Chicago: University of Chicago Press.

Page, Ruth. 2011. *Stories and social media: Identities and interaction*. London: Routledge.

Paivio, Allan. 1986. *Mental representations: A dual coding approach*. New York: Oxford University Press.

Palonen, Emilia. 2008. "The city-text in post-communist Budapest: Street names, memorials, and the politics of commemoration." *GeoJournal* 73 (3): 219–30.

Pavel, Thomas. 1986. *Fictional worlds*. Cambridge, MA: Harvard University Press.

Pearce, Celia. 2009. *Communities of play: Emergent cultures in multiplayer games and virtual worlds*. Cambridge, MA: MIT Press.

Pearce, Margaret W. 2008. "Framing the days: Place and narrative in cartography." *Cartography and Geographic Information Science* 35 (1): 17–32.

Pearson, Joseph. 2010. "Nazi victims and stumbling blocks to memory." The Needle: Sharp on Berlin. http://needleberlin.com/2010/08/23/nazi-victims-and-stumbling-blocks-to-memory/ (accessed December 3, 2013).

Perec, Georges. 1975. *Tentative d'épuisement d'un lieu parisien* [An attempt at exhausting a place in Paris]. Paris: Christian Bourgeois.

Piatti, Barbara. 2012. "Vom Text zur Karte: Literaturkartographie als Ideengenerator. [From text to map: Literary cartography as idea generator.] In *Kartographisches Denken* [Cartographic thinking], edited by Christian Reder, 270–79. Berlin: Walter de Gruyter. http://www.literaturatlas.eu/2012/08/30/literaturkartographie-als-ideengenerator/ (accessed December 5, 2013).

Piatti, Barbara, Hans Rudolf Bär, Anne-Kathrin Reuschel, and Lorenz Hurni. 2008. "Die Geographie der Fiktion: Das Project 'ein literarischer Atlas Europas.'" [The geography of fiction: The literary atlas of Europe project.] *Kartographische Nachrichten* 58 (6): 287–94.

Piatti, Barbara, Hans Rudolf Bär, Anne-Kathrin Reuschel, Lorenz Hurni, and William Cartwright. 2009. "Mapping literature: Toward a geography of fiction." In *Cartography and art*, edited by William Cartwright, Georg Gartner, and Antje Lehn, 177–92. Berlin: Springer. ftp://cartography.ch/pub/pub_pdf/2009_Piatti_Geography_of_Fiction.pdf (accessed December 5, 2013).

Pitt Rivers Musuem. 2013. Introduction to the displays. http://www.prm.ox.ac.uk/pittrivers.html (accessed February 4, 2013).

Pocock, Douglas C. D. 1981a. *Humanistic geography and literature: Essays on the experience of place*. Totowa, NJ: Barnes and Noble.

———. 1981b. "Place and the novelist." *Transactions of the Institute of British Geographers*, New Series 6: 337–47.

———. 1988. "Geography and literature." *Progress in Human Geography* 12 (1): 87–102.

Potteiger, Matthew, and Jamie Purinton. 1998. *Landscape narratives: Design practices for telling stories*. New York: John Wiley.

Powell, Jessica. 2006. *Literary Paris: A guide*. New York: Little Bookroom.

Preziosi, Donald. 1979. *The semiotics of the built environment: An introduction to architectonic analysis*. Bloomington: Indiana University Press.

Price, Patricia L. 2004. *Dry place: Landscapes of belonging and exclusion*. Minneapolis: University of Minnesota Press.

———. 2010. "Cultural geography and the stories we tell ourselves." *Cultural Geographies* 17 (2): 203–10.

Prieto, Eric. 2013. *Literature, geography and the postmodern poetics of place*. New York: Palgrave Macmillan.

Prince, Gerald. 1987. *A dictionary of narratology*. Lincoln: University of Nebraska Press.

———. 1988. The disnarrated. *Style* 22 (1): 1–8.

Propp, Vladimir. 1968. *Morphology of the folk tale*. Translated by L. Scott, revised by A. Wagner. Austin: University of Texas Press.

Proulx, E. Annie. 1996. *Accordion crimes*. New York: Scribner.

Proust, Marcel. 1981 [1913–27]. *Remembrance of things past (A la recherche du temps perdu)*. Translated by C. K. Scott Montcrief. New York: Random House.

Pynchon, Thomas. 2004 [1997]. *Mason and Dixon*. New York: Picador.

Radford, Andrew D. 2010. *Mapping the Wessex novel: Landscape, history and the parochial in British literature, 1870–1940*. New York: Continuum.

Raento, Pauliina, and Cameron J. Watson. 2000. "Gernika, Guernica, Guernica?: Contested meanings of a Basque place. *Political Geography* 19: 707–36.

Ravelli, Louise J. 2006. *Museum texts: Communication frameworks*. New York: Routledge.

The Red Violin. 1999. DVD. Directed by François Girard. Santa Monica, CA: Lionsgate.

"Redrawing the map of Europe." 2010. *The Economist*. http://www.economist.com/node/16003661 (last accessed April 2, 2015).

Regier, Alexander. 2010. The magic of the corner: Walter Benjamin and street names. *Germanic Review* 85: 189–204.

Rehabilitation Department Unit for the Commemoration of Fallen Soldiers, Ministry of Defense, State of Israel. 2003. *Mount Herzl military cemetery visitors' trail*. Tel Aviv: Rehabilitation Department Unit for the Commemoration of Fallen Soldiers, Ministry of Defense, State of Israel.

———. 2004. *The interconnecting trail walk*. Tel Aviv: Rehabilitation Department Unit for the Commemoration of Fallen Soldiers, Ministry of Defense, State of Israel.

Rendell, Ruth. 2012. *The vault*. London: Arrow Books.

"The revenge of geography." 2003. *The Economist*. March 15: 19–22. http://www.economist.com/node/1620794 (accessed March 9, 2015).

Richardson, Alan. 2010. *The neural sublime: Cognitive theories and romantic texts*. Baltimore: Johns Hopkins University Press.

Ricoeur, Paul. 1981. "Narrative time." In *On narrative*, edited by W. J. T. Mitchell, 165–86. Chicago: University of Chicago Press.

Rimmon-Kenan, Shlomith. 1983. *Narrative fiction: Contemporary poetics*. London: Routledge.

Robbe-Grillet, Alain. 1963. *Pour un nouveau roman*. Paris: Gallimard, coll. Idées.

———. 1981 [1957]. *Jealousy*. Translated by Richard Howard. New York: Grove Press.

Robie House Interior Restoration Project. 2013. http://gowright.org/robie/ (accessed January 1, 2013).

Rose-Redwood, Reuben. 2008a. "From number to name: Symbolic capital, places of memory, and the politics of street renaming in New York City." *Social & Cultural Geography* 9: 431–52.

———. 2008b. "Sixth Avenue is now a memory: Regimes of spatial inscription and the performative limits of the official city-text." *Political Geography* 27: 875–94.

Rose-Redwood, Reuben, Derek H. Alderman, and Maoz Azaryahu. 2010. "Geographies of toponymic inscriptions: New directions in critical place-names studies." *Progress in Human Geography* 34: 453–70.

Rose-Redwood, Reuben and Derek H. Alderman. 2011. "Critical Interventions in Political Toponymy." *ACME: An International E-Journal for Critical Geographies* 10: 1–6.

Ross, Michael. 2003. *The Jewish friendship trail: Guidebook to Jewish Boston history sites*. 2nd ed. Belmont, MA: BostonWalks Publishing.

Rounds, Jay. 2002. "Storytelling in science exhibits." *Exhibitionist* 21 (2): 40–43.

Rubenstein, Mary Jane. 2014. *Worlds without end: The many lives of the multiverse.* New York: Columbia University Press.

Russell, Alison. 2000. *Crossing boundaries: Postmodern travel literature.* New York: Palgrave.

Ruston, Scott. 2010. Storyworlds on the move: Mobile media and their implications for narrative. *Storyworlds: A Journal of Narrative Studies* 2 (1): 101–19.

Ryan, John, George Dunford, and Simon Sellars. 2006. *Micronations: The Lonely Planet guide to home-made nations.* London: Lonely Planet Publications.

Ryan, Marie-Laure. 1991. *Possible worlds, artificial intelligence and narrative theory.* Bloomington: University of Indiana Press.

———. 2001. *Narrative as virtual reality.* Baltimore: Johns Hopkins University Press.

———. 2004a. "Cyberspace, cybertexts, cybermaps." *Dichtung-Digital: Journal für Digitale Ästhetik* 31. http://www.dichtung-digital.org/2004/1-Ryan.htm (accessed March 9, 2015).

———. 2006. *Avatars of story.* Minneapolis: University of Minnesota Press.

———. 2007. "Diagramming narrative." *Semiotica* 165 (1–4): 12–40.

———. 2009. "Space." In *Handbook of narratology,* edited by Peter Hühn, John Pier, Wolf Schmid, and Jörg Schönert, 420–33. Berlin: Walter de Gruyter.

———. 2011. "Peeling the interactive onion: Layers of user participation in digital narrative texts." In *New narratives: Stories and storytelling in the digital age,* edited by Ruth Page and Bronwen Thomas, 35–62. Lincoln: University of Nebraska Press.

Said, Edward. 1975. *Beginnings: Intentions and methods.* New York: Basic Books.

Saitta, Dean J., Mark Walker, and Paul Reckner. 2006. "Battlefields of class conflict: Ludlow then and now." *Journal of Conflict Archaeology* 1 (1): 197–213.

Samuel, Raphael. 1994. *Theatres of memory,* Vol. 1. London: Verso.

Sandweiss, Martha A. 1987. "Laura Gilpin and the tradition of American landscape painting." In *The desert is no lady: Southwestern landscapes in women's writing and art,* edited by Vera Norwood and Janice Monk, 62–73. New Haven, CT: Yale University Press.

Saunders, Angharad. 2010. "Literary geography: Reforging the connections." *Progress in Human Geography* 34 (4): 436–52.

———. 2013. "The spatial event of writing: John Galsworthy and the creation of *Fraternity.*" *Cultural Geographies* 20 (3): 285–98.

Schlichtmann, Hansgeorg. 1999a. "Cartosemiotics." In *Semiotics encyclopedia online,* edited by Paul Bouissac. http://www.semioticon.com/seo/C/cartosemiotics.html (accessed June 27, 2012).

———. 1999b. "Map semiotics around the world." Paper presented at the annual meeting for the International Cartographic Association, Ottawa, Canada.

Schneider, Andrea Kupfer. 1998. *Creating the Musée d'Orsay: The politics of culture in France.* University Park: Pennsylvania State University Press.

Schneider, Ralph. 2001. "Toward a cognitive theory of literary character: The dynamics of mental-model construction." *Style* 35 (4): 607–40.

Schulten, Susan. 2001. *The geographical imagination in America, 1880–1950.* Chicago: University of Chicago Press.

Sebald, W. G. 1996. *The emigrants.* Translated by Michael Hulse. New York: New Directions.

Segel, Edward, and Jeffrey Heer. 2010. "Narrative visualization: Telling stories with data." *IEEE Transactions on Visualization & Computer Graphics* 16 (6): 1139–48.

Serrell, Beverly. 1996. *Exhibit labels: An interpretive approach*. Walnut Creek, CA: AltaMira Press.

Sherman, Daniel J., 1995. "Objects of memory: History and narrative in French war museums." *French Historical Studies* 19 (1): 49–74.

Shortridge, James R. 1991. "The concept of the place-defining novel in American popular culture." *Professional Geographer* 43 (3): 280–91.

Speer, Nicole K., Jeremy R. Reynolds, Kheena M. Swallow, and Jeffrey M. Zacks. 2009. "Reading stories activates neural representations of perceptual and motor experiences." *Psychological Science* 20: 989–99.

Spielvogel, J. Christian. 2013. *Interpreting sacred ground: The rhetoric of national Civil War parks and battlefields*. Tuscaloosa: University of Alabama Press.

Stadtkreis Mannheim. 1945. "Umbenennung von Straßen, Plätze und Schulen." *Military Government Gazette* 15, July 21. Stadtkreis Mannheim, Militärische Regierung.

Stafford, Barbara. 1984. *Voyage into substance: Art, science, nature, and the illustrated travel account, 1760–1840*. Cambridge, MA: MIT Press.

Stangl, Paul. 2010. "Locating protest in public space: One year in San Francisco and Los Angeles." *California Geographer* 50: 37–57.

Stanzel, Franz K. 1984 [1979]. *A theory of narrative*. Translated by Charlotte Goedsche. Cambridge: Cambridge University Press.

Stein, Sabine, and Harry Stein. 1993. *Buchenwald: A tour of the memorial site*. Weimar, Germany: Buchenwald Memorial.

Steiner, Wendy. 2004. "Pictorial narrativity." In *Narrative across media: The languages of storytelling*, edited by Marie-Laure Ryan, 145–77. Lincoln: University of Nebraska Press.

Stevenson, Robert Louis. 2001. *Treasure island*. Introduction by David Cordingly. New York: Modern Library.

Stewart, George Rippey. 1975. *Names on the globe*. New York: Oxford University Press.

Stiebel, G. 2000. *Masada national park*. Jerusalem: Israel Nature and Parks Authority.

Stockhammer, Robert. 2007. *Kartierung der Erde: Macht und Lust in Karten und Literatur*. Munich: Wilhelm Fink Verlag.

Studio Daniel Libeskind. 2013. http://daniel-libeskind.com/projects/imperial-war-museum-north (accessed February 4, 2013)

Stump, Roger W. 1988. "Toponymic commemoration of national figures: The cases of Kennedy and King." *Names* 36: 203–16.

Swift, Jonathan. 2001. *Gulliver's travels*. London: Penguin Books.

Tagliabue, John. 2011. "Both hero and traitor, but no longer on the map." *New York Times*. January 3: A8.

Tally, Robert T., Jr., ed. 2011. *Geocritical explorations: Space, place, and mapping in literary and cultural studies*. New York: Palgrave Macmillan.

———. 2013. *Spatiality: The new critical idiom*. New York: Routledge.

Theban Mapping Project. 2013. http://www.thebanmappingproject.com/ (accessed January 1, 2013).

Till, Karen. 1999. "Staging the past: Landscape designs, cultural identity and erinnerungspolitik at Berlin's Neue Wache." *Ecumene* 6 (3): 251–83.

Tinderbox. 2010. Locative hypertext: Project [murmur]. http://www.eastgate.com/locative/ #item_17 (accessed March 11, 2013).

Todorov, Tzvetan. 1969. *Grammaire du Décameron*. The Hague: Mouton.

Tolman, Edward. 1948. "Cognitive maps in rats and men." *Psychological Review* 55 (4): 189–208.

Tretter, Eliot. 2011. "The power of naming: The toponymic geographies of commemorated African-Americans." *Professional Geographer* 63 (1): 34–54.

Trubek, Anne. 2011. *A skeptic's guide to writers' houses*. Philadelphia: University of Pennsylvania Press.

Tuan, Yi-Fu. 1975. "Images and mental maps." *Annals of the Association of American Geographers* 65 (2): 205–13.

———. 1977. *Space and place: The perspective of experience*. Minneapolis: University of Minnesota Press.

———. 2013 [1979]. *Landscapes of fear*. Minneapolis: University of Minnesota Press.

Tufte, Edward R. 1997. *Visual explanations: Images and quantities, evidence and narrative*. Cheshire, CT: Graphics Press.

Turner, Mark. 1996. *The literary mind*. New York: Oxford University Press.

Tversky, Barbara. 1991. "Spatial mental models." *Psychology of Learning and Motivation* 27: 109–46.

———. 1996. "Spatial perspective in descriptions." In *Language and Space*, edited by P. Bloom, M. Peterson, L. Nadel, and M. Garrett, 463–92. Cambridge, MA: MIT Press.

Urry, John. 2002. *The tourist gaze*. 2nd ed. Thousand Oaks, CA: Sage.

U.S. Holocaust Memorial Museum. 2013. http://www.ushmm.org/museum/a_and_a/ (accessed February 4, 2013).

Vermeule, Blakey. 2011. *Why do we care about literary characters?* Baltimore: Johns Hopkins University Press.

Village Homes. 2013. "How our streets got their names." http://www.villagehomesdavis.org/public/about/street_names (accessed July 2, 2014).

Virtual Gettysburg. 2013. http://www.virtualgettysburg.com/ (accessed January 1, 2013).

Visual Travel Tours. 2013. http://visualtraveltours.com/ (accessed January 1, 2013).

Walking Papers Media. 2013. http://walkingpapersmedia.com/ (accessed January 1, 2013).

Walton, Kendall. 1990. *Mimesis as make-believe: On the foundations of the representational arts*. Cambridge, MA: Harvard University Press.

Weinberg, Jeshajahu, and Rina Elieli. 1995. *The Holocaust Museum in Washington*. New York: Rizzoli.

Weissberg, Liliane. 2001. "In plain sight." In *Visual culture and the Holocaust*, edited by Barbie Zelizer, 13–27. New Brunswick, NJ: Rutgers University Press.

Welter, Volker M. 2010. "Museum architecture and gallery design." In *Encyclopedia of library and information sciences*, 3rd ed., edited by Marcia J. Bates and Mary Niles Maack, 3689–3701. Boca Raton, FL: CRC Press/Taylor and Francis.

Wertheim, Margaret. 1999. *The pearly gates of cyberspace: A history of space from Dante to the Internet*. New York: Norton.

Westphal, Bertrand. 2011. *Geocriticism: Real and fictional spaces*. Translated by Robert T. Tally Jr. New York: Palgrave Macmillan.

White, Hayden. 1981. "The value of narrativity in the representation of reality." In *On narrative*, edited by W. J. T. Mitchell, 1–24. Chicago: University of Chicago Press.

Wilken, Rowan, and Gerard Goggin, eds. 2015. *Locative media*. New York: Routledge.

Witcomb, Andrea. 2003. *Re-imagining the museum: Beyond the mausoleum*. New York: Routledge.

Wolf, Mark J. P. 2012. *Building imaginary worlds*. London: Routledge.

Wolf, Werner. 2002. Das Problem der Narrativität in Literatur, Bildender Kunst und Musik: Ein Beitrag zu einer Intermedialen Erzähltheorie. In *Erzähltheorie transgenerisch, intermedial, interdisziplinär*, edited by Vera Nünning and Ansgar Nünning, 23–104. Trier: Wissenschafltlicher Verlag.

Wood, Denis. 1987. "Pleasure in the idea / The atlas as narrative form." *Cartographica: The International Journal for Geographic Information and Geovisualization* 24 (1): 24–45.

———. 1992. *The power of maps*. London: Routledge.

———. 2010. *Everything sings: Maps for a narrative atlas*. Los Angeles: Siglio.

Woodwards Mount Waverley. 2013. http://www.woodards.com.au/?pagecall=misc&pagemode=contactOffice&agentID=3518 (accessed July 2, 2014).

Yad Vashem, The Holocaust Martyrs' and Heroes' Remembrance Authority. 2007. *Visitors guide*. Jerusalem: Yad Vashem, The Holocaust Martyrs' and Heroes' Remembrance Authority.

Yeoh, Brenda. 1992. "Street names in colonial Singapore." *Geographical Review* 82: 313–22.

———. 1996. "Street-naming and nation-building: Toponymic inscriptions of nationhood in Singapore." *Area* 28: 298–307.

Young, James. 1993. *The texture of memory: Holocaust memorials and meaning*. New Haven, CT: Yale University Press.

———. 2000. *At memory's edge: After-images of the Holocaust in contemporary art and architecture*. New Haven, CT: Yale University Press.

Zerubavel, Yael. 1995. *Recovered roots: Collective memory and the making of Israeli national tradition*. Chicago: University of Chicago Press.

Zonn, Leo, ed. 1990. *Place images in media: Portrayal, experience, and meaning*. Savage, MD: Rowman & Littlefield.

Zoran, Gabriel. 1984. "Towards a theory of space in narrative." *Poetics Today* 5 (2): 309–36.

Zunshine, Lisa, ed. 2010. *Introduction to cognitive cultural studies*. Baltimore: Johns Hopkins University Press.

INDEX

A la Recherche du temps perdu [*Remembrance of Things Past*] (Proust), 38, 40n1
Aarseth, Espen, 104–5
Abbott, Edwin, 39
abolitionist movement, and narrative, 216
Absalom, Absalom (Faulkner), 61
Alber, Jan, 24
Alice in Wonderland (Carroll), 38, 135
alternate reality games (ARGs), 121, 132–35; and boundary fiction-reality, 135; as chaotic storytelling, 133; dissolution of magic circle, 133; and mystery stories, 133, 134; rabbit-hole, 135; riddles, 133; use of multiple media, 133; and TINAG convention, 133–34; "The Lost Ring," 135
anagnoresis, 120
Angel Island (San Francisco Bay) and political narrative, 217
Applebaum, Ralph, 192
architecture, and narrative in museum design, 13–14, 181, 183, 196–200, 203–4, 213
Arendt, Hanna, 189
Aristotle, 120
Arlington National Cemetery (Virginia), 13, 177
Art museum, 183–84
Atlas of Literature, The (Bradbury), 46

Atlas of the European Novel (Moretti), 46
Auel, Jean, 61
Augé, Marc, 22
augmented reality, 135
Austen, Jane, 47
authenticity, 182
authorship, of landscape and museum narratives, 165, 179, 216
autobiography, 2, 52, 115

Bakhtin, Mikhail, 21
Bal, Mieke, 17n1
Balzac, Honoré de, 30, 38
Barrett, Andrea, 45n2
Barthes, Roland, 17
Baudelaire, Charles, 126
Beacon Hill (Boston), and intersecting narratives, 173, 175, 174 fig. 7.5
Belgium , 73, 193, 197
Benjamin, Walter, 148
Bentham, Jeremy, 125
Berlin, 143, 145, 148–51, 155–56, 185, 191–93, 198–202, 205, 215–16, 218, 146 fig. 6.2, 149 fig. 6.4, 152 fig. 6.6, 192 fig. 8.3
Berlin Alexanderplatz (Döblin), 156
Biberkopf, Franz, 156
Bildungsroman, 32

247

Birmingham (Alabama), 161, 162 fig. 7.1, 166, 214
Bismarck, Otto von, 143, 149
Bjornson, Richard, 76
Blue Highways (Heat-Moon), 32
Bodenhamer, David 224
Bonaparte, Napoléon, 69–70, 145, 151, 165, 70 fig. 3.7
Borges, Jorge Luis, 44n1, 102
Boston, Massachusetts, 33, 155, 166, heritage trails and narrative, 173, 175, 175 fig. 7.5
Bracher, Frederick, 52
Bradbury, Malcolm, 46
British Ordnance Survey maps, 60
Bronx (New York city), 155
Buchan, John, 118
Buchenwald concentration camp (Germany), 174, 176 fig. 7.6, 180, 213, 217
Buddenbrooks (Mann), 30

Cairo Trilogy (Mahfouz), 156
Carnock (Scotland), 116–17
Carroll, Lewis, 44n1, 135
Carter, Jennifer, 183, 188
Castle, The (Kafka), 38
CAVE, 203
Certeau, Michel de, 125
Cervantes Saavedra, Miguel de, 45
Chase County (Kansas), 32–35
Chatman, Seymour, 17
Chesterton, Gilbert Keith, 155
Child, Lee, 144
Choose Your Own Adventures stories, 49
Chronicle of a Death Foretold (García Márquez), 75–94; importance of topographical layout, 78; master map, 79–80; organization of space in concentric circles, 83
chronotope, 21, 22
Churchill Museum (London), 189
cinema in the mind, 98
circulation path, 13–14, 181, 186–187, 189–91, 196, 199, 200–204
City of Memory, 115n7
city-text, 145–50, 152
civil rights movement, 148, and significance of protest sites, 214, and Birmingham, Alabama, 161, 162 fig. 7.1, 166, 215
Clarke, Samuel, 19n1
Cloud Atlas (Mitchell), 26
cognitive mapping, 10, 64, 75–100, 179, 208; conception of, 76–77; defined for chapter 4, 77; and memory, 97; and reading process, 97–99; turned into graphic maps, 95. See also mental map
collaborative writing, 15
collection-based museum, 13, 182
Collot, Michel, 208–9
Colonial Williamsburg (Virginia), 182, 213
commemoration(s), 141–43, 146, 148–50, 152–55, 159
commemorative street names, 141, 143, 144, 159
Complete Works of T. S. Spivet, The (Larsen), 45n2
computer games, cheats, 112; and emotional attachment to worlds, 113–14; *EverQuest*, 113; *Liberty City*, 113; mimetic design, 105; *Ms. PacMan*, 105–6, 106 fig. 5.1; *Myst*, 114; *Myst Online: Uru*, 114; *PacMan*, 104; *Second Life*, 109, 114; and space, 104–5, 110–11; strategic design, 105, 107, 108; *Tetris*, 104; *The Sims*, 110, 111; *World of Warcraft*, 105, 106, 107 fig. 5.2, 113 fig. 5.4, 118; as worlds, 106–7; *Zanzarah*, 107, 108 fig. 5.3. See also narrative design of computer games
Conan Doyle, Arthur, 42
Conrad, Joseph, 34
"Continuity of Parks" (Cortázar), 24
Count of Monte Christo, The (Dumas), 156
Cowan, James, 45n2
Crime and Punishment (Dostoevsky), 47
Crusoe, Robinson, 38
Cummins, Charles, 118, 118 fig.5.6
cyberspace, 101, 136
Czech Republic or Czechoslovakia, 73, 157, 158 fig. 6.7, 165, 195 fig. 8.4, 197, 202, 205

Dachau concentration camp (Germany), 217
Dampier, William, 50
Dante Alighieri, 61, 61n10
Debord, Guy, 126
Deleuze, Gilles, 43, 105, 105n2; and smooth vs. striated space, 105
Dennerlein, Katrin, 17, 26
dérive (Debord), 126
description, viewer-relative, absolute and object-relative, 84; and anchors, 84
Dicks, Bella, 179
diegetic levels, 24
digital humanities, 14, 223–24
digital media, 11, 74, 101–38, 180, 203, 220–21, 223–24; properties, 10; spatiality, 103; as way to connect narrative to physical space, 127–32
Dillard, Annie, 67n12

discourse, contrasted with narrative, 2, 84; discourse space (Chatman), 17
discovery tours, 180
disnarrated (Gerald Prince), 219
Divine Comedy (Dante), 61, 61n10
Dodge, Martin, 102
Doležel, Lubomír, 63
Don Quixote (Cervantes), 32, 47
Dong, Aixia, 129–31, 132
Dora, Veronica della, 66
Dostoevsky, Fedor, 47
double coding theory of information storage, 96
Dubliners (Joyce), 19
Dumas, Alexandre, 156
Duvert, Elizabeth, 28

Earth Children (Auel), 61
Economist, The, 73, 74 fig. 3.9
Einstein, Albert, 21
emotional conception of space, 39–43; in Kafka's *Metamorphosis,* 64
England, 20, 25, 47, 50, 64, 72, 169, 173, 186, 193, 197, 204
Eugénie Grandet (Balzac), 30
Eveline (Joyce), 8, 16, 18–23, 37, 60, 64, 212
Exhibition sequence , 13, 183, 193, 199,
Exhibition space, 13, 186, 189, 193–95, 199–203

fabula, 18n1
fantastic texts. *See* maps and mapping
Fauconnier, Gilles, 17, 35
Faulkner, William, 8, 28–29, 60–61, 61n8
Ferguson, Erika, and Mary Hagerty, 84, 96, 97, 97n7
Ferguson, Priscilla Parkhurst, 155
Feyerabend, Paul, 187
fictional geography, 20–21
Fitzgerald, Francis Scott, 63
flânerie (Baudelaire), 126
Flatland (Abbott), 39
Flaubert, Gustave, 48
fMRI imaging, 209
focalization, 20
Forster, Edward Morgan, 16
Foucault, Michel, 125
Frank, Anne, 38
Frank, Joseph, 5, 139
Franklin Roosevelt Museum (Washington, DC), 181
Franklin, Benjamin, narrative about in Philadelphia, 168
Freed, Ingo James, 198

Friedman, Susan Stanford, 17
Friel, Brian, 45n2

games, geocaching, 47; magic circle, 103, 133; table-top role-playing games, 134. *See also* computer games; gameworlds
gameworlds, 11, 108–113
García Márquez, Gabriel, 75–94
"Garden of Forking Paths, The" (Borges), 102
Gaulle, Charles de, 143, 151
Geneva, 71–73, 72 fig. 3.8
Genette, Gérard, 17, 20
geocriticism, 209–210
geographic information science (GIScience), 224
geographic information system (GIS), 223
geohumanities, 224
geo-tagging, 222
German Historical Museum (Berlin), 183, 191, 193–95, 202
German worker's movement, 151
Germany, 153–54, 175–76, 176 fig. 7.6, 192, 196, 200, 202, 210, 214, 216, 218; Nazi leaders, and regime, 149–50, 153–54, 175 fig. 7.6, 191, 201, 204
Gettysburg National Battlefield (Pennsylvania), 171, 172 fig. 7.3, 204, 213–16, 222
Gibson, William, 101
Gosh, Amitav, 61
Glass Palace, The (Gosh), 61
Goldsmith, Kenneth, 125
Google, Earth, and maps, 11, 116–119, 118 fig. 5.6, 222–23
Great Gatsby, The (Fitzgerald), 62–64, 63 fig. 3.4
Greimas, Algirdas Julien, 48
Guattari, Félix, 43, 105, 105n2; and smooth vs. striated space, 105
Guide to the Lakes (Wordsworth), 67n12
Gulliver's Travels (Swift), 9, 38, 50–54, 61n9, 78; and travel writing, 50; extradiegetic maps in, 50, 51 fig. 3.2; inconsistent geography of, 53

Hamlet, 4
Hardy, Thomas, 8
Harrison, Todd, 131–32
Harvey, David, 6, 43
Heart of Darkness (Conrad), 34
Heat Moon, William Least, 32–35
Herman, David, 16, 17, 27
Heroes Square (Budapest), 215
Herrnstein Smith, Barbara, 139, 187, 202
Herzl, Theodor, 143

Hitler, Adolf, 146, 150, 153–54
Hobbit, The (Tolkien), 156
Hogarth, William, 70
Holmes, Sherlock, 4
Holocaust History Museum (Jerusalem). *See* Yad Vashem
Holocaust Memorial Center (Budapest), 197–98
Homer, 9, 42, 84
Houellebecq, Michel, 45n2
Huizinga, Johan, 103
Human Comedy (Balzac), 38
hypertext, 102

identity discourse, 140–41
Imperial War Museum (London), 189
Imperial War Museum North (Manchester), 191, 196
Independence Hall (Philadelphia), 181
In Flanders Field Museum (Ypres/Ieper), 193, 197
Inferno (Dante), 61n10
islands, as favorite objects for the imagination, 57
Israel Defense Forces Museum (Tel Aviv), 187, 188 fig. 8.1
Israel, 55, 159, 169–70, 187, 190, 205, 151 fig. 6.5

Jameson, Fredric, and spatial turn, 2, 206; and cognitive mapping, 77
Jenkins, Henry, 108
Jerusalem, 14, 61–62, 166, 169–70, 198, 200, 203, 201 fig. 8.5
Jewish history, 189, 199–201
Jewish Museum (Berlin), 14, 192, 198, 192 fig.8.3
Johnson, Mark, 19, 35
Johnstown flood (Pennsylvania), 165
Joyce, James, 8, 16, 18–25, 26, 60–61, 64, 156. *See also* "Eveline"

Kafka, Franz, 38, 64
Kaplan, Frédéric, 137
Karp, Ivan, 204
Katriel, Tamar, 187
Kazimiroff, Theodore, 155
Kennedy, John F., in Berlin, 215, Sixth Floor Museum and Dallas, 13, 177
Kerouac, Jack, 32, 43
King, Martin Luther, Jr., 143, 148, 214
Kitchin, Rob, 102

L'Education sentimentale (Flaubert), 48
La Carte et le territoire (Houellebecq), 45n2

La Picara Justina (anonymous), 47
La Vie mode d'emploi [*Life as a User's Manual*] (Perec), 61
Labov, William, 6, 8, 27–28, 123, 130
Lakoff, George, 19, 35
landscape narrative 12–13, 160–179; authorship, 178; definition, 163; terminology, 161–62; types, 12–13, 163–77; prototypes, 166–67; examples, 161–79
Larsen, Reif, 32, 45n2
Lazarillo de Tormes (anonymous), 47
Least Heat-Moon, William, 9, 32–35
Lefebvre, Henri, 6, 43, 105
Leibniz, Gottfried, 19n1, 148
Les Trucs, 11, 121–27, 122 fig. 5.7, 127; narratives produced by players, 123–24
Libeskind, Daniel, 199–202
Lidice (Czech Republic), 205, 206 fig. 8.6
Lincoln, Abraham, 148, 215, and Gettysburg Address 215–16, memorial (Washington, DC) 215; and Springfield (Illinois), 169, 190, 202
Linde, Charlotte, 6, 8, 27–28
Literary Atlas of Europe, 211
literary geography, 7–8
literary tourism, 47
Little Bighorn Battlefield (Montana), 167, 168 fig. 7.2, 178, 180
Little House on the Prairie (Wilder), 47
locative narrative and media, 11, 47, 127–32, 135–36, 220–21
Loci mnemonic technique, 28
London, 143, 155, 159, 186, 189, 196, 209, 217
Lonely Planet guides, 59
Loper, Bert, 67
Lopez, Barry, 67n12
Lord of the Rings (Tolkien), 8, 24, 156
Lotman, Jurij, 9, 35–37
Ludlow massacre (Colorado), 165
Lusitania, R. M. S., and memorialization, 165
Luther, Martin, and locative symbolism of his ninety-five theses, 214
Lutwack, Leonard, 40n1

Macdonnell, John, 67, 69
Magna Carta, 216
Mahfouz, Naguib, 156
make-believe, 134
Mann, Thomas, 30
Mannheim (Germany), 153–54
Mányi, István, 197
Mapmaker's Dream, A (Cowan), 45n2

INDEX • 251

maps and mapping, 9–11, 15, 28, 32–36, 44–56, 58–62, 65–68, 69–72, 74–77, 80, 83, 85–89, 91, 94–100, 103, 113–25, 127, 136–37, 140, 142, 145, 147, 157, 167, 172–73, 179, 185, 204, 210–11, 213, 216, 219, 221–24; of fantastic texts, 25, 38, 210–11. *See also* cognitive mapping; narrative maps; readers' maps; storytelling through maps
Márquez, Gabriel García, 10. See also *Chronicle of a Death Foretold*
Marriage à la Mode" (Hogarth), 70
Masada (Israel), 159, 170–71, 205
Mason and Dixon (Pynchon), 45n2
master narratives, 12
Mayes, Frances, 67n12
McCloud, Scott, 74
McDiarmid, Angus (Diarmid Mogg), 116, 116 fig.5.5
McGonigal, Jane, 133
McPhee, John, 67n12
Memory Maps (web site), 11, 115–17
memory, short term vs. long term, 97–98
mental map, 9–10, 21, 29, 45, 63–64, 67, 75–77, 83, 85, 95–100
mental models of space. *See* cognitive mapping, mental maps
Mercedes-Benz-Museum (Stuttgart), 196, 204
metalepsis, 24
Metamorphosis, The (Kafka), 64, 65 fig. 3.5
micronations, 59–60
Microtruc, 121
Mikkonen, Kai, 32
Minard, Charles Joseph, 70, 70 fig. 3.7
minimal departure, principle of, 20
Mitchell, David, 26
mobile computing, 47
Moll, Herman, 50–51, 52
Moore, John Robert, 52, 53
Moretti, Franco, 46–49, 49 fig. 3.1, 223
Mormon Trail (United States.), 171, 174 fig. 7.4
[murmur], 47, 127–32, 135, 220, 130 fig. 5.8
Murray, Janet, 101, 103
Muschamp, Herbert, 198
Musée d'Orsay (Paris), 196
Museums, architecture, 13, 182, 196; and narrative, 12–13, 14, 159, 179–80, 200, 202–4, 212, 215; space, 14, 138, 180–81, 183, 186, 190
Museum of American History (Washington, DC), 1833
Museum of Communism, (Prague), 157
"My First Book" (Stevenson), 54

Nagel, Thomas, 45
namesake(s), 143, 153, 155–56, 218
narrative design of computer games, embedded narrative, 109–10; emergent narrative, 110; journey, 109; in MMORPGs, 111–13; world design, 111
narrative maps, of Dante's *Divine Comedy*, 61–62; extradiegetic, 50; genealogical relations to narrative, 59–62; immersive function, 58; of hypertext, 48–49; inserted by publisher, 61; intradiegetic, 55; of Middle Earth, 60; as part of the writing process, 60; as prop in game of make-believe, 61; of spatial context, 46–47; of spatial form, 48–49; of storyworld, 50–59; strategic function, 58; of Yoknapatawpha county, 60. See also *Gulliver's Travels*; readers' maps; storytelling through maps; *Treasure Island*
narrative, across media, 137, 210, 216; and architecture, 195, 198–99, 203; differences by media type, 2, 14, 17, 102–103, 140, 170, 177–79, 202, 210, 216, 218, 219–20; dimensionality, 4–5, 16, 46, 102, 203; experience, 11, 103, 182; future research directions, 215–24; in games, 104; in geography, 7–8, 14, 139, 206, 211; master, 12; museum, 182, 188–89, 204; performative elements, 5, 30, 60, 96, 123, 144–45, 186, 190, 208, 213, 215; political dimensions and examples, 215–16; and protest, 158, 166, 213–14; space defined, 3–4; structure, 3, 6, 12, 32, 139, 141, 148, 184–85, 191, 196–97, 202; turn 2, 13, 206; universe, 24; used in geography, 2. *See also* description; geography; narrative design of computer games; narratology; plot; point of view
narrativity, 9, 11–12, 16, 28, 35–36, 65n11, 70, 122–23, 137, 139, 141–42, 145–46, 156, 158–60, 197, 225
narratology, and geography, 2–6; future research directions, 207–11, and space, 17
National Museum of the American Indian (Washington, DC), 196
National Memorial on Vitkov Hill (Prague), 195, 195 fig. 8.4, 197, 202
Natural History Museum (London), 186
nature tours, 179; walks, 212; writing 4, 8
Nebraska, place names, 144, 156, and Mormon Trail, 173
Neues Museum (Berlin), 185
Neuromancer (Gibson), 101
new media. *See* digital media
New York, 46n4, 63, 115n7, 155–56, 173, 212, 215

New York Times, stories about street names, 154–55
Newton, Isaac, 19n1
Nibelungenlied, 210
Nitsche, Michael, 108, 108 fig. 5.3
non-places, 22

O'Casey, Sean, 155
Occupy Wall Street protest, 214
Odyssey, The (Homer), 9, 32, 38–40, 43; as prototype for sequential narrative, 166
"On Exactitude in Science" (Borges), 44n1
On the Road (Kerouac), 32, 43
Oral history, 2, 221
Owen, Charles, 66
Oxford (England), Pitt Rivers Museum, 186

Padrón, Ricardo, 54, 57
Page, Ruth, 128
Paivio, Allan, 96
palimpsest, 150
Palmach Museum (Tel Aviv), 190, 190 fig. 8.2, 202, 204
parataxis, 184, 188, 190–91, 201
Parcel 301 (Budapest), and Hungarian uprising of 1956, 162 fig. 7.1, 177
Paris, 143, 145, 148, 151, 155, 146 fig. 6.2
Parsifal (Wagner), 140
"Partial Magic in the Quixote" (Bores), 44n1
Pearce, Celia, 114
Pearce, Margaret W., 66, 69
Pearson, Joseph, 219
Perec, George, 61, 125
Philadelphia (Pennsylvania), 169, 182, 189; President's House controversy, 216–17
Piatti, Barbara, and Literary Atlas of Europe, 211–212
Pitt Rivers Museum (Oxford), 185
place, definition of 6–7; place-defining novels, 4, 8; sense of, 6–7
place names, 140–142, 158–59, 205, 211; in fiction, 19. *See also* toponyms
plot, and boundary crossing, 36; plotless texts, 36; spatial conception of, 36; and symbolism of space, 37–39
Pocock, Douglas, 8
Poe, Edgar Allan, 55, 156
point of view, 27
Portrait of the Artist as a Young Man, A (Joyce), 26
Potteiger, Matthew and landscape narrative, 163
Powell, John Wesley, 67

Prague (Czech Republic), 157, 158 fig. 6.7, 195, 195 fig. 8.4, 197, 202, 211
PrairyErth (Heat Moon), 9, 32–35
Prince, Gerald, 18n1
Project Gutenberg, 223
Proust, Marcel, 38, 40n1, 42
Prussia, generals and kings, 143, 145, 150–51, 165
Purinton, Jamie, and landscape narrative, 163
Pynchon, Thomas, 45n2

readers' maps, 62–65; and character movements, 92–93; of *Chronicle of a Death Foretold,* 85–90; and inventory of storyworld, 85–87; and mapping style, 89–92; as representation of cognitive maps, 95; and spatial relations, 87–89; and story space, 94; and symbolic meaning, 94; of *The Great Gatsby,* 62–64; of *The Metamorphosis,* 64
Reinventing Comics (McCloud), 74
Rendell, Ruth, 143
representation of space, aperspectivist, 26; and character movements, 21–22; in film, 17n1; levels of, 23–25; microlevel, 25–31; and narrative devices, 81–83; perspectivist, 26. *See also* narrative; description; setting; spatial frame; story space; storyworld; tour vs. map description
Rhine River (Germany), and *Nibelungenlied,* 210
Rimmon-Kenan, Shlomith, 17
River Guide of the Grand Canyon, 67
Robbe-Grillet, Alain, 28–29
Rockne, Knute, 33, 35
Routes and paths, in narrative, 159, 163
Rubenstein, Mary Jane, 19n1
Russell, Alison, 34
Ruston, Scott, 135
Ryan, Marie-Laure, 24

Safdie, Moshe, 200
Said, Edward, 202
Saussure, Ferdinand de, 48
screens (electronic and computer), 5
Sebald, Winfried Georg, 30–31
Selected Works of T. S. Spivet, The (Larsen), 32
Selma (Alabama), 148, 166, 214
Sendak, Maurice, 74
Servants of the Map (Barrett), 45n2
setting, 24
Shakespeare, William, street name in Chicago, 156
Sixth Floor Museum (Dallas) and assassination of John Kennedy, 13, 177

INDEX • 253

Soliloquy (Goldsmith), 125
Space, as backdrop to plot, 1, 97, 100, 207; in *Chronicle of a Death Foretold*, 77–94; chronotopic, 99; as container, 66; as context and reference for text, 4, 138, 164, 180; definitions, 6–7; and digital media, 101–37; dimensions of, 39; division into dichotomies and trichotomies, 43; everyday, 139, 219; in film and television, 219; Marxist theories of, 19; mental models of, 95–96, 98–100; of museums, exhibits, and exhibitions, 180–205; and narrative theory, 16–43, 224; as network, 18–19, 21; occupied by text, 160, 207; postmodern conceptions, 219; progression or sequence through, 69, 166–69, 177, 212; public vs. private, 22; as setting for storytelling, 213; 60, 77; and Stolpersteine, 217; as surrogate for time, 139–40, 161; symbolic meanings, 22, 209; taken by text, 4–5, 138, 160, 180; space, topographic, 99; urban, 127–32, 141, 143, 145, 147, 155, 216. *See also* emotional conception of space; representation of space; strategic conception of space
Spacing (magazine), 132
spatial arrangement, 13–14, 141, 159, 182, 184, 186–87, 190, 196, 199
spatial art, 139
spatial form of text, 5–6; dimensionality of text, 5–6, 9, 32, 48–49, 49 fig. 3.1, 102–3, 138, 181, 183, 208; of text 160–61; space taken by text, 4–5, 138, 160, 181
spatial frames, 24
spatial humanities, 14, 223–24
spatial media, 141
spatial metaphors, 16, 32, 35, 101
spatial orientation, 143, 155, 186
spatial practice (Lefebvre), 105
spatial turn, 2, 207
"Speckled Band, The" (Conan Doyle), 42
Stanzel, Franz, perspectival and aperspectival spaces, 6, 25–26
Stations of the Cross, 166–67
Stevenson, Robert Louis, and *Treasure Island*, 9, 54–59, 56 fig. 3.3
Stockhammer, Robert, 59, 60
stolpersteine [stumbling blocks], 218
story space, 24
storyline, 12–14, 109, 141, 159, 161, 173, 182–87, 189–95, 201–4, 213
storytelling, 2, 4, 5, 12; and atlases, 65–66n11; and cartographic language, 67, 69; chaotic, 133; chronological, 189, 191; cinematic, 190; in *Geneva Urbs* etching, 71; in landscape, 173, 177; through maps, 65–74; through Memory Maps, 115–17; in Minard's map of Napoleon's Russian campaign, 69–70; in "Redrawing the Map of Europe," 73–74; and museum architecture, 180, 196–200; oral, 130; on-site, 132, 136; about place, 127; and place-making 135; in *River Guide to the Grand Canyon*, 67; and stories of linear progression, 69; vs. storytelling with maps, 74; and temporal sequence, 70; in *The 21 Steps*, 117–21; use of language in, 72; toponymic, 139–59, 218; venues, vehicles and media of, 139–40, 163, 178, 179, 190, 203, 211, 219, 224; visual, 202
storyworlds, 2, 20, 24, 138, 211–12, 225
strategic conception of space, 39–43; in Kafka's *Metamorphosis*, 64
street names, as commemoration, 142–45; as city-text, 145–50; as news stories, 153–55, as literature, 155–56. *See also* toponyms
Surrealism, 126
Swift, Jonathan, 9, 50–54
Sylvie and Bruno (Carroll), 44n1

Tally, Robert T., Jr, 209
Tate Modern (London) art gallery, 196
Tel Aviv (Israel), 143–45, 147 fig. 6.3, 148, 153, 165, 187–88, 190, 202, 204, 213
temporal sequence, 9, 27, 140, 161, 163, 166, 178, 184, 202
Tentative d'épuisement d'un lieu parisien (Perec), 125
Theban mapping project, 222
Themed neighborhood, 148
Todorov, Tzvetan, 17
Tolkien, J. R. R., 8, 24, 60, 61, 156, 212
Tolman, Edward, 76
Topographie des Terrors (Berlin), 205
toponymic history, 12, 142, 146, 148–49, 152
toponyms, 11–12, 138–59, examples, 142 fig. 6.1, 146 fig. 6.2, 147 fig. 6.3, 149 fig. 6.4, 151 fig. 6.5, 152 fig 6.6, 158 fig. 6.7
Toronto (Canada), 128–32, 144
Tour, 212; ghost, 213; guided or spoken, 212–13; vs. map description on macrolevel, 31–35; on microlevel, 27–31. *See also* mental maps; cognitive mapping
tourist gaze, 179
Trafalgar Square (London), 159, 217
Translations (Friel), 45n2
transmedial texts, 211
travel literature, 4

treasure hunt, 120
Treasure Island (Stevenson), 9, 54–59, 56 fig. 3.3; genesis of, 54; lacking sense of place, 58
Tuan, Yi-Fu, 6, 41, 43, 76; and *Landscapes of Fear*, 41
Turner, Mark, 17, 35
Tversky, Barbara, 97n7
Twenty-one Steps, The (Cummins), 11, 117–121, 118 fig. 5.6, 125, 136

United States Holocaust Memorial Museum (Washington, DC), 14, 192, 198, 202
United States of America, 14, 32, 87, 143, 154, 156, 159, 167, 169, 173, 190, 217
Urban orientation, and street names, 141–43, 150
Urban space. *See* space, urban
Urry, John, 179

Velvet Revolution, 157
Vertov, Dziga, 31
Via Dolorosa (Jerusalem), 166
Vichy regime, 154
Vienna (Austria), 46, 145
virtual reality, and narrative, 136, 221, 223; and spatial immersion, 203, 221; and virtual worlds, 103

Vítkov Hill (Czech Republic), 195, 195 fig. 8.4, 197, 202

Wagner, Richard, 140, 210
Waletzky, Joshua, 123, 130
"Walking in the City" (de Certeau), 125
Wallace, Sir William, 165
Walton, Kendall, 61
Washington DC, 14, 32, 177, 182, 192, 197–98, 202–3, 215
Washington Square (New York City), 156
Washington, George, 217
Weinberg, Jeshajahu, 186
Welter, Volker, 197
Westphal, Bertrand, 209
Wilder, Laura Ingalls, 47
Wolf, Mark J. P., 60
Wood, Denis, 65n11, 66
Wordsworth, William, 67n12
world creation, 59–60
World War I, 43, 154, 193–94, 197
World War II, 35, 66, 154, 185, 201

Yad Vashem (Jerusalem), 14, 169, 197, 200–201, 200 fig. 8.5, 203
Yosemite National Park (California), 163, 213

Zoran, Gabriel, 21, 24, 98, 99
Zuran Hill (Czech Republic), 165

THEORY AND INTERPRETATION OF NARRATIVE
James Phelan, Peter J. Rabinowitz, and Robyn Warhol, Series Editors

Because the series editors believe that the most significant work in narrative studies today contributes both to our knowledge of specific narratives and to our understanding of narrative in general, studies in the series typically offer interpretations of individual narratives and address significant theoretical issues underlying those interpretations. The series does not privilege one critical perspective but is open to work from any strong theoretical position.

Narrating Space / Spatializing Narrative: Where Narrative Theory and Geography Meet
MARIE-LAURE RYAN, KENNETH FOOTE, AND MAOZ AZARYAHU

Narrative Sequence in Contemporary Narratology
EDITED BY RAPHAËL BARONI AND FRANÇOISE REVAZ

The Submerged Plot and the Mother's Pleasure from Jane Austen to Arundhati Roy
KELLY A. MARSH

Narrative Theory Unbound: Queer and Feminist Interventions
EDITED BY ROBYN WARHOL AND SUSAN S. LANSER

Unnatural Narrative: Theory, History, and Practice
BRIAN RICHARDSON

Ethics and the Dynamic Observer Narrator: Reckoning with Past and Present in German Literature
KATRA A. BYRAM

Narrative Paths: African Travel in Modern Fiction and Nonfiction
KAI MIKKONEN

The Reader as Peeping Tom: Nonreciprocal Gazing in Narrative Fiction and Film
JEREMY HAWTHORN

Thomas Hardy's Brains: Psychology, Neurology, and Hardy's Imagination
SUZANNE KEEN

The Return of the Omniscient Narrator: Authorship and Authority in Twenty-First Century Fiction
PAUL DAWSON

Feminist Narrative Ethics: Tacit Persuasion in Modernist Form
KATHERINE SAUNDERS NASH

Real Mysteries: Narrative and the Unknowable
H. PORTER ABBOTT

A Poetics of Unnatural Narrative
EDITED BY JAN ALBER, HENRIK SKOV NIELSEN, AND BRIAN RICHARDSON

Narrative Discourse: Authors and Narrators in Literature, Film, and Art
PATRICK COLM HOGAN

An Aesthetics of Narrative Performance: Transnational Theater, Literature, and Film in Contemporary Germany
CLAUDIA BREGER

Literary Identification from Charlotte Brontë to Tsitsi Dangarembga
LAURA GREEN

Narrative Theory: Core Concepts and Critical Debates
DAVID HERMAN, JAMES PHELAN AND PETER J. RABINOWITZ, BRIAN RICHARDSON, AND ROBYN WARHOL

After Testimony: The Ethics and Aesthetics of Holocaust Narrative for the Future
EDITED BY JAKOB LOTHE, SUSAN RUBIN SULEIMAN, AND JAMES PHELAN

The Vitality of Allegory: Figural Narrative in Modern and Contemporary Fiction
GARY JOHNSON

Narrative Middles: Navigating the Nineteenth-Century British Novel
EDITED BY CAROLINE LEVINE AND MARIO ORTIZ-ROBLES

Fact, Fiction, and Form: Selected Essays
RALPH W. RADER. EDITED BY JAMES PHELAN AND DAVID H. RICHTER.

The Real, the True, and the Told: Postmodern Historical Narrative and the Ethics of Representation
ERIC L. BERLATSKY

*Franz Kafka: Narration, Rhetoric,
and Reading*
EDITED BY JAKOB LOTHE, BEATRICE
SANDBERG, AND RONALD SPEIRS

Social Minds in the Novel
ALAN PALMER

*Narrative Structures and the Language
of the Self*
MATTHEW CLARK

*Imagining Minds: The Neuro-Aesthetics of
Austen, Eliot, and Hardy*
KAY YOUNG

*Postclassical Narratology: Approaches and
Analyses*
EDITED BY JAN ALBER AND MONIKA-
FLUDERNIK

*Techniques for Living: Fiction and Theory
in the Work of Christine Brooke-Rose*
KAREN R. LAWRENCE

*Towards the Ethics of Form in Fiction:
Narratives of Cultural Remission*
LEONA TOKER

Tabloid, Inc.: Crimes, Newspapers, Narratives
V. PENELOPE PELIZZON
AND NANCY M. WEST

*Narrative Means, Lyric Ends: Temporality in
the Nineteenth-Century British Long Poem*
MONIQUE R. MORGAN

*Understanding Nationalism: On Narrative,
Cognitive Science, and Identity*
PATRICK COLM HOGAN

*Joseph Conrad: Voice, Sequence,
History, Genre*
EDITED BY JAKOB LOTHE, JEREMY
HAWTHORN, JAMES PHELAN

*The Rhetoric of Fictionality: Narrative
Theory and the Idea of Fiction*
RICHARD WALSH

*Experiencing Fiction: Judgments,
Progressions, and the Rhetorical Theory of
Narrative*
JAMES PHELAN

*Unnatural Voices: Extreme Narration in
Modern and Contemporary Fiction*
BRIAN RICHARDSON

Narrative Causalities
EMMA KAFALENOS

*Why We Read Fiction: Theory of Mind and
the Novel*
LISA ZUNSHINE

*I Know That You Know That I Know:
Narrating Subjects from* Moll Flanders
to Marnie
GEORGE BUTTE

Bloodscripts: Writing the Violent Subject
ELANA GOMEL

*Surprised by Shame: Dostoevsky's Liars and
Narrative Exposure*
DEBORAH A. MARTINSEN

*Having a Good Cry: Effeminate Feelings and
Pop-Culture Forms*
ROBYN R. WARHOL

*Politics, Persuasion, and Pragmatism:
A Rhetoric of Feminist Utopian Fiction*
ELLEN PEEL

*Telling Tales: Gender and Narrative Form
in Victorian Literature and Culture*
ELIZABETH LANGLAND

*Narrative Dynamics: Essays on Time, Plot,
Closure, and Frames*
EDITED BY BRIAN RICHARDSON

*Breaking the Frame: Metalepsis and
the Construction of the Subject*
DEBRA MALINA

Invisible Author: Last Essays
CHRISTINE BROOKE-ROSE

*Ordinary Pleasures: Couples, Conversation,
and Comedy*
KAY YOUNG

*Narratologies: New Perspectives on Narrative
Analysis*
EDITED BY DAVID HERMAN

*Before Reading: Narrative Conventions
and the Politics of Interpretation*
PETER J. RABINOWITZ

*Matters of Fact: Reading Nonfiction over
the Edge*
DANIEL W. LEHMAN

The Progress of Romance: Literary Historiography and the Gothic Novel
DAVID H. RICHTER

A Glance Beyond Doubt: Narration, Representation, Subjectivity
SHLOMITH RIMMON-KENAN

Narrative as Rhetoric: Technique, Audiences, Ethics, Ideology
JAMES PHELAN

Misreading Jane Eyre: *A Postformalist Paradigm*
JEROME BEATY

Psychological Politics of the American Dream: The Commodification of Subjectivity in Twentieth-Century American Literature
LOIS TYSON

Understanding Narrative
EDITED BY JAMES PHELAN AND PETER J. RABINOWITZ

Framing Anna Karenina: *Tolstoy, the Woman Question, and the Victorian Novel*
AMY MANDELKER

Gendered Interventions: Narrative Discourse in the Victorian Novel
ROBYN R. WARHOL

Reading People, Reading Plots: Character, Progression, and the Interpretation of Narrative
JAMES PHELAN

www.ingramcontent.com/pod-product-compliance
Lightning Source LLC
Chambersburg PA
CBHW021847300426
44115CB00005B/55